*Counselling skills*
# IN SOCIAL WORK PRACTICE

## Second edition

# Counselling skills
# IN SOCIAL WORK PRACTICE
## Second edition

*Janet Seden*

**Open University Press**

Open University Press
McGraw-Hill Education
McGraw-Hill House
Shoppenhangers Road
Maidenhead
Berkshire
England
SL6 2QL

email: enquiries@openup.co.uk
world wide web: www.openup.co.uk

and Two Penn Plaza, New York, NY 10121–2289, USA

First edition 1999. Reprinted 2000, 2001
Second Edition 2005

A catalogue record of this book is available from the British Library

ISBN 0335 21649 8

Library of Congress Cataloguing-in-Publication Data
CIP data applied for

Typeset by Refinecatch Limited, Bungay, Suffolk
Printed in the UK by Bell & Bain Ltd

*To Roy, Deborah, Charlotte, Matthew*
*and all the family, with much love*

# Contents

# Preface to the second edition

This book is one of a series that considers the relationship between counselling skills and the professional concerns of a specific group, in this case social workers. This second edition responds to changes in social work education as the requirements for the degree in social work bring a welcome emphasis on communication, human development and reflective practice as central to social workers' roles with people who use services. The key roles and standards, to which the discussion is linked, will become familiar to people on social work degrees and those teaching them, but perhaps not to others, so it is important to say that these categories build on knowledge, values and skills developed over time for social work practice.

Counselling and social work theory have shared a developmental pathway, drawing from the psychological and sociological theories that inform interpersonal work. Social work like counselling is concerned with the promotion of wellbeing and responds to what people say they want as far as possible. Unlike counselling, social work is concerned with combating social inequalities in the socio/political environment. Social workers also have legal responsibilities to certain groups of people defined by the social policy concerns of governments and this can involve compulsory interventions.

It is clear from research and consultation with people who use services that social workers need at least the basic counselling skills, and sometimes more advanced ones, to carry out the complex tasks they face. Exactly what is needed depends on where someone is employed but the failure to use the most fundamental listening and responding skills is often a contributory factor when things go wrong. These are skills that service users identify as important in social workers: the capacity to listen, hear and respond respectfully. This basic and core ability to hear the reality of others and respond reflexively cannot be emphasized enough.

This book examines counselling skills, starting with active listening and responding, and considers the ways these and other counselling skills can sensitively and appropriately contribute to good social work practice. Human beings communicate with each other all the time but social workers have to be sure that their manner of communication conveys respect and that they, and a diversity of others, interconnect effectively. They are accountable not just for their actions, but also for the way they speak and interact and cannot just rely on habits and experience, they need skills in communicating and relating.

Social work is a multidisciplinary, inter-agency activity, with professionals collaborating to provide services. One of the barriers to effective collaboration has been differences of language, background, attitudes and values. While this has the advantage of bringing several perspectives to a situation so that someone's circumstances may be considered holistically, there is also the risk of professionals guarding their territory and of conflict about ways of resolving problems. As all professionals need counselling skills (the ones here will be familiar to nurses, education staff and a range of other professionals) they have the advantage of being a common and unifying approach to use to resolve differences and work out how to collaborate. High quality interpersonal skills are fundamental to the capacity to network and build partnerships.

My own experience (as probation officer, generic social worker, children and families' social worker, social work and social care lecturer, counsellor and counsellor trainer) has shown me the commonalities and differences of approach between social workers, counsellors and others in the application of skills. The material in this book has been taught to a range of professionals including social workers, health professionals, teachers, clergy, support workers, nursery officers, therapists, community and youth workers, voluntary sector workers and others. Transferable skills like these provide a basis for a common approach.

However skills are never fixed in the way they are applied. They are dependent on many contextual factors. As far as possible service users should lead and have 'voice' and 'choice'. In this book the focus is on the skills needed by practitioners. This is not because people using services are passive, far from it, but because social workers are accountable for their own attitudes and responses to what people bring to them. They have a professional responsibility to communicate and relate to the best of their abilities. If counselling skills are learnt and then used reflexively in practice they can enable social workers to be more responsive to service user's agendas and be used to enhance service user choice, each time, in each context. They are not meant to be used rigidly, prescriptively or oppressively, but rather flexibly, responsively and ethically to avoid discrimination and the harm which is possible when social workers intervene wrongly in the lives of others. Social workers always have to take care with the power inherent in their role and the authority given by legal mandates.

Here, counselling skills are seen as tools to underpin a range of theories, methods and frameworks for social work, as such they are not neutral but depend on the ability of practitioners to use them to enhance the experiences of others. The book is therefore as much about social work contexts as counselling skills and the two are continually viewed in relationship with each other.

Terminology is always important. Counsellors usually refer to those they work with as 'clients'. Where I am quoting from counselling materials or someone's narrative I have left this word unaltered. Otherwise I have adopted the terms in the Framework for Social Work Education in Scotland where:

> The term '**people who use services**' means any individual group, community or organisation who receive social work services. This term will include some people who do not want or ask for these services, for example people who are on probation or parole.

> The term '**carer**' means people who provide informal, unpaid care to a member of the family or to another person and who work in partnership with social workers to deliver a service. As part of their learning students must gain the understanding and skills they need to separate the conflicting interests that some people who use services and some carers have, in order to offer appropriate support.

> The term '**social worker**' is defined in the Regulation of Care (Scotland) Act 2001 as 'a person who has an entitling professional qualification in social work'.
>
> (www.scotland.gov.uk: accessed 4 April, 2004)

The term 'service user' stands for 'people who use services'. The term paid carer or care worker is used to distinguish carers employed by agencies or individuals from 'carers'. I have used social worker and professional interchangeably. I have also used the words 'worker' and 'practitioner' to describe people in employed roles in health and social care. Sometimes 'professionals' include others beside social workers (such as teachers, nurses, doctors).

Social work has been subject to media and moral panic from society over the years, and yet, day in, day out, many social workers carry out their tasks in a caring, competent and effective way which rarely seems to be publicly acknowledged. Significant events like moving from home to residential care or hospital, losing a child, liberty, income or citizenship are some of the significant life events where social workers become involved. The practice examples show social practitioners who are committed to carrying out their everyday tasks well with children, families and adults, in the organizations where they are employed.

The examples are drawn (with consent) from real situations, reworked and rewritten for publication. They illustrate the practical use of counselling skills in social work and can be studied and learned from. They were contributed by beginning and experienced practitioners who hold recognized social work qualifications and included work in children's and adult services, criminal justice and voluntary sector practice. Context shapes every piece of work, but the choices that are made about process distinguish best practice from basic bureaucratic competence.

The general theoretical and methodological material used is drawn from my own experience, research and teaching material, and some from a commissioned literature review completed for the Department of Health. The full version is published as *Studies which inform the development of the Framework for the Assessment of*

*Children in Need and their Families* (Department of Health 2000). Thanks for agreement to draw on this work are registered here.

Acknowledgments are also due for assistance and permission to use their work to: Kimberley Absalom, Pauline Anstead, Juliet Bewley, Julie Brooks, Lorraine Chapman, Toni Fox, Sandra Holyoake, Elizabeth Lawrence, Liz McKenzie, Sarah Morris, David Neville, Sarah Orgill, Moira Phillips, Arlene Price, Pamela Shenton, Chris Shotton, Andy Smith, Martin Shaw, Richard Taylor, Martyn Vail and Claire Wilkinson.

Thanks are also due to those who completed the questionnaire mentioned in chapter 1. I remain indebted to Michael Jacobs for teaching me much of what I know about counselling and acting as mentor to the first edition and to Professor Jane Aldgate for encouragement to write. I would also like to acknowledge the value of working on course teams with many colleagues at The Open University whose insights, experiences, perceptions and challenges are a great impetus to learning more.

Janet Seden, Leicester, 17 July, 2004

# Note on the questions and activities for self development

While this new edition is not primarily a self teaching manual or part of an open learning course, at the suggestion of reviewers, it seemed useful to offer some activities and questions that could be used by individuals or groups to facilitate learning and the practice of skills. These can be found at the end of chapters 1–7 and at the end of each section in chapter 8. They assume that the reader has an interest in health and social care and probably some knowledge of health and social care practice. Continuing professional development is an important component in a practitioner's career and taking responsibility for self development is key. Readers of this book will already be interested in counselling skills and social work and the Questions and Activities provide a way of looking at their own skills reflectively.

Learning is more than absorbing information; it involves active experimentation, trying ideas out in practice from which to develop new insights and skill. Frances and Woodcock (1982: 1, 2) suggest a three-stage approach to self-development: exploring the present (auditing and evaluating what you know); visioning the future (assessing what you wish to achieve); bridging the gap (devising strategies and activities to achieve your goals). In this book I have suggested that noticing the skills of others and learning from them is helpful and so is reflection 'in' and 'on' your day-to-day practice. The activities and questions for self-development provide a way of organizing this in relation to the material in the book. There are several ways of using them:

1. As an individual. After you have read each section, complete the activities, drawing from the chapter content and your own practice experiences. Keep a learning log and actively work on improving your counselling skills and relationships in your work setting.
2. Find a colleague who will become a 'critical friend'. Work together on your skills and ask them for feedback and ideas for improvement. You could also seek service user feedback and evaluation of your practice.

3. Work in a group. Use the activities with others so that you can compare and contrast your experiences and exchange ideas.
4. Use the questions and activities with people that you supervise/teach.
5. Lead a team development session.

Whatever you choose to do, interpersonal skills such as those used by counsellors can always be improved and developed by practice, feedback and reflection. As contexts changed skills may need to be adapted to new situations. Service users are consistent in their view that they want social workers who will:

listen actively to what individuals, families, carers, groups and communities have to say;

build honest relationships based on clear communication;

be good at starting, continuing and closing relationships.

(Extracted from: *Statement of expectations from individuals, families, carers, groups and communities who use services and those who care for them* (NISWE for Topss 2003b).

# Chapter 1

## Counselling skills and social work: a relationship

Mrs Andrews, aged 67, was trying to obtain some help for her elderly relative Mr Yelland, aged 87, who lived several miles away. He was becoming frail and less able to manage to care for himself, needing assistance with washing, dressing, shopping and cooking. His doctor had suggested a home carer could be provided through social services. Mrs Andrews was very concerned about Mr Yelland, especially as she was caring for her sick husband, aged 71. This meant she couldn't visit her uncle, who had no other relative nearby and had been 'like a father' to her. She consulted the local advice centre who found the telephone number of a social worker for older people in the area where her uncle lived. She phoned feeling rather anxious, and although the worker who took her call was courteous and efficient, they requested information by a series of rapid questions. Mrs Andrews was informed that a referral had been taken, that a telephone call would be made to ascertain if Mr Yelland wanted a visit and that someone would go and see him. The call ended and Mrs Andrews began to worry whether she had done the right thing. She had managed to pass on the information but now felt upset. She had been unable to say how concerned she felt, or to explain how difficult it was for her uncle who had always been well and independent, not to be able to manage simple tasks. She had not been able to share how worried she was that he was forgetting things, that he might mind about a visit or that he was not caring for himself properly. She wondered how he would feel about a stranger visiting his home and what was behind all the questions the social worker asked. She had a sleepless night worrying about what she had done.

Meanwhile, in another city Mrs Dalgleish, aged 67, was trying to obtain some help for her elderly relative Mr Ennis, aged 85, who lived several miles away. He too was becoming frail and unable to care for himself. He needed assistance with washing, dressing, shopping and cooking. She was very concerned about him, especially as she was caring for her sick husband, aged 71, and couldn't visit Mr Ennis, who had no other relative any nearer. She consulted the local advice centre who found the telephone number of a social worker for older people in the area where her uncle lived. She telephoned feeling rather anxious. The worker at the end of the telephone was courteous and efficient, but after asking for some basic information asked her how she thought her uncle would react to the referral. Mrs Dalgleish felt relieved to be able to share her concerns. She was helped by the social worker acknowledging the difficulty of this potential change for Mr Ennis. It was also helpful that, beginning to feel that the worker understood, she could share that she was also concerned about her uncle's forgetfulness and lack of care for himself. The social worker explored these concerns and finished by offering to read back what she had written down so that Mrs Dalgleish could be sure it was correct. She also checked what times of day might be best to call Mr Ennis, whether he was expecting to hear from social services and whether he could easily use the telephone. The social worker said that she understood Mrs Dalgleish's worries about talking to a stranger about her relative and explained that in any case they needed her to contact him and check that he was agreeable to a visit from them. Mrs Dalgleish was reassured by this understanding and the attention given to details. Mrs Dalgleish was informed that a referral had been taken, that a telephone call would be made to ascertain that Mr Ennis did want a visit, that someone would go and see him, and that she would be contacted about the outcome. She was also reassured by the social worker that Mr Ennis' wishes would be ascertained and respected. The call ended and Mrs Dalgleish began to feel it would be alright. She had done the right thing. She telephoned her uncle to let him know what would be happening.

In the everyday interactions between professionals and the people who consult them the detail of what is said and then done really matters.

As Coulshed says, 'If case management is to succeed as a strategy for organising and coordinating services at the level of the individual client it has to concentrate on the minutiae of interactions between helper and helped' (1991: 44). Counselling skills play a pivotal role in this.

Relationship, one person interacting with another, is at the heart of all social work in health and social care settings. Counselling and communication skills are used every day to build such relationships in order for the work to happen. All social work processes: interviewing, assessment, planning, interventions, evaluations, take place in the context of meeting people, their worries and their life crises. The quality of what happens relies heavily on conversations between people. Poor services are often marked by conflict and hostile relations between service users, their families and the workers. Quality services rely on the ability to build a co-operative partnership where social workers and service users participate together. Relationship-building skills remain the bedrock of quality in practice, especially when people who need a service are anxious, angry, distressed or upset because of their situation.

Skill can be defined simply as the ability to 'do something well'. This definition works well enough for some practical tasks. However what is 'done well' in a social work context is more complicated to judge. Whether a communication is 'good' depends on how it is received in the situation and what is conveyed to the other person. A skilful communication enhances the other person's experience and their ability to respond and participate. What is skilful creates a sense of working together. Using these criteria, Mrs Dalgleish's social worker was more skilled than the person who took the call from Mrs Andrews.

As these brief scenarios show, communication is the everyday currency of human interaction, but the context in which communication takes place changes the meanings of words and what lies behind them. Both social workers had more power than the woman requesting help because they could give or withhold a service. The experience of telephoning social services was new for both women who were understandably apprehensive. The social worker might have been nervous about her abilities but had a responsibility to take the call professionally and competently and to enable the caller's concerns to be her priority. It is essential that social workers take responsibility for developing and improving those skills which enable them to build relationships. This enables them to provide a professional service for which they can be accountable.

From babies to older people, everyone communicates. When there is a specific impairment that impedes communication creative ways and means to overcome this can be found. Much communication skill is commonplace in that it is learned in the process of socialization. Each person learns a communicating style from parents and others in the cultural environment where they grow up. Professional workers, however, meet people from a range of cultures, backgrounds and abilities. They need therefore to be open to learning how to improve their interactions with a whole range of 'others'. The skills developed over the years for training counsellors to build good relationships and use them in therapeutic processes provide a useful starting place for applying skills to social work practice.

### Contexts for practice

At one time, it would have seemed obvious that social workers use counselling and casework in their tasks (Perlman 1957; Biestek 1961; Hollis 1964; Mayer and Timms 1970; Roberts and Nee 1971). However from the 1980s onwards, a preoccupation with markets, commissioners, providers, resources and outcomes (Taylor-Gooby and Lawson 1993) might have led an observer to the conclusion that such skills were no longer needed. Social workers employed in local authorities may have entered the profession thinking that they would focus on the kind of assistance given by counsellors to their clients. Instead, they found themselves overwhelmed by work of a more bureaucratic and directive kind in order to meet the requirements of the procedures in social services departments.

Harris (2002) outlines how the new right under Margaret Thatcher and then John Major was committed to the reform of the welfare state. They introduced business thinking into the organization of social services, arguing their case from economic necessity. This was followed by the modernization agenda of new Labour (Department of Health 1998a, 2000a, 2001b). This collection of changes is often referred to as 'managerialism'. Waine and Henderson (2003: 51) define this as 'an overarching set of changes introduced in the UK from the 1980s onwards that

involve providing effective services at lower cost through the application of management techniques borrowed from business and industry'.

This trend sets up a tension for professionals who find their work shaped and
contextualized by this 'managerialist' policy framework. The indicators of this
business based framework are identified by Harris as:

- **Competition:** The belief that competition among providers results in
  more economical, efficient and effective services.
- **Contracts:** The use of contracts ensures that control resides with the purchaser, who has the power to make decisions and see them carried through.
  The provider has to implement the purchaser's decisions.
- **Performance indicators:** Business-oriented measurable standards and
  pre-set output measures are found increasingly in the monitoring of social
  work.
- **More work:** The underlying message, rarely explicitly articulated but con-
  tained within business thinking and pursued through capitalist models of
  managing social services is that social workers should work harder.
- **Increased scrutiny:** Information technology systems allow detailed
  specification of social work tasks and checks on their completion. Much of
  this control is expressed in computerized manuals, directions and guidelines that limit discretion and set up standardized and repetitive systems
  with tightly defined criteria for eligibility for services; standardized assessment tools; interventions, which are often determined in advance from a
  limited list; minimization of contact time and pressure for throughput.
- **Gatekeeping and rationing:** Business thinking requires social workers
  to see themselves as micro-managers of resources who carefully control
  access to and ration the distribution of services.

(2003: 36)

Harris suggests that this trend to 'business thinking' has demoralized social
workers leaving them working to find ways to 'emphasize the variability and
unpredictability of services users' needs' (2003: 37).

While the policy environment has this particular 'managerialist' shape,
other ideas concerning citizenship, human rights, and service user voice have also
become very important. First, it can be recognized that everyone needs or uses
services at some point in their lives. The provision of health and welfare services is
not just for the 'unfortunate'. Second, some people are more reliant on services
than others and this is often because of powerful forces of exclusion and disadvantage (Connelly and Seden 2003). Third, we are all citizens and as such entitled to
have a voice about the services offered to us by the state. Fourth, all activities by
service providers can be scrutinized in the light of the Human Rights Act 1998.
'Listening to People' and 'Valuing People' are concepts which also form part of
policy rhetoric and which need to become integrated into practice. The consultation paper *A Quality Strategy for Social Care* says that it is important to focus on
what people want from services and suggests that, as citizens, what people expect is:

- High standards at all levels in service delivery throughout the whole workforce.
- Responsiveness, speed and convenience of service delivery.
- Appropriateness — services tailored to individual need, with respect for culture and lifestyle.
- Services that build on people's abilities and help them to participate fully in society.
- Services that involve the user, so that choices are informed and respected.
- Strong safeguards for those at risk.

(Department of Health 2000a: 6)

Consultation with service users, participation, partnership, citizenship, rights and the power of user organizations are as much part of dialogue in social work as the language of 'business'. This concern with the voice and actions of service users on their own behalf provides a significant challenge to bureaucratic and managerialist environments for practice (Henderson and Atkinson 2003; Seden and Reynolds et al. 2003). Social workers find themselves operating in the space between 'top down' directives and the 'bottom up' needs and views of people who use services.

Legal mandates remain significant in defining the boundaries of social work practice. Law carries the values and philosophies that influence society's approaches to the care and control of some citizens by others. It gives local authorities powers (things they must do) and duties (things they may do at their discretion) which are frequently delegated to social workers. The Children Act 1989, NHS and Community Care Act 1990, Criminal Justice Act 1991, Mental Health Acts and subsequent legislation and amendments have dominated the thinking of the profession about role and function. A new entrant to social work will find that they need to understand the impact on their work of a wide range of statute law, case law, and the regulations, guidance, directions, policy and procedures that flow from them. This includes European law in the Human Rights Act 1998 and may on occasions include other international law. Throughout their professional life they will be expected to respond to changes in the law, policy and procedures. Whatever kind of agency a practitioner is employed by, voluntary, private, local authority, fieldwork or group care, the law will provide a framework of roles and responsibilities for every aspect of their activity. This is far less the case for counsellors both in private and public roles.

The organizational framework for practice also changes. Social work services for adults, in the early twenty-first century, are part of Primary Care Trusts, and The Children Bill (2004) provides for the creation of Children's Trusts. Social workers increasingly work within multidisciplinary and multi agency structures. Whatever the shape of the organizations where they are employed, social workers continue to work at the interface between the individual, their needs and aspirations and the particular social, political and economic concerns of public policy. As they work with people in their families and environments they make assessments, interventions and referrals and commission a range of specialist services, many in the voluntary and private sector, including some which offer counselling based on casework. Some workers still make therapeutic relationships and provide direct counselling services themselves (Barnes 1990). In the varied, everyday activities of social work and care it is impossible to function without offering some level of personal work. Social workers become involved with people needing support in a crisis, change, transition or loss; protection from self or others; help to deal with disadvantage or injustice; in fact any combination of life changing events depending on the particular circumstances (Seden and Katz 2003).

Many social workers still want to 'care', often motivated by the wish to 'help people' and 'make a difference'. The mandate to safeguard people from harm and to promote their welfare is embedded in the legislation under which social workers carry out their tasks. Brechin writes that to care is:

> to accept a host of moral responsibilities for your own and others wellbeing. It is to accept that people matter. At the extreme, care can sustain or extinguish life itself. Even at its most routine, it can influence how people live their lives and the kind of people they become. Caring therefore really matters. It is fundamental to the pact of being human.
>
> (1998: 1)

Counselling skills, used to communicate and build relationships are central to care. Work with children, young people and adults, with colleagues in multi disciplinary teams, in partnerships across agencies, and activities for continuing professional development all require attention to the detail of speaking and relating. The core business of social work is still 'people' and 'talk'. Communicating, face to face, on the telephone, by email, by letter and in written reports remains a key skill. This is underpinned by the values of conveying respect and combating discrimination and disadvantage, using a knowledge base which has been developed from the social sciences over the second half of the twentieth century and redefined as society changes. Social work moves into the twenty-first century with a distinctive contribution to offer society and a more secure knowledge base on which to draw for practice.

### The relationship between counselling and social work

The relationship between counselling and social work has always been complex and interactive. As two distinct activities they share some theoretical origins and ways of thinking. Professionals who qualified in the 1960s and 70s were grounded in casework principles based on psychodynamic theoretical underpinnings. Since those times social work training has moved in other directions adopting social learning (behavioural) theories, ecological and systems theories and a range of derivative practice methods (Seden 2001 and 2005).Through the radical and Marxist approaches of the 80s and the development of anti-discriminatory and anti-oppressive practice in the 90s it has reclaimed the original pre-occupation with social inequalities, injustice and social exclusion, working with people's own strengths and abilities using advocacy and empowerment strategies, despite a climate of resource constraint.

By the mid-1990s, however, casework appeared to be less prioritized then empowerment ideologies and functionalism. The idea of a therapeutic relation-ship appeared to be subsumed to bureaucratic priorities. Some social workers might have argued that counselling skills were no longer relevant to social work practice and that the focus on the struggles of the individual was pathologizing. This tension was possibly more about ideology than practice, and a renewed cer-tainty about the value base of the profession has also brought renewed recognition of the centrality of communication and counselling skills to reflective social work practice.

The National Occupational Standards for Social Work (Topss 2003a) identify six key roles in which the 'key core skill of communication (verbal and written), alongside application of number and information technology skills' is embedded within the requirements for qualifying training. Both basic and more advanced counselling skills will be needed for professionals to carry out the six key roles and as they move from qualifying to post qualifying and advanced practitioner awards. In this book I will show how these well-tested skills contribute to assessing, plan-ning and reviewing when social workers act to support and safeguard people. They are, if used reflectively, absolutely fundamental to achieving partnership with service users and colleagues within and across agency boundaries and networks.

Just as the knowledge base for social work practice has developed and been refined over the years by practitioners and academics, the discipline of counselling has also developed (McLeod 1998; BACP 2004). Counselling services and the methods used by counsellors have become more diverse. Psychodynamic counsel-ling remains a major theoretical approach, but many others also flourish (for example, person-centred, cognitive-behavioural, integrative). Counselling practice has been re-evaluated for its relevance to women, black people, lesbian, gay and bisexual people, younger and older people and those who are disabled. Counsel-ling training, like social work training, has re-examined its ideologies and practice as society's attitudes and values have changed. Paternalistic and discriminatory ideologies and models have been challenged and approaches re-examined. Theory and practice in the two areas of work remain complementary.

At the same time, there is still a lack of clarity about the boundaries between the activities of social work and counselling. At one extreme all direct work with clients in social work agencies is labelled counselling, while at the other some social workers regard counselling as entirely a matter for specialist referral or the commissioning of services. Both extremes fail to negotiate the boundaries between the two disciplines adequately. The reality is that social workers in some situations take on a counselling role and counselling skills can be applied to a variety of social work tasks. Workers in Community Mental Health Teams use counselling skills in undertaking assessments and providing services. Supportive counselling and skills for communicating remain central to work with children and their families in agencies like Sure Start, Connexions and CAMHS (child and adolescent mental health services) and work with adults.

The boundary confusion is not helped by the fact that individual social workers may take on a number of roles in relation to a particular person, so that the counselling element of the working contract needs to be distinguished, clarified and contracted openly in relation to the overall package of work being undertaken (Hill and Meadows 1990). For instance a social worker may agree to temporarily take the role of offering brief counselling to a young person about a particular aspect of their life (for example, education, contact with a parent) or they may commission that from someone else. What matters is that the young person knows what is offered, by whom, and has an informed choice about the arrangements.

The historical interaction between counselling and social work is analysed by Brearley (1991) who traces the ways the two activities intertwined and influenced each other in terms of skills, knowledge and values and how the two disciplines have also developed distinct identities and training pathways. She writes:

> the Barclay report identified counselling as one of the two main activities of social workers, the other being social care planning, and the report acknowledged the interlocking nature of these activities. The particular, perhaps unique, challenge faced by social workers is to offer counselling in a way that is integrated appropriately with a variety of other approaches in the overall work with a given client often within the same interview

She continues:

> A logical categorization of the counselling dimensions of social work would therefore be as follows:
>
> • counselling skills underpinning the whole range of social work
> • counselling as a significant component of the work, carried out in conjunction with other approaches
> • counselling as a major explicit part of the job description.
>
> (1991: 30)

This book focuses on the relationship between counselling skills and social work practice, the first two of Brearley's categories. My own experiences as probation officer, generic social worker, children and families' social worker, social work and social care lecturer, counsellor and counselling trainer make me acutely aware of both the commonalities and differences of approach at a practice level between social workers and counsellors in the application of skills to their work. Social workers can be unclear about the counselling skills that apply to social work and what the major specialist counselling approaches offer to people. Counsellors can be unduly critical of the legally mandated and bureaucratic task-centred parts of social work, without appreciating the counselling and other inter-personal skills needed to facilitate these complex and difficult human inter-actions. When operating, as I have done, across the two professional areas it is clear that there is overlap in practice skills, shared values and shared knowledge, as well as differences about how professional mandates and ethics determine the content of the work with people.

The lack of clarity about the role of counselling in social work practice is perhaps an outcome of the symbiotic relationship with the newly emerging social work profession, which in its early days was seeking to identify which areas of expertise distinguished it from other professional activities. This was most clearly the case in the second half of the twentieth century when casework literature from America dominated social work. In the 1990s it became possible to assert that the distinctiveness of social work might be identified more by a value base, within legal mandates, than by particular sets of methods.

## Social work and counselling in the twenty-first century

It is impossible to discuss the place of counselling skills in social work without considering them in relation to the requirements for a qualification in professional social work (Training Organisation for the Personal Social Services (Topss) 2003a, b, c and the framework for social work education in Scotland). There are now National Occupational Standards for social workers and social work is defined as:

> A profession which promotes social change, problem solving in human relationships and the empowerment and liberation of people to enhance well-being. Utilising theories of human behaviour and social systems, social work intervenes at the points where people interact with their environments. Principles of human rights and social justice are fundamental to social work.
> (International Association of Schools of Social Work and the International Federation of Social Workers)

A holistic model of social work is promoted which describes six key roles (standards in Scotland) underpinned by values and ethics, which are:

1. Prepare for, and work with individuals, families, carers, groups and communities to assess their needs and circumstances.
2. Plan, carry out, review and evaluate social work practice, with individuals, families, carers, groups, communities and other professionals.
3. Support individuals to represent their needs, views and circumstances.
4. Manage risk to individuals, families, carers, groups, communities, self and colleagues.
5. Manage and be accountable, with supervision and support, for your own social work practice within your organization.
6. Demonstrate professional competence in social work practice.

There is detailed guidance on what is expected under these headings and the occupational standards are accompanied by a Code of Practice for employees and a separate one for employers. There is also a 'Statement of Expectations' developed from consultation with 'individuals, families, carers, groups and communities who use services and those who care for them'. The expectations are summarized under the headings: communication skills and information sharing; good social work practice; advocacy, working with other professionals, knowledge and values. There are also subject benchmarking statements for social policy and social work degrees which training providers must meet (Topss 2003 a, b, c). There is detailed documentation accompanying the same six major areas of practice (standards) which apply in Scotland.

The International definition of social work provides an ecological perspective which suggests social workers are engaged with people who are themselves interacting with their environments. It also reminds social workers that they are there to promote change and to enhance wellbeing. The principles that guide practice are those of respecting rights and promoting social justice. These aspirations are unlikely to conflict with the ethics of doctors, counsellors or other professionals with whom social workers collaborate, but social workers have a distinct role in keeping a focus on people's expressed needs, understanding the impact on people of economic and social inequalities and offering social support. They have powers and duties to intervene on behalf of the state to safeguard both adults and children from harm. They have key roles in building networks to provide services and working in multidisciplinary teams and agencies.

Counselling has been disserviced and misunderstood within social work when the term 'counselling' is used without clarity about its meaning. This can be seen in some social work literature, ever since the Barclay Report included counselling as a function of social work without further definition. It can be assumed that personal support and listening on casework principles is what is meant, but to anyone with specific counselling training, this is too simplistic. Counselling, like social work, is not one way of working. It includes several major schools of thought and practice, with differing theoretical underpinnings. It is important to stress that approaches to counselling practice are diverse, as the literature can demonstrate (Mearns and Thorne 1988; Egan 1990; Jacobs 1995a, b; Davies and Neale 1996; Lago and Thompson 1996; Corey 1997; Heron 1997; McLeod 1998).

Given the variety of possible approaches, the provision of counselling as a generic term can be very misleading. It is important that people know exactly what is being offered and the premises on which a particular service is based. Therefore, if social workers are commissioning counselling services for people they need to know, at least at a basic level, how the different therapeutic schools operate (for example, the differences between psychodynamic, person-centred and cognitive-behavioural counselling). If they have no such knowledge they are not in a position to help others to make informed choices about the therapies on offer and what approach might be most helpful. Social workers might in some circumstances advise a service user to think carefully before entering a complex therapeutic process for which they may not be suited.

This may be particularly important when commissioning a service for someone with a mental health issue or a child who needs post abuse counselling and support. Trusting a counsellor can be very difficult and not all counselling is help-ful or straightforward as accounts written by people who have experienced it evi-dence (Donna; Nicklinson; Spring in Malone et al. 2004). Counselling is a very varied set of activities, which is the outcome of its developmental history and the role society has given it (McLeod 1998). This makes it difficult for the public and those, like social workers, who might refer people to counsellors to know exactly what to expect from a counsellor or therapist without further exploration. There are however useful accounts on which to draw for information (Corey 1997; Jacobs 1995a, b; McLeod 1998; Walker 1995a, b; BACP website).

### Training deficits in social work

It is still rightly assumed that some counselling is done by social workers, but a study of beginning practitioners' readiness for practice (Marsh and Triseliotis 1996a, b) indicates that basic social work skills is an area where the respondents would have liked more training. Fifty one per cent said that too little time on their course had been spent on social work skills, by which they meant those techniques and actions by which tasks are processed, including communication skills. 'Coun-selling approaches and interpersonal skills appear to be widely taught' (1996b: 52) but students apparently remain unclear about how these relate to the pragmatic tasks undertaken in their workplaces. The study also found that the students inter-viewed split off theory from agency task and reported that this link was not made well by teachers. 'The reality for many respondents was that the actual application of theory to practice was very poorly done and proved to be one of the weakest parts of the course' (1996b: 60).

The authors describe the type of counselling taught as largely relying on Rogerian perspectives or Egan's goal-centred psychodynamic mode:

> The definition of counselling itself varies widely, depending on the perspec-tive from which it is being defined and practised. Approaches can range from total non-directiveness at one end of the continuum (if such a thing is at all possible) to degrees of direction and even challenge at the other end. In fact it is difficult to see how any sort of social work activity or interaction can take place without some form of 'counselling' taking place, unless the word is reserved exclusively for some kind of esoteric/therapeutic approach
>
> (1996b: 54)

The study provides more evidence of the lack of clarity in social work training on the distinction between counselling skills for social work practice, specialist coun-selling approaches and psychosocial casework, the latter being absent from the training of the respondents in the study. Counselling is used but, in common with other theoretical models, it remains a problem for trainees and newly qualified practitioners to understand how, for what purpose and when specific approaches are relevant. Experienced practitioners still struggle with this issue, although successful or failing practice outcomes begin to define what works. This book seeks to make the links between counselling skills and their use in practice more explicit.

Many qualified social workers seek further counselling and psycho-therapeutic training, often at personal expense, to enhance their work and skills. They also write in professional journals arguing for more time and attention to be given to these areas of practice, which they feel are marginalized. Gwen Bird writes:

> If social workers are to be deeply interested in the quality and character of people's perceptions of their close relationships, as David Howe and Diana Hinnings say (Recovering the Relationship, 31 July–6 August) then social work training might well have something to learn from the training which psycho-dynamic counsellors undergo. Real understanding and empathy for human suffering and misery caused by relationship difficulties is born out of a professional training which includes two fundamental elements.
>
> First, an in depth study of the theory which underpins early psycho-logical, emotional and social development, such as the work of Donald Winnicott, John Bowlby and Melanie Klein for example, together with the study of more modern writers such as Michael Jacobs and Anthony Storr. Second, comprehensive self-awareness training that enables a practitioner to work from a position of strong inner stability, and not as Howe and Hinnings point out, cause them to be 'phased by the emotional ups and downs of difficult cases' or 'react defensively'. Combining these two major elements in my own training with experiential work has enabled me to work with a feeling of confidence which is the result of understanding each client in a holistic way
>
> (1997: letter)

This theme is echoed by people who use services. They regularly identify that social workers do not listen and do not understand. Jane Reeves found in a study of the views of young mothers in the care system that they valued social workers who communicated clearly. The failure to do so created barriers:

> The overriding message from all of the young women who participated in this research was that they valued their autonomy, which is, of course, much more difficult to achieve when a baby is at risk. However, unclear messages, ambiguity about who was the focus of the social work interest and undelivered promises, all provoked resistance from the young women. The ability to listen, to make a connection and have fun were felt to be the best ways to encourage co-operation.
>
> (2003: 44)

Forbat and Nar studied how carers from ethnic minorities view services for the carers of people with dementia. They found that 'being listened to and under-stood' was crucial for the carers. 'Staff who took time to ask questions and hear complex and long stories of how the family were coping were seen as the most helpful' (2003: 39).These findings confirm previous ones and it is of great concern that people using services are still identifying that only some social workers are proficient in such crucial and basic skills. If people who use services value time spent in this way, it is a resource that could be provided simply by frontline managers authorizing social workers to spend more time listening. There would be an increase in service user satisfaction and the social worker's sense of wellbeing at work. There might be financial savings if social workers listened more as an outcome would not commission unwanted or unsuitable services.

It is absolutely clear that social workers need to have at least basic counselling skills for communicating and relating and preferably to have more advanced ones, even if it is not necessary for all social workers to be qualified to counsel in depth. Exactly what is required depends upon the setting where the social worker is employed. This book examines these skills and discusses the way that they might, if used sensitively and appropriately, underpin good social work practice.

The basic skills can be identified as:

- attention giving; active listening; non-critical acceptance;
- paraphrasing; reflecting back; summarizing and checking;
- ability to use different kinds of questions; minimal prompting; alternatives to questions;
- empathic understanding; linking; immediacy;
- challenging; confronting; work with defences;
- goal setting; problem solving; focusing techniques;
- knowledge about own and other's use of body language;
- avoidance of judging and moralistic responses;
- boundary awareness; structuring techniques; the ability to say difficult things constructively;
- the ability to offer feedback; techniques for defusing, avoiding the creation of and managing hostility;

Such skills are well documented in literature across a range of approaches to counselling and interviewing (Egan 1990; Jacobs 1982; McLeod 1998; Nelson-Jones 1981). They are essential to the counselling process and also in facilitating social work tasks such as giving benefits advice, interviews and assessment with adults, children and their families. They can be used in planning, carrying out, reviewing work and many other core social work functions at the office, in care establishments and people's own homes.

When planning the first edition of this book, the use of these skills was verified through a survey of social workers. These were practitioners chosen because they had completed a university based counselling course and were also qualified and practising social workers. It showed them to be using counselling skills regularly. Those selected for the survey had completed experiential counselling studies training, to merit level or above, over three years. They were working in a range of settings, including mental health teams, children and families teams, adult services fieldwork and group care. The questionnaire was only sent to people who had clearly demonstrated knowledge of counselling skills practice alongside social work practice. Respondents were asked to indicate the use in their daily social work practice of the skills listed. Twenty five out of thirty responded and the outcome is shown in Table 1.1. All the figures are percentages of the total of returned questionnaires.

This sample shows listening skills to be the most used, and challenging/confronting the least, although every skill is used to a considerable extent. It was impossible without follow up interviews to make inferences about the comparative use of skills, for example, between listening and challenging or the use of skills for specific purposes. However the survey confirms that qualified and competent practitioners in both counselling and social work consistently use counselling skills to underpin and carry out their day-by-day social work roles and tasks.

While this book focuses on skills for practice, it is also important to consider that in the area of interpersonal skills, technical proficiency alone is not enough. The attitudes and qualities of the practitioner are also important for achieving good outcomes. This was first asserted by Truax and Carkhuff (1967: 141): 'Research seems consistently to find empathy, warmth, genuineness characteristic of human encounters that change people for the better'. This use of the self in relationship as the prerequisite for changing the other person is strongly restated in the person-centred approach and psychodynamic approaches to counselling

**Table 1.1** Use of counselling skills in daily practice by social workers

| | Percentage using skill | | | |
| --- | --- | --- | --- | --- |
| *Skill* | *Always* | *Often* | *Sometimes* | *Never* |
| Attention giving | 71 | 29 | 0 | 0 |
| Listening | 93 | 7 | 0 | 0 |
| Active listening | 57 | 43 | 0 | 0 |
| Use of empathy | 28 | 64 | 8 | 0 |
| Acceptance | 57 | 28 | 15 | 0 |
| Genuineness | 28 | 57 | 15 | 0 |
| Paraphrasing | 30 | 35 | 35 | 0 |
| Reflecting back | 30 | 34 | 36 | 0 |
| Summarizing | 38 | 38 | 24 | 0 |
| Questions/exploration | 20 | 60 | 20 | 0 |
| Minimal prompts | 21 | 54 | 25 | 0 |
| Challenging | 7 | 43 | 50 | 0 |
| Confronting | 0 | 56 | 44 | 0 |
| Linking | 7 | 50 | 43 | 0 |
| Immediacy | 7 | 53 | 40 | 0 |
| Work on defences | 7 | 40 | 53 | 0 |
| Goal setting | 28 | 36 | 36 | 0 |
| Problem solving | 36 | 64 | 0 | 0 |

where the conditions for therapeutic relationships are explored in detail (Jacobs 1982; Mearns and Thorne 1988).

What appears to make the difference between effective and ineffective therapists is the degree of warmth and respect towards individuals which the practitioner demonstrates. Carl Rogers (1961) formulated this as the core conditions for person-centred practice: congruence, advanced accurate empathy and unconditional positive regard. These core conditions have equally always underpinned analytic/psychodynamic therapy and social casework (Biestek 1961). Whatever counselling theory is used, it is the personal relationship and facilitating qualities of the worker that are valued, as much as skills and theoretical models, by recipients of services. This has been known ever since the Truax and Carkhuff research and there has been no contrary evidence to invalidate this finding. Current research into social work delivery finds contemporary evidence to similar effect. Hardiker and Barker (1994) found social workers relying on casework and counselling skills to facilitate complex work in cases of significant harm under the Children Act 1989. Aldgate et al. (1997) found that the clients valued the personal support, as it was viewed, of the social workers who planned respite care services as much as they appreciated the service provided.

This kind of finding is also seen in other research studies (Department of Health 2001a; Forbat and Nar 2003; Reeves 2003). In many social work settings more advanced skills can considerably enhance worker performance and confidence (for example, work with bereaved people, abused young people, people suffering from depression or other mental health difficulties, substance users or offenders). The narrative examples of practitioners' work, which appear throughout this book, show the varied use of beginning and advanced skills in everyday social work practice.

### Choice and control

Social workers and counsellors both work towards helping individuals develop, adjust to a change in life circumstances, or find new opportunities and resources. The key difference is that while people come for counselling through choice, those using social work services are often compelled by societal or legal mandates to address a particular area of their lives, or are driven to ask for help by poverty or some other type of disadvantage. The dimension therefore that clearly differentiates counselling from social work is context. Counsellors do not have to engage with service delivery or directly with their clients' social environments. They can offer confidentiality in a distinctive way, and can operate in neatly contracted hourly sessions within discrete agencies.

Counselling is defined as follows by the British Association for Counselling and Psychotherapy. The definition begins:

> Counselling takes place when a counsellor sees a client in a private and confidential setting to explore a difficulty the client is having, distress they may

be experiencing or perhaps their dissatisfaction with life, or loss of a sense of direction and purpose. It is always at the request of the client as no one can properly be 'sent' for counselling.

By listening attentively and patiently the counsellor can begin to perceive the difficulties from the client's point of view and can help them to see things more clearly, possibly from a different perspective. Counselling is a way of enabling choice or change or reducing confusion. It does not involve giving advice or directing a client to take a particular course of action. Counsellors do not judge or exploit their clients in any way . . .

(BACP 2004: for a full definition see www.bacp.co.uk)

The key elements of the process are:

- Service provided when you want to make a change in your life.
- An opportunity to make sense of your individual circumstances.
- Contact with a therapist who helps identify the choices for change.
- Support for the individual during their process of change.
- The end result leaving you better equipped to cope for the future.

(www.bacp.co.uk: 5 March 2004)

These guidelines can apply to some parts of a social worker's contract with a service user and there is some resonance with the social work task. However, social workers exercise their counselling skills in very specific legal and procedural frameworks. People can be 'sent' for social work; information, advice and directions are given. Social workers are rarely entirely free to refuse to work with someone even if they are violent or hostile. The responsibilities that social workers have and the frameworks in which counselling takes place are different.

Social workers do engage with service users to try and work to agreed goals together, for example in: programmes to address offending behaviour; helping parents with childcare; supporting young people leaving care; making care plans with adults. However, actions such as applying for an Emergency Protection Order under the Children Act 1989 or arranging a compulsory admission to hospital under a Mental Health Act lead social workers to intervene directly and with compulsion in people's lives in a way counsellors do not. Social workers cannot offer complete confidentiality to individuals either because, subject to the requirements of the Data Protection Act 1998, information is often shared between agencies.

Paradoxically, the societal constraints that lead people to becoming users of social work services, and the compulsory nature of some of the work, means that social workers are often working with some of the most distressed, disadvantaged and troubled people in the community; people who might benefit from an in-depth counselling approach. Likewise, teams of social workers find themselves suddenly involved in post-disaster counselling or situations which demand intensive input when emotions are running high. This means a need for interpersonal skills of the highest order. Many practising qualified social workers identify the need for further training. Certainly the basic counselling skills, once acquired, are quickly put into practice:

One new social worker described this:

> I remember on my first day I interviewed: first, a very abusive large man who needed furniture for a new flat and whose anger with a benefits refusal was being directed at me; second, a woman living alone with four young children whose electricity was about to be disconnected and who in contrast was weepy, distracted and desperate; third, a terrified and shocked young couple who had just been subjected to a terrible experience of racist abuse, in which their flat had been vandalised and covered in graffiti because she was a black woman living with a white man; fourth an elderly man who seemed confused about why he had come and who finally told me he had ants in the kitchen and didn't know how to get rid of them. That was only the morning!
>
> (communication to the author)

All those people needed practical assistance and also, in different ways, wanted understanding related to the way they were feeling. They wanted time to talk as well as practical assistance or information as to where to obtain resources or what action to take next. They all were helped by the use of counselling skills in facilitating the interview but none wanted counselling as such.

## Key points

- Good communication and relationships remains at the heart of effective practice with individuals, families, carers, groups, communities and colleagues.
- Social work takes place in a managerial and legal framework within which good interpersonal skills are essential.
- Work with crisis, change and life events involves social workers in counselling roles.
- Practitioners evidence the usefulness of counselling skills and would like training opportunities to develop them.
- The outcomes of research into effective practice repeatedly give the message that people want social workers who can listen to and support them.
- Practical counselling skills are relevant to all social work whatever the practice context.

## Questions and activities: for self development or discussion groups

**1** Reflect on the discussion of counselling and counselling skills in this chapter. Note how they are relevant to your work.

**2** Think of a time when you needed a service or imagine that you need one now.

Jot down the qualities and skills that you would want from someone who is helping you. Make a few notes on what you would not want the person to be like. Now look at the notes again, if you were the social worker would you have the desirable qualities and skills? How might you improve your skills?

3  Look at Table 1.1 and audit your own skills against the skills listed. Identify those that are familiar/less familiar. Reflect on how, when and where you use them effectively.

# Chapter 2

# Counselling skills for communication and building relationships

Communication skills have always been important in the caring professions. However, examples of poor communication between professionals and from practitioners to people using services have led to a renewed focus on the importance of careful, clear and sensitive communicating. Poor communication has contributed to problems which can lead to service users being harmed or receiving inadequate care. Social workers therefore need to develop better communication skills with service users, their colleagues and when working across agency boundaries. The failure of professionals across a range of disciplines to communicate with each other effectively has been highlighted in several inquiries into deaths or injury that might have been avoided.

For example, it is not enough to transmit information without checking that it is received. Sometime important information has simply not been passed on to the person who needed it. It is easy to take communication 'for granted' perhaps because there is so much going on around us. However, often what is thought to be communication is not communication at all and in professional settings assumptions can be costly if the effectiveness of communication remains unstudied and unevaluated. Communication in social work is a complex process, with the aim of engaging the service user (and often others) with a plan of action to achieve a specified goal. This chapter shows how counselling skills are the foundation for communicating with others, even when the situation is imposed on the people involved rather than chosen by them. In social work people have to relate to each other simply because one person is a service user and the other the professional involved. The fact that they have not chosen to be with each other often creates an initial barrier. Also the way the people involved use language and communicate may be very different. The skills here may appear to be straightforward but they need to be learned, practised in training, developed and refreshed for effective use in real situations. As one student wrote while reflecting on practice:

combining a practical and realistic approach to theory and employing sound,

taught interviewing techniques is the most competent and skilful approach
... it seems the more practice you get, the more confident you become, and
with this your confidence grows, so you become an effective and skilful
helper.

(Smith 1994)

Many of the skills needed to underpin human interactions derive from the practice
of social casework (Richmond 1922; Perlman 1957; Hollis 1964) and have subsequently been developed by others (Coulshed 1991). Social casework has its origins in psychoanalysis and the associated literature that has permeated the helping
professions including medicine, counselling, education and pastoral care. A core of
derivative listening, attending and other counselling skills have been found useful
in a range of communication and relationship tasks. Communication in social
work practice involves far more than imparting information. It is a process where
thoughts, feelings, ideas and hopes are not only exchanged between people, but
also need to be understood together. Verbal and non verbal communications are
used to:

- transmit and share information;
- establish relationships;
- exchange ideas and perceptions;
- create change;
- exchange attitudes, values and beliefs;
- achieve service user and practioner goals.

## Recognizing the other's way of communicating

Communication does not take place in a vacuum. Social workers need to be sensitive to each other person and their wider contexts for a successful exchange of
understandings. Each person's interactions with their own social environment
have shaped the way they see and interpret the world. The challenge is to learn to
make sense of what each person brings to each encounter, as the first practice
example in this chapter illustrates. Practitioners have to respect the values and
beliefs of others as far as is consistent with their professional authority and
function.

Meanings must be carefully checked and in each exchange care needs to be
taken to be aware of, and reduce, the blocks to communication that can come from
the many differences between individuals such as: authority and power; language;
ability and disability; personality; background; gender; health; age; race; and class.
Other barriers may impede communication, such as: environment; the pressure of
limited available time; the involvement of other people; the physical environment; or interruptions. Genuine communication is only achieved if the barriers
are considered and worked through or removed. This is a part of developing an anti
oppressive and anti discriminatory approach to communication.

Lago and Thompson writing about cultural barriers to communication in counselling, suggest a range of possible dimensions to consider:

> language, time, context, purpose of meeting, views and attitudes towards each other, location of meeting, customs/rituals, smell, age, touch, disability, decoration, adornment, jewellery, personal institutional power, expectations, perceptions of previous personal history, context of meeting, why they are meeting, conventions of greeting and meeting behaviour, gender, notions of acceptable/unacceptable behaviour, system of ethics/morals, interpersonal projections, political differences, personal theories of communication, physical appearance, height, weight, non verbal behaviour.
>
> (1996: 40)

Each meeting between two human beings, each carrying their prejudices, cultural conditioning and agendas, can be seen to have complex dimensions. Lago and Thompson (1996: 41) suggest that the 'counsellor may have considerable difficulty in fully offering one of the core therapeutic conditions as defined by Rogers (1961) for successful therapy to occur, that of acceptance or non-judgementalism and argue that awareness of the cultural dimensions of counselling should not be used to conceal prejudice or racism within the counsellor.

These dimensions of diversity mean social workers need to be flexible in their practice. The addition of social work authority through role and law adds a critical dimension to the human encounters which take place in a variety of office and home settings. The concern of social workers to avoid discrimination in carrying out their roles makes it especially important to diminish communication barriers as far as possible. However, this has to be balanced with awareness of role and function, as well as caution about concealed or unacknowledged power on the part of the worker. Aspects of this are considered next.

First, social workers are daily working with people who are made vulnerable because of age or disability (abused children; confused older people; the mentally ill) or through circumstances (denial of rights; eviction; bereavement; asylum seeking). This makes it important not to use communication skills to cajole, manipulate or persuade someone into a course of action which they may not want or to pacify someone whose rights are being negated. At the same time if a social worker's duty to society or some-one else's safety, for example a child, means difficult things have to be said skills are needed to communicate this honestly so that the realities and consequences of legally sanctioned actions are understood. The possibility of the misuse of delegated power through verbal abilities is an ethical consideration of the utmost importance. For example, if the service user's view of their needs does not match the resources available, an honest appraisal of the mismatch and what might be done is different from trying to persuade the person into the available resource.

Second, sometimes people ask for social work services on a voluntary basis but frequently there is an element of compulsion or social control. This means that social workers cannot, as counsellors can, choose only to work with people who are motivated towards the process in which they are engaged. This adds barriers of reluctance, hostility and resistance to many encounters. The ability to communicate and establish relationships, to establish purpose and to engage people in effective working in these circumstances needs acutely developed and refined skills, especially as anxiety and anger are likely to be very much in evidence. There will need to be communication about the nature of the relationship, the service user's powerlessness and their possible lack of choice about who the worker is, if it is not to impede the relationship.

Third, social workers need to develop skills for communicating with people whose ability for verbal communication is either reduced or not fully developed. This includes people with dementia, adults with learning disabilities and adults with a range of impairments such as hearing loss. Social workers need to be able to communicate effectively with children and young people. Learning to interview children therapeutically and when required to establish video evidence for a court hearing, is a specific skill. Social workers also need abilities in using facilitated communication methods such as Makaton and, at the very least, need to know how best to ensure that communication is two way.

Fourth, service user consultation is central to social work practice. Attending and listening to what is said and finding creative and empowering ways to make sure that action follows is very important. It is the social worker's responsibility to develop the skills for a level of communication which empowers the service user to make their views known. This means finding out how the person communicates, preparing for the meeting and bringing in any resources that will be helpful such as interpreters (Chand 2000; French and Swain 2004).

Communication is therefore an interactive process involving the giving, receiving and checking out of meaning. It occurs on many levels and care needs taking to ensure it is really happening. It is crucial that interviewers tune into the potential barriers created by factors such as age, class or ethnicity. Communication is a process of which the outcome is engagement, the beginning of a further process where the parties are able work together, to be involved, to achieve mutual understanding, to hold attention and to contract to a purpose.

Communication skills are fundamental to all professional activities and the failure of doctors or nurses to communicate well is at the root of many complaints in the NHS (East 1995; Moore 1997; Smith and Norton 1999). Consequently more attention is being paid to communication skills in doctor and nursing training. Social workers in hospitals frequently find themselves using their own counselling skills in communication to clarify miscommunication and the subsequent lack of engagement. Social workers aim for the active involvement of the person, so that they can be empowered to change their own situation or have more control and knowledge within it. The practice example, Mr Mistry, shows how a block in communication was producing conflict between a patient and his doctor and how it was resolved through the use of counselling skills by a hospital social worker.

## Practice example: Mr Mistry

Mr Mistry was a hospital patient being cared for on a medical ward. He was a black man born in India, and his first language was Gujerati. The social worker was a white woman, born in Britain, whose first language was English. The doctor was a white man, born in Britain, but of Eastern European ancestry. His first language was English. Mr Mistry was in hospital after a stroke. He had completed his drug therapy and was described as medically stable by the doctor. He was referred to the social worker because he was reluctant to comply with further treatment, which included physiotherapy and occupational therapy. He refused to go to the gym for exercise. The doctor described the patient as having become 'lazy' and adopting the 'classic sick role'. The social worker explored this with the doctor (*open-ended questions*) and found the doctor thought that the patient enjoyed the sick role and liked the idea of people doing everything for him, including dressing and feeding him. The conclusion from this was that Mr Mistry would be best placed in a nursing home, where he could remain dependent and be looked after by other people.

The social worker's first step was to visit Mr Mistry with an interpreter to check that this understanding was accurate. Mr Mistry clearly stated that he did not want to go into a nursing home, and that he wanted to go home. He knew that as he lived alone he would need to be able to wash, dress and feed himself in order to be safe. In this interview he did not appear to be enjoying the sick role and seemed to want to return home as soon as possible (*skills used here: active listening, attending, listening to body language, use of interpreting service, checking, so enabling worker and patient to communicate, empathy*).

At the end of this interview there was a contradiction between what Mr Mistry said and the original referral information. At the next meeting, the worker shared her puzzlement over what was happening (*immediacy*) with Mr Mistry. She asked 'how was it that if he wanted to get better, he didn't comply with the treatment?' (*exploratory open-ended question*). He replied that he had complied, as he had taken all his tablets. The worker then understood that he saw medicine as treatment. He thought that the doctor no longer believed that he was ill and was sending him to the gym for exercise to prove it. There was a block in communication and understanding between Mr Mistry and the ward. He had not been enabled to participate in the follow up treatment.

The social worker decided to observe the interaction between the doctor and the patient. She reflected on the use of language between the two people. Her conclusions were that the doctor's approach and the language he used were moralistic, judgemental and authoritarian. Mr Mistry was labelled as lazy. This view had been arrived at quickly, without checking Mr Mistry's mind-set, in an authoritarian mode of knowing best. The worker considered that this style of communication came from a controlling parent ego-state (*ego-psychology/ transactional analysis theoretical model*). This was possibly arousing resistance *(a defence)* in Mr Mistry. As she reflected upon Mr Mistry's language, he was using phrases like 'I will not' and 'he cannot make me', reflecting the kind of responses which can come from the dependency of childhood, and which may be aroused in adults through illness and helplessness. The anger and resistance that can accompany such feelings where there is a parental attitude in the helper, reinforce the difficulties of dependency (*child ego-state*).

The worker recognized that neither party was being helpful to each other and were instead reinforcing polarized attitudes. The more the doctor acted as a controlling parent, the more Mr Mistry refused the prescribed activities. This analysis enabled the worker to focus clearly on the way in which the doctor and patient were reinforcing their miscommunication. She arranged a meeting between the doctor and Mr Mistry and herself. She invited the doctor to explain the treatment and the benefits of it: it would build up muscles; improve the ability to walk; enable Mr Mistry to gain strength before being at home alone. She asked Mr Mistry to explain that he refused the treatment because he thought that he needed to be really fit to use a gym, and that rest was the best cure. He thought that the doctor regarded him as fit. (*Here the worker used her empathy for the views of both people to set up a meeting to clarify and summarize the actual intentions of both people, using counselling skills in mediation as she challenged the authority model constructively.*) At this meeting, the two 'sides' were able to exchange information and perceptions as one adult to another. Mr Mistry was able to hear and understand that physiotherapy was offered to increase his possible rehabilitation. The doctor began to understand that Mr Mistry's reluctance to use the gym was for reasons, not from laziness or unexplained reluctance (*challenge to perspectives, the enabling of the lowering of defences on the patient's part*).

This example demonstrates the time and attention that may be needed to enable true communication. It also shows the problems that can arise if statements are heard unreflectively and assumptions made. The worker, by her early involvement of the interpreter, had checked that two way communications could happen between herself and Mr Mistry for whom English was a second language. She reduced the power imbalance between the hospital and Mr Mistry who was able to have his voice heard. By valuing both people equally and by *attentive listening* she established where the misunderstanding was, and examined the frames of reference of both people carefully. She used her skills (*listening, summarizing, use of questions, empathy*) to facilitate a meeting to work out a solution. She did this by her *immediacy* and understanding to facilitate a three-way conversation that unblocked the impasse and enabled Mr Mistry to receive the services to which he was entitled in a dignified and adult mode. She had also avoided an unnecessary and inappropriate admission to residential care

The social worker's analysis of her actions demonstrated her knowledge, values and skills. She explored the cultural context in which she was working and considered how far her theoretical model was applicable. There was a clear cultural difference between the doctor's belief that the patient would improve with active rehabilitation and the patient's belief that he should rest and pass the time quietly to improve. There were power differentials created by role and status. Her part was to remain non-judgemental and objective while working both to support someone and provide a service for the hospital. The worker also discussed the boundaries of her role with Mr Mistry and the doctor, so as to be explicit about their transactions. The counselling skills she used enabled accurate two-way communication.

### Interviewing

Much social work communication takes place through interviewing, either in offices, on the telephone or in the person's home. The social work interview has been described in various ways. Davies (1985) calls it a 'conversation with a purpose', while Hugman (1977) argues for social workers to 'act natural'. Personal attributes such as warmth, flexibility and creativity have been considered a good base from which to begin. Social work literature on communication and relationship argues for a combination of warmth, empathy and positive regard with skills which have been developed through supervised practice (simulated or actual). Compton and Galaway (1989: 334) offer a framework, describing the social work interview as, 'a set of communications with four special characteristics: (1) it has a context or a setting; (2) it is purposeful and directed; (3) it is limited and contractual; (4) it involves specialized role relationships'.

There are many useful books to help students with the theoretical structuring and purposes of this process (Breakwell 1990; Heron 1997; Nelson-Jones 1981; Rollnick 1996; Trevithick 2000). Social work programmes are expected to teach basic skills and practice placements to assess them. The difficult part for trainees is to transfer learning to practice in the beginning stages, although interviewing techniques remain the subject of a lifetime's practice and development. Research does show that interviewing skills can be taught and developed through the practice and rehearsal of micro skills (Dickson and Bamford 1995) and can be transferred into the workplace (Ryan, Fook and Hawkins 1995). The next section explores basic counselling skills in more detail for social workers seeking to develop the kind of communication skills which facilitate good practice.

### Exploring counselling skills further

*Listening*

In social work this is an active process, and not just a series of 'nods' and the overuse of 'mms' that might provoke hostility and impatience in the service user. The guidelines offered by Jacobs (1985: 13) on the details of how to listen well are helpful here:

- listen with undivided attention, without interrupting;
- remember what has been said, including the details (the more you listen and the less you say the better your memory);
- listen to the base line (what is not openly said but possibly is being felt);
- watch for non verbal clues to help you understand the feelings;
- listen to yourself and how you might feel in a described situation, as a way of further understanding (empathy);
- try to tolerate pauses and silences that are a little longer than is usual in conversations. Avoid asking lots of questions to break silences;
- help yourself and the other to feel comfortable and relaxed with each other. Keep calm even when you don't feel calm.

Such checklists are helpful in guiding actions and combined with supervised live practice can substantially improve practitioner's skills. However, many people think when they read such guidelines that this is what they already do, only to be amazed to find in simulated practice that, for example, they find silence less easy to tolerate than they thought, or are not clear how to paraphrase well or are prone to say something just to fill the gaps in the conversation. This ability to listen properly, and hear accurately by focusing on the other person way is an essential basic skill for work with people.

Cornwell (1990) writes about listening as part of the context of empowering practice. She argues that 'if listening is selective it disallows the other person choice in setting the agenda . . . if listening is open with positive unconditional regard and lack of negative judgement, this offers the gift of space and the discharge of internal pain leading to a sense of control over the self which is empowering'. The importance of 'active listening' and 'attending' being 'focused' and 'really hearing' what the other person is communicating cannot be overemphasized. Also the only way to be sure that you have heard and understood is to check back with the other person. It is not enough to assume that because you heard physically that you also understood.

It is also useful to identify some of the features of ordinary conversation which are not so helpful in professional interviews. An interesting formulation of these is described by Townsend (1987: 21). They are:

- daydreaming (losing attention, thoughts wandering);
- labelling (putting the other person into a category before hearing the evidence);
- scoring points (relating everything you hear to your own experience);
- mind reading (predicting what the other person is thinking);
- rehearsing (practising your next lines in your head);
- cherry picking (listening for a key piece of information and then switching off);
- interrupting (being unable to resist giving advice);
- duelling (countering the speaker's verbal advances with parries and thrusts of your own);
- side stepping sentiment (countering expressions of emotion with jokes or clichés).

If you think back honestly on your recent everyday conversations you are likely to find examples of times when you have done all of this. In everyday conversation this happens all the time but in your professional life more care is needed because of the power of your role. Accurate and good listening in an interview context has to be different. It tries to understand and hear the experience of the other; keeps an open mind about what may said next; waits until the other has finished speaking and reflects upon it before responding; does not select what will be important in advance; keeps focused on the other's agenda; does not label or stereotype; does not advise until advice is requested and a full picture is obtained; does not make provocative or challenging comments thoughtlessly; makes space for the other to express and clarify feeling.

It is possible to imagine the distorted assessment of possible harm to a child; or the inaccurately constructed care plan for an adult which comes from an interview where the social worker has 'cherry picked' or 'labelled'. It is all the more important that people are heard accurately by social workers because by the time they reach the agency, they are often angry or frustrated by the labelling or hostility they have met elsewhere. There are times when, after listening carefully to the person's story, the social worker cannot offer a service, or needs to make a referral. However, the person who has been thoughtfully heard finds this more acceptable than the person who feels dismissed and 'brushed off'. Listening skills can assist the worker to give a personal and non-bureaucratic response without compromising the agency remit. Difficult information can be heard better in an atmosphere which is kept calm and constructive by the social worker. Sadly, failure to communicate well, with individuals or between agencies, is all too frequently identified as a cause of things going wrong, as in the Climbié inquiry (Laming 2003) amongst others.

### Responding

Social workers also need to be able to give skilled and accurate responses. Initially responses may be non verbal, but it is crucial to begin to offer more than token monosyllables to indicate that the speaker is being heard and understood. Counselling skills such as summarizing, reflecting and paraphrasing are very useful indeed to check that information is correctly understood and recorded and to ensure that the services offered meet the expressed need and that you have understood the other person's meaning. Learning to do this accurately takes time and practice. The skills listed by Jacobs (1985) can be used to begin to move an interview forward, to clarify or explore more fully:

- be as accurate as possible in describing feelings/ideas that you perceived (not just depressed or angry);
- use your empathic understanding to make this accurate, although tentatively, you could be wrong;
- keep questions to a minimum unless you need precise information (in which

case ask precise questions); if you want to open up an area use open questions; if you wish to prompt use rhetorical questions; avoid questions beginning why;
- use minimal prompts (mm, yes, or repeat the last few words);
- paraphrase, summarize or reflect accurately as: a way of prompting; an indication that you have been listening; a way of checking that you have heard accurately;
- avoid making judgements or loaded remarks;
- where possible link reported experiences, events, reactions and ideas;
- avoid changing the subject or interrupting unnecessarily;
- avoid speaking too soon, too often or for too long.

These basic counselling skills can be used in social work interviews in order to gather information, to enable the person to communicate their needs and concerns, to assess what the agency might offer and to pave the way for action or problem solving. Remember that your professional role means that your responses will be given more weight than in ordinary conversations. The benefit of using these techniques is that they will enable you to keep a focus on the other person and their strengths. A focus on accurate reflection and paraphrase prevents you from 'putting words into the person's mouth' or making your own assumptions. An ability to facilitate people to tell their own stories is essential for sensitive work like the disclosure of abuse.

### Questioning

Much social work involves gathering initial information from which to make an assessment and/or to provide a service and/or to take some action. Many interventions arise from a personal crisis in the person's life to which social workers are expected to respond quickly. This makes it all the more important to cultivate sound interviewing and interpersonal skills. Some of the forms which social workers need to complete with people are long and time consuming. Interviews therefore need to be shaped to elicit necessary information as efficiently as possible. In these circumstances, honesty about the need to ask a series of questions is facilitative, since obtaining the information otherwise takes too long. Some areas of work such as benefits advice require detailed questioning and information collection. Explanation of the purposes and outcomes of given information, such as who will see it or with whom it may be shared, is very important.

Social workers inevitably have to talk more and be more active in their interviews than most counsellors. In order to remember detailed information social workers often make notes and fill forms out with people present. Explicit reference to this process and obtaining co-operation in checking and agreeing detail is valuable. It is also good practice to invite the other person to fill in forms with you, so that they can see what is recorded and areas of agreement or disagreement can be identified as you go along. Counselling skills such as the use of paraphrase, summary and immediacy can be employed in this process. This facilitates an interview and it can feel more conversational if strings of interrogatory and intrusive questions are avoided. Questions which are phrased carefully or alternatives to questions may be used to obtain information. For example the interviewer can say, 'Could you tell me about' or 'It would be helpful for me to know more about' instead of firing blunt questions to obtain information.

It is essential to be able to distinguish between closed and open questions. Closed ones are needed for asking about specific topics. For example, 'Are you working at the moment?' invites the answer Yes or No. A question like, 'Are you on medication?' flows better when rephrased, 'Can you tell me what medication you are taking at the moment?' This is a less closed question and is less interrogatory in its phrasing. It also means you do not have to ask two questions, the person can either say none or if the answer is yes give the details. They can also indicate if they would rather not give the information or ask why it is needed.

Interviewers who use open questions find the interview progresses better if these can begin with 'How?' 'What?' 'When?' rather than 'Why?' Questions beginning 'Why?' can sound both accusing and overly authoritarian, with echoes of schooldays and childhood (Why are you late? Why didn't you do your homework?). This is particularly important to remember when working with children and young people. People are often unsure of the direct reasons for their actions. They can answer a question like 'Why?' more easily if a less direct invitation to speak like 'tell me about the day when the incident happened' or 'Because?' is used to enable them explore motivations. Giving a narrative account is easier for most people than answering a question. Listening to someone's story can often tell you more than asking direct questions.

These techniques centre on the careful use of language and phrasing. They still promote explicit interviewing, but phrase questions in ways that can reduce hostility and anxiety. Judgements, loaded remarks and expressions of moralizing are to be avoided because they create defensiveness. It is better if social workers can avoid confronting people with aspects of themselves, such as offending behaviour or maltreatment of a child, in a way that is clumsy or unplanned. Either of these will be counterproductive. That does not mean social workers fail to challenge or confront, it does mean that words are chosen carefully. This is particularly crucial because 'difficult messages' are hard to hear. You might want to ask the person to repeat back to you what they think you said and agree what is to be written down and recorded. Personal disapproval or dislike of the service user is something to be taken to supervision, not to be openly expressed. The use of open interviewing is essential in situations where evidence for court or information for a meeting such as a case conference is needed. Particular care needs to be taken not to ask leading questions or put words into people's mouths.

### *Body language*

While cultural diversity about what is and is not acceptable in terms of eye contact, touch, dress and so on needs to be considered carefully in each situation, there are some basic areas to keep in mind. For example, it is usually best to ensure that a comfortable distance is observed between the interviewer and interviewee. Arrange not to be interrupted unnecessarily. Consider the informality and/or formality of the room. Looking distracted, yawning and peering at your watch and other lapses of concentration give clear negative messages. Facial expression is important since frowns, or smiles, at inappropriate moments carry the wrong message. The lower tones of the voice generally carry better and are calming. Speaking quietly and very clearly to small children is more effective than saying too much, too fast, in a shrill tone. Also great care needs to be taken to understand the extent to which a child's speech and understanding have developed. These guidelines from counselling literature are all useful when transferred across to social work settings. Assertiveness, attention to body posture, facial expressions, breathing and seating are all factors that can facilitate the environment and decrease anger, hostility, anxiety or tension. Interviewing in other people's homes means negotiating distractions like radios, televisions, pets, and neighbours. Social workers need to take care that the climate is right for an effective interview and must be prepared to address distractions in an assertive but sensitive way. It is also useful to ask who is in the home before you commence the interview and whether they should be there. If you have good reason to think that there is a risk of physical violence towards yourself or another, it is best to plan for someone else to be present and to have considered how to keep the environment safe by thinking about the physical lay out and where exits and other staff who could help you are.

The following account shows how a new practioner used her skills with a young offender. An initial relationship had to be built through skilled communication in order to establish a basis for future cooperative work. She had to listen, attend, respond and confront and challenge, a combination of skills that are frequently needed in social work.

### Practice example: Dean

Dean was a young adult with a wife and baby who left a magistrates' court subject to a community sentence made for drinking and driving. This was a second offence. The major objectives facing the worker were to *confront* the offender with the impact of this offence on his family and the community, and to look at the risks he was taking. He had to be seen weekly. At the first interview the major task was to *check out* that Dean understood what was expected of him in terms of attendance at meetings and participation in the programme. He was offered the opportunity to give his own thoughts and reactions to events. A joint plan of action was created.

Firstly, information was given carefully, to show a clear understanding of process (*checking, paraphrasing, summarizing*). Dean was asked to give his perspective on his situation (*use of empathy*). He was encouraged to identify his own strengths (*ego support*) and say where he needed help (*linking, problem solving, goal setting*). His initial playing down of the offence was discussed and reframed (*challenge*). The worker treated Dean as an individual (*genuineness, acceptance*) and valued him as a person, while not minimizing the drinking while driving (*attentive listening*). To explore the potential causes and effects of the offence *open questions* were used. At the beginning of the interview the worker endeavoured to put Dean at ease and tried to give *body messages* of *attentiveness* and *active listening*. The court had already passed sentence, so moralistic and judging responses could be avoided. The practitioner said:

> I reflected back his own feelings and behaviour. I was aware of the need to challenge where appropriate and motivate Dean into accepting responsibility and recognising the impact that his offence caused his victims.

The outcome was that Dean could accept the dangers of drink/driving and acknowledge the need to control his alcohol intake for the sake of his wife and child and the community. He did not re-offend during the work. He dealt with some practical issues around housing and employment which had been causing anxiety and therefore drinking. He attended a group for motoring offenders. The worker, as is usual in such work, employed a variety of approaches; individual work, group process and practical assistance. All these were based on communication and the building of a relationship

Whatever the long term outcome, in the short term purposeful and boundaried interactions, based on carefully chosen techniques and skills enabled the worker to meet agency objectives. Dean gained verbal and cognitive awareness of himself and his behaviour. Such communication skills are crucial to sustaining a working social work relationship from the initial contact onwards. Careful listening, observing and responding to yourself and the other person enable exchanges of meaning which make the work effective. The use of such skills is particularly important in clarifying expectations and challenging and maintaining the authority role that exists while seeking to work to a client's strengths and own goals for their life. In particular the worker was able to assess Dean's motivation and create a relationship which sustained a partnership approach to problem solving.

### Frameworks for interviewing

Social workers are usually employed to work within clear legal or agency mandates and the job usually involves that practical problem solving is undertaken. The matters which people bring are as frequently defined by others as by themselves. Issues of risk to the self or public feature highly. The accountability with which the social worker is invested on behalf of society is very important and society's investment in this is sometimes demonstrated vigorously, when things go wrong, in the media and through public inquiries. This accountability has led social workers to organize their interviewing into frameworks which help achieve the agency's and service user's identified goals. Frameworks can be really helpful, and do not have to feel 'unnatural' if used flexibly. The following frameworks, based on particular psychological theories about human behaviour have been widely used to facilitate interviews. A brief summary is offered here which can be followed up, using the references provided.

### Solution focused therapy

This approach derives from the work of De Shazer (1985, 1988). The worker's focus is on enabling people to identify their own established solutions to difficulties and supporting them to sustain change. The emphasis is less on problems and more on reinforcing coping strategies which have already succeeded for the client. This approach has also been applied to work to safeguard children (Turnell and Edwards 1999; Turnell and Essex, forthcoming).

### Motivational interviewing

This approach is described by Rollnick (1996). It is essentially a practical eclectic approach, with the worker assisting the client to recognize and build on their own abilities to change. Five principles for intervention are described in detail: express empathy; develop discrepancy; avoid argumentation; roll with resistance; support self efficacy. This work has been found particularly relevant in agencies where a major focus of the work is helping people to change from behaviour which is bringing them into conflict with the law or other people (offending behaviour, drug and alcohol use).

### Humanistic frameworks

Heron (1997) presents six intervention styles for face-to-face helping. These are prescriptive; informative; confronting; cathartic; catalytic; supportive. These detailed responses are related to choices about intervention made by therapists and clients together to meet need. The approach clarifies for practitioners which kinds of intervention are most useful in which situation.

### Cognitive frameworks

Cognitive approaches are effective in both social work and psychotherapeutic interventions. Examples can be found in the work of Roberts (1995) Ryle (1995) and Corey (1997). In recent years research has shown the effectiveness of such ways of working with offenders and other specific groups of people (McGuire 1995). Jones and Ramchandani (1999) have made applications of these theories to working with children who have been sexually abused and their carers.

The basic counselling skills discussed here can be used to underpin all these different approaches for interviewing and engaging people and building on their existing strengths and coping capacities. The next practice example shows how a social worker used counselling skills to communicate and work with a family within the legal framework of the Children Act 1989 to promote welfare and safeguard a child.

### Practice example: Daniel

Daniel's step-father and birth mother had applied to adopt him, giving the step-father full parental responsibility, together with the birth mother. The formal role of the social worker is to assess whether the granting of such an application is in the child's best interest. There is a duty between the application and the hearing date to: make inquiries and be satisfied as to the welfare of the child; advise the prospective adopters about the full legal implications of such an order, its effects on them and the child; advise on alternative courses of action. A written report gives information to the court about: the family; their circumstances; the likely outcome of the proposed adoption; the child's welfare and any alternative action that might be better for the child. Part of the social worker's responsibility is to ascertain the feelings and wishes of children and to ensure that they are informed of changes that affect them. They therefore also need skills in communicating with children.

Daniel was quite young (6) and the family were finding it difficult to tell him about his origins and why the mother and 'father' were applying to a court to adopt him. The worker knew from research and practice that making the child clear about his identity and origins was best policy in this situation. She shared this information with the adults and offered to work with them to make sure their son was aware of his life circumstances including the proposed adoption.

Initially she used *empathy* to think what the process might be like for the family. She worked with the parents to construct a story book which in picture and simple word form could be read to Daniel. It was designed as an open-ended project so that he had his storybook with all the important events chronicled and on which he could build later with his parents. With the adults the social worker allowed space in her communications (*use of silence*) which meant the family could think and reflect and respond. She used *open ended questions* when exploring their domestic arrangements and parenting roles and capabilities, in order to avoid being oppressive. She involved everyone in discussions so that communication in the family stayed open. With Daniel she played, read and drew, at all times trying to use simple, clear language without jargon. Thus she was able to discuss, *listen, empathize and counsel* through their different concerns.

Families in this situation are often surprised by unanticipated social work attention, and resistant. The adults were anxious about telling the child that he was born to the mother prior to the marriage and about his birth father. However, sensitive use of personal skills combined with honesty about process and careful use of power meant that the family became engaged in the process, and gained through it. The worker's counselling skills were a valuable tool in enabling her to put into operation the values of empowerment on which she based her practice. She was thus able to communicate effectively with the family. At each stage, she considered what she needed to achieve and what skills would best achieve the outcome. She used authority in a skilled way to ensure that Daniel and his family were able to cooperate with her in achieving what the family wanted and in a way that met the child's assessed need to know about his early history.

### Skills for direct work with children

Communication skills are essential in all social work, but particular ways of working are needed to involve children. The worker in the practice example above read to and played with the child and made a storybook about his life so far with him. The Children Act 1989 requires practitioners in all settings to find out about and take account of children's wishes and feelings at all stages of their work. Additionally the UN rights of the child (adopted by the UK) and the children's rights movement have given the importance of direct engagement with children further impetus. All practitioners who find they are working with children need to be able to:

- listen to children and elicit their thoughts, feelings, wishes and views;
- talk with and involve children to build a working relationship for partnership work;
- talk to children and give information about events in their lives;
- engage in work which helps children with processes that happen to them, for example, moving home, starting a new school, changing foster placement;
- communicate in a way which is appropriate to their age, ability, understanding and background;
- communicate sensitively with children around complex and painful issues in their lives;
- interview children and young people when writing reports or collecting evidence for court.

This has been highlighted again by the failure of professionals to safeguard Victoria Climbié (Laming 2003) where social workers and others failed to carry out the basic elements in their roles, including communication. Lord Laming, while recognizing that good practice guidelines for interviewing children should be observed comments:

the guidelines do not prevent a simple exchange of conversation with the child, the content of which should be properly recorded. Seeing, listening to and observing the child must be an essential element of an initial assessment for any worker, and indeed any member of staff routinely working with children, and this can be of great importance when dealing with child protection cases.

(2003: 238)

There is a clear message here that all workers involved with children need the skills to observe them and to talk with them often enough to find out how they are and how they view their situation. Margaret Crompton (1990) writes that, 'Direct work with children is done every day by ordinary people in ordinary agencies'. There are several useful resources for learning to communicate better with children (Aldgate and Simmons 1988; Crompton 1990; Jones 2003, 2005; Lancaster and Broadbent 2003; NSPCC 1997; Wickham and West 2002). There are a range of methods to communicate with disabled children depending on the specific impairment.

The challenge for childcare workers is to face their responsibility to children, to really see them and hear them and to seek the necessary skills for the work which also means understanding the child's developmental capacity, cultural situation and having the skills to work with other agencies. There are times when it is better to find out who a child knows, trusts and likes to talk to. However, the person who receives an urgent referral must be skilled enough to intervene in a crisis. None of this necessarily prejudices evidence gathered through more formal interviewing carried out by designated professionals in preparation for court proceedings. Communication with children themselves and their families is fundamental in social work practice and process in children and families work (Aldgate and Seden 2005).

These principles of good practice could also apply to work with vulnerable adults. Professionals working with adults also need good basic communication skills and also need to be aware of the work of authors such as Killick (2004) and Kitwood (2004) on understanding dementia, Sinason (1992) and Hollins and Sinason (forthcoming) on learning disabilities and writers such as French and Swain (2004) who write about the importance of going beyond the usual communication skills creatively when necessary and staying willing to learn. French and Swain argue that listening to disabled people must be collaborative, so that the disabled person has power. There must be willingness to remove barriers and be flexible in order to respond to the person's experiences and feelings in a genuine way.

When it comes to communication skills, the first point is to attend to the person and to listen carefully. Attentive listening is what leads to appropriate understanding and interventions. Professionals need to work on their skills, both basics and more specialized. Every day communication with service users is everybody's business.

### Key Points

- Communication skills are fundamental to understanding and intervening.
- Communication takes place in cultural and social contexts.
- Barriers to communication need to be recognized and minimized.
- Basic counselling skills and the linked frameworks provide a sound base for practice.
- Direct work with children and adults needs good preparation and attention to detail according to the circumstances.

### Questions and activities: for self development or discussion groups

1 Start a communication skills diary. Make notes when you think communication in your practice has gone well and when it is less successful. Note any good practice you observe in a colleague's practice. Analyse what made specific communications successful. Note the learning points that you might apply to a future practice situation.
2 Turn to the basic counselling skills identified by Jacobs (see pp. 26–27). Choose one to practice and develop. If you audited your skills against Table 1.1 at the end of chapter 1, choose something where you thought yourself less effective. When you are satisfied with your practice in that skill choose another and develop your skills incrementally.
3 Turn to Townsend's list of features of communication behaviours that are unhelpful (see p. 26). Think about times you may have blocked communication in one (or more) of those ways. Are there any pointers there for things to avoid for improving your working practices?

# Chapter 3

# Assessment: relevant counselling skills

Chapters 1 and 2 considered the relationship between counselling and social work and outlined how the basic communication and relationship-building skills which underpin counselling remain relevant when applied appropriately to social work processes, whatever the political, economic and social contexts. The next six chapters each consider a component of social work practice as articulated in the six key roles in the National Occupational Standards for social work (Topss 2003a) and six standards for qualifying social work in Scotland (www.scotland.gov.uk) Each chapter also draws from the associated benchmarking, codes of practice and other guidance associated with the degree in social work where relevant.

Each topic is examined from social work's knowledge and theory base. Alongside this, practice examples and a discussion of linked counselling skills for communication and relationship building continue to show how these can be embedded in the day-to-day actions of professionals and promote better practices. This chapter considers the assessment of individuals, their families, carers groups and communities and the skills needed to prepare for assessment (Key Role 1, Standard 1) of people's needs and circumstances.

Assessment is central to social work and should be viewed as a process, not as an isolated event. It is in itself an intervention that may create change. It is not static, re-evaluation happens within the process as it goes along. The outcome of assessment is usually the provision of services and it is frequently used by agencies as the gateway to resources. Assessments are to be undertaken in partnership with service users; however, it can be questioned how much this can be reality when social workers have the power and resources for a range of interventions and services users do not.

The bureaucratic approach can sometimes be heard in offices as social workers speak of going to 'do an assessment'. This is surprising as the same social workers might notice and deplore the medical habit of referring to patients as the 'bodies' or 'conditions'. In this chapter the terms 'assessment' and 'assessment process' are used to describe work with people in their social contexts, with the underlying view that there is a person at the heart of what is happening whose needs and views should lead in partnership with the practitioner. Social workers are 'going to meet with a person who is being assessed' and whose needs must be kept at the front of all their thinking. The language of 'doing an assessment' used as shorthand may unthinkingly lead to an administrative approach to people which lacks respect.

Assessments in social work start from the needs of or the concerns about a person. The principles which underpin the *Framework for the Assessment of Children in Need and their Families* (Department of Health et al. 2000: 10) start with the person at the centre. Assessments (my italics with adults in mind):

- are child centred *(person-centred)*;
- are rooted in child development *(human growth and development)*;
- are ecological in their approach;
- ensure equality of opportunity;
- involve working with children in families *(carers and relevant others)*;
- build on strengths as well as identify difficulties;
- are inter-agency in their approach to assessment and the provision of services;
- are a continuing process not a single event;
- are carried out in parallel with other action and providing a service;
- are grounded in evidence based knowledge.

Assessment is the foundation of planning and decision making and therefore a cornerstone of professional activity in health, education, voluntary sector provision, housing, benefits agencies and other services available to the public. Assessments may be made briefly on the telephone, in response to daily events in group care settings or be extended and comprehensive over a period of time in complex situations. Assessments both as process and outcome have to be understood together by a range of people involved with the person(s) at the centre and this is a challenge to the communication skills of everyone involved. A key issue for coordinating the services that might result from an assessment is the extent to which the service user and all the professionals concerned can share the same language.

Assessments are usually guided by written frameworks, which vary according to the task as social workers assess: people's needs for services; whether someone might harm others; whether someone is vulnerable to harm from others or themselves. Several theories and models have influenced practice. These are now discussed, in particular the tension between the assessment of need and the anxieties social workers carry for society about risky situations. This discussion is important because it links to the use of certain counselling skills while taking the role of assessor.

## The origins of social work assessment

Casework writing borrowed from medicine and devised the concept of 'social diagnosis' (Richmond 1922; Hollis 1964). This model for assessment, which concentrated on the individual, remained in general use until the early 1970s, but increasingly there began to emerge recognition of the extent to which individuals were influenced by their social circumstances. Haines describes social work assessment as 'the ability to assess a social situation and intervene in whatever seems to be the most effective way'. He conceptualizes the social work process as 'assessment, action and evaluation' in which the purpose of assessment is:

> to gather as much information as possible about the situation and form some opinion about its meaning for the client and its implications for action
>
> (1975:16):

In the late 1970s Curnock and Hardiker conceptualized assessment as a filter by which practitioners weigh and sift information to plan their interventions. The stages in the assessment are described as:

- acquisition of information;
- studying facts and feelings;
- balancing and formulating;
- strategies in goal setting;
- intervention.

This model of assessment was constructed from empirical research with practitioners in probation, child care and mental health settings from the observation of practice which was then analysed. It is noticeable that gathering information is only the beginning of assessment and weight is given to the meanings derived from the information and the decisions for intervention that follow. They found social workers using:

- frameworks;
- communication;
- balance sheets of risks, needs and resources;
- goal-setting strategies.

Curnock and Hardiker (1979) show how assessment involves a range of activities including analysis.

Assessment is informed by theory frameworks which guide the practitioner. Interview schedules are devised which reflect these and are suitable for the task. Compton and Galaway (1989) also contribute to understanding assessment. They suggest (1989: 414) that 'the ultimate purpose of assessment is to contribute to the understanding necessary for appropriate planning'. The phases of assessment are described as:

- purpose and process;
- doing the assessment;
- exploring the problem;
- putting meaning to the situation;
- feelings and facts.

Such frameworks become helpful practical tools for practitioners. Others were developed by Pincus and Minahan (1973), Specht and Vickery (1977), Coulshed (1991), Meyer (1993). These remain influential in and continue to be applied to a range of tasks (Taylor and Devine 1993; Sinclair et al. 1995). These frameworks essentially describe the ways in that practitioners interact with the public to gather relevant information and formulate ways of achieving specified outcomes. These elements are retained in the key roles and standards for the social work degree.

While the frameworks for undertaking assessments are well established, the purposes and theory bases have sometimes developed in different directions. The main shift in the ideology of assessment since 1970 has been a move away from a diagnostic focus towards understanding the perspectives of the client within a holistic and needs-led framework (White and Epston 1989; Meyer 1993; Lloyd and Taylor 1995). These approaches build on the identified strengths of individuals rather than looking for dysfunction. They emphasize assessing what is present in terms of the person's strengths and social workers look for the successful ways of problem solving that people have already developed (De Shazer 1985). In some models, the service user's narratives or stories determine the process (Franklin and Jordan 1995; Laird 1995).

Models of assessment range from diagnosis of dysfunction through problem solving to the newer designation of clients as 'expert' about and 'actor' on their own situations. The existence of different approaches sets up a tension between diagnostic (exclusion/pathology) and social (inclusion/strengths) approaches. This can be reconciled because in practice the use of different approaches may relate more to the context of assessment, and its legally defined purpose, than to the assessment process itself. Also assessment takes place in a continuum of circumstances relating to the balancing of 'needs' and 'risks of harm'.

In some situations social workers are asked to assess and respond to 'need', but it may become apparent during the assessment that immediate action to safeguard someone must be taken because of circumstances that occur. Conversely, while carrying out an assessment about serious concerns a social worker may identify needs which, if met, significantly reduce the possibilities of harm. For example, a woman's children could become immediately safer if she left a violent partner to live with supportive friends. Conversely, a situation that seemed safe can be jeopardized by the arrival of someone known to have a history of assaulting people. While some assessments are entirely about 'need' and some more sharply focused on 'protection' many situations are a complex mix of 'needs' and 'risks' impacting on a range of people. Thus, assessment is often a complex, changing and uncertain process and the relationships with the key people involved need to be open, honest and reciprocal if a situation is to be appraised realistically. Such relationships may be as crucial as the assessment model in determining outcomes.

The task of balancing need with the possibility of harm is the most difficult part of assessment in social work, so it is helpful if social workers are able to acknowledge the shifting nature of the situations they meet and work openly with people to identify how situations are being perceived. Because social work practice has been so very concerned with two predominating approaches, risk assessment and needs-led assessment, it is worth examining them further before considering how counselling skills contribute to the process of assessment.

### A focus on risk assessment

In children's services there has been a pre-occupation with models for risk assessment that have tended to stress family dysfunction rather than strengths. This is largely a reaction to the way that public anxiety about preventing child deaths has permeated social workers' thinking. Attention to the highly publicized 'failures' to protect some children from harm has led the professions to develop checklists of indicators and predictors which claim to measure the safety of a child within a family.

To some extent, there has been similar concern in adult services about the safety of vulnerable groups of older or disabled people and concern about the 'risks to themselves and the dangerousness' of some people with mental illness, which continues in the debates about Mental Health legislation and 'care in the community' policies. The Probation Service has always been concerned to assess the possible danger to the public from the release of some offenders into the community. Consequently, much attention has been given to the development of scales to assess the 'risks' to children from parental dangerousness; the 'risks' offenders pose to the community; and the 'risks' some adults pose to themselves and others (Prins 1995; Kempshall and Pritchard 1997; Cooper 2003).

So far, risk assessment scales only offer a range of predictors and factors based on what in the past has contributed to dangerous actions. They map the factors which, when aggregated, indicate cause for concern. However, despite increasing sophistication in the ability to devise scales and evaluate them, the variables involved and their interrelationships are very complex, so that any decision making based on them still requires a high level of professional judgement and qualitative assessment (Schon 1983; Dowie and Elstein 1988; Schaffer 1990; Lindsey 1994; Yelloly and Henkel 1995; Jones et al. 2005).

### Risk assessment revisited

Research into the effectiveness of risk assessment tools in child welfare shows the limitations of the approach because of the problem of undifferentiated data (Wald and Woolverton 1990; English and Pecora 1994; Corby 1996). A review of ten risk assessment models (Lyons, Wodarski and Doueck 1996) suggests that caution about use is needed until more evaluation is available. Gaudin et al. (1996) conclude that models for risk assessment are only developed enough to be useful in guiding the management of individual cases.

Doueck et al. (1992) and Murphy Berman (1994) identify that risk assessment procedures vary on a number of dimensions, are complex to compare against each other, and need to take account of variables such as the purpose of the assessment and the nature of the decisions to be made. Dalgleish and Drew (1989) and Dalgleish (1997, 2003) discuss how the analysis of risk is separate from the judgement about what is an acceptable degree of risk, and from subsequent decision making. Decisions should take account of the experience, expectations, motivations and history of the social worker which impacts on assessments and must be made explicit in 'aspects of the judgements and decisions made by child protection workers in uncertain and risky situations'.

Work to evaluate the usefulness of such assessment scales continues. Lescheid et al. (2003) suggest that there is still no clear evidence that such frameworks can be empirically verified. Krane and Davies (2000: 3) go further and suggest that risk assessment systems have the potential to 'entrench oppressive relations of gender, race and class in child welfare practice with mothers'. Jones et al. (2005) provide a framework for linking assessment, analysis and decisions, based on a review of the available research evidence.

### Moving to a needs-based model

The refocusing of Children's Services in England has led to an assessment system based on an ecological and developmental model (Department of Health et al. 2000; Horwath 2001; Ward and Rose 2002; Aldgate et al. 2005). The accompanying guidance collates the most recent research into the needs of children and their families (Department of Health 2000c). *The Framework for the Assessment of Children in Need and their Families* places each child at the centre of a triangle comprised of their individual developmental needs, the capacity of their parents or main carers to look after them and the family and environmental factors that may be available to support them. This approach provides a systematic way of analysing, understanding and recording what is happening to a child within the family and wider community from which professional judgements can be made.

To work with the framework, social workers require an understanding of child development, family dynamics, and the role of communities. Good communication skills are vital to communicate with families using the framework for identifying needs and planning interventions. Checklists, questionnaires and scales are all helpful mapping tools to use with service users to assess what their goals and courses of action might be might be. These can be used in an open way which enables partnership working to achieve the best outcomes (Joyce 2003).

Frameworks need to be used flexibly to avoid creating increased stress for the person assessed and adversarial relationships between them and the social worker.

They also have to be evaluated for their cultural bias and implicit moral and political judgements. As Parton has argued (1998) 'uncertainty and ambiguity' are 'pervasive' and decisions need to be 'defensible'. Factors have to be weighed against information obtained and the knowledge available in the specific context. However, social workers still need to make judgements based on conceptual links between knowledge and assessment (Howe et al. 2000). Decisions may be made on the basis of a partnership relationship with service users (co-operation, willingness to use resources, implement protective actions).

The skills of the assessor are the crucial factor. Healey (1998: 911) discusses the importance of the context of social work decision making arising from assessments and suggests that problems 'lie not in the judgement itself but rather in the lack of reflexivity in the way the judgement has been developed and applied'. Whatever assessment framework is used meanings are arrived at by social workers, service users and other professionals. To operate skilfully in these complex situations, practitioners need the basic counselling skills outlined in Chapter 2 to underpin their work.

The next practice example shows a social worker assessing the factors that impact on a young woman's anorexia in order to plan the way social services and the health services respond. There is a balance to be achieved between meeting 'need' and 'minimizing harm'. The social worker's understanding of attachment theory (Howe 2003) and the developmental stage of early adulthood informs her judgement that, if possible, Sophie's needs are best met through staying with her family. However, whenever Sophie is at home she loses weight to levels which put her health and development at severe risk. It is thought that the dynamics in the family are perhaps contributing to this. The assessment is an attempt to work with the family to find a way forward. However, there is a tension between safeguarding Sophie from harm and keeping the family intact.

### Practice example: Sophie

Sophie (13) had anorexia nervosa. The symptoms of this illness were first noticed at the age of 11. She was referred to social services because the clinician who was seeing her thought she was at risk of neglect. Her parents did not seem able to help her retain her weight gain after she was discharged from the in-patient clinic. A social work assessment was requested to ascertain what factors in the home environment might be impeding Sophie's health and development.

The social worker's assessment began with the parents to consider their capacities for care, their management of their daughter's situation and the general family relationships. A feature of Sophie's situation, already identified, was her substantial jealousy of her four-year-old sister. While the same social work assessment was taking place, Sophie was supported by individual therapy with her NHS specialist.

The initial phase of the assessment was to compile a family history. This took time and needed patience and persistence on the part of the social worker to gain information that was relevant. The parents were feeling sensitive to the potential implication of 'blame' for their child's illness, rather than seeing the assessment as an opportunity to understand past events and plan for change. Their feelings therefore needed to be understood and managed by the practitioner.

To keep the parents engaged with the process the worker chose to start with *active listening, paraphrasing, summarizing and using closed and opened questions* to check information and to explore. The practitioner felt it was important to remain open-minded and accepting despite the *challenges* from the parents. At this stage, decisions about which techniques to use affected what information was given and by whom. If the worker had interrupted too often or focused too soon she might have closed down the parent's narrative and missed important information. At the same time some focus on parenting was kept, *using summary and paraphrase* to avoid repetition and becoming stuck. This required skill and judgement alongside awareness of the potential selectivity of the process.

Once this was done, the next stage was to use *non-critical acceptance* to set the scene for greater understanding of the impact of certain relationships and behaviours on family functioning. This stance was important because if the parents had felt judged further, they would have become defensive and less open to considering options for change. As the process developed the practitioner *challenged* the couple in respect of the way they were focusing outside the family to scapegoat and blame the agencies involved for Sophie's difficulties. The worker began making *links* between some of their past experiences and behaviours, and current ways of parenting their daughters, to assist them with exploring future ways of addressing issues such as rivalry between the two children.

At this stage the practitioner's therapeutic approach to assessment 'crashed' because senior managers, at the instigation of the clinician involved, started to consider legal proceedings as a way to 'make' the family care more appropriately for Sophie. The practitioner argued against this by saying that it did not seem right to take the family to court at this stage. This view was supported by her immediate managers, but led to a loss of confidence between the clinician and the local authority. The outcome was that clinical care was arranged more locally and a less coercive approach adopted. This was maintained until finally Sophie returned to health at home and to school on a full-time basis.

The purpose of the assessment was to clarify the relevant issues and the outcome became the basis for planning with new clinicians, Sophie, the family and social services. Counselling skills such as *empathic understanding and genuineness* enabled the practitioner to maintain a working alliance with the family in the face of many challenges to its continuance. However, *challenging and confrontation* were seen as vital in asking the parents to look at family dynamics. The worker emphasized that in their future work with therapists they would need to work honestly with their issues if they were to achieve change and understanding that could benefit their daughter. She worked hard to enlist their co-operation and increase their understanding of Sophie's position in the family.

This assessment, undertaken within a legal framework, required finely tuned personal skills. Reliance on assessment procedures alone would not have enabled the social worker to build a working alliance with the family in a way that led to a less intrusive intervention to promote Sophie's optimal development and safeguard her from harm in keeping with the Children Act 1989. In this example the social worker is making use of an interviewing framework outlined by Gerard Egan and cited by Francesca Inskipp:

### Stage One

The helper develops a warm relationship which enables the client to explore 'the problem' from their own frame of reference. Together the worker and client move on to focus on specific concerns. The skills associated with this phase are:

1. Attention giving;
2. Listening;
3. Active listening;
       communicating, empathic understanding;
       non-critical acceptance;
       genuineness;
       by
       paraphrasing;
       reflecting feelings;
       summarizing;
       focusing, helping the client to be specific;

### Stage Two

Is concerned with developing new understandings. The client is helped to see themselves and their situation in a new perspective. The worker and client focus on what might help the client to cope more effectively. They consider what strengths and resources the client might use. The skills used are:

All the skills of Stage One plus:

1. Communicating deeper empathic understanding and hunches, 'hearing the music behind the words';
2. Helping the client recognize themes, inconsistencies;
3. Giving information;
4. Sharing the helper's feelings/and or experiences;

5. 'You-me talk' — what is happening between (immediacy);
6. Goal setting.

### Stage Three

Is where the client is helped to consider possible ways to act, to look at costs and consequences, to plan action, implement it and evaluate it. This is a goal setting phase and uses:
> All the skills of Stages One and Two plus:

1. Creative thinking and brainstorming;
2. Problem solving and decision making;
3. Using learning theory to plan action;
4. Evaluating.

(1986: 20)

This formulation of counselling skills into a progressive action framework is a useful one for social work practice. It provides a sufficient range of skills, if taught in detail in practice sessions, to equip practitioners for most social work interviews, with clear 'stop off' points, depending on the task or level of intervention. It can also be integrated with the use of assessment frameworks. Most social workers find themselves undertaking some supportive counselling in the course of their more complex assessments for which these skills are sufficient.

Those social workers who offer more specialized counselling require more specific knowledge and skills and more supervised practice. While a skills list looks daunting, the only way to develop the ability to use such skills reflexively and holistically is to learn what they are and take the opportunity to practice each discretely, to observe its impact on others, and to think about ways of improving. Such micro skills practice has been demonstrated to be effective (Dickson and Bamford 1995) and is core training for counsellors. As Marsh and Triseliotis (1996) show this kind of skills practice is not consistently offered within social work education.

The practitioner in the example used a social casework approach and an interviewing framework to carry out her part of the assessment of Sophie and her family. She benefited from her knowledge of human growth and development in considering Sophie's needs and the relationship issues with her sister and her parents. She also took account of the parent's defences; used the skill of immediacy to manage challenge; managed her own anxiety and the high emotions in the family. These three areas are explored further next.

## Understanding defences

A psychodynamic explanation of behaviour which can be useful is an understanding of 'defences', as this can enable social workers to avoid unproductive and heavy confrontation. Psychodynamic counsellors work from the premise that when people are upset, angry or afraid they behave defensively and become 'resistant' to change or other new ideas. In working with this behaviour, they recognize that there are reasons for this kind of reaction which can be understood, and that if understanding and acceptance are shown this enables the person to lower their defences.

Defences and resistance are seen as 'natural' ways of avoiding discomfort, anxiety and threat. Acceptance of these ideas into social work practice gives practitioners an understanding of some of the hostility and reluctance to work with them that they may meet. There is also the hope that by using some counselling skills they can lower resistance and build a more co-operative relationship, whatever the nature of the work. Jacobs (1988: 81–9) outlines the kinds of defences that might be encountered, but the most frequently seen by social workers in complex work and experienced as 'resistance' are probably:

- Denial: not accepting the reality of your own part in something difficult or painful;
- Projection: placing your own feelings on to someone else, perhaps blaming them;
- Rationalization: explaining something away.

Jacobs argues that what matters is not precise understanding of the defence that is operating, but rather the capacity to understand that the resistance you are meeting will only be lowered by using counselling skills. Sometimes acceptance is enough to enable the lowering of a defence, sometimes a gentle means of confrontation can be used which:

1. looks for the resistance/defence that is present;
2. draws attention to it;
3. suggests an explanation which:

    i.   recognizes the person's anxiety;
    ii.  if possible identifies the feeling or thought which is being resisted;
    iii. invites the person to confirm or reject the interpretation.

Alternatively, the anxiety is recognized and the person invited to suggest what feelings or thoughts are being resisted.

(Adapted from Jacobs 1998: 90)

Skill in facing people with these concerns in a constructive way can avoid both 'blocks' and hostility. Another name for such skill is 'immediacy'.

## Using immediacy

This is the skill of commenting directly on the process which is happening between the worker and the other person(s). The worker comments directly on what they observe or feel is happening. It is an advanced skill, best learned through practice and reflection. It is based on competent basic listening and responding skills and a willingness to be open and genuine, framing the words honestly in a calm way. It involves the practioner in monitoring carefully their own feelings and being prepared to practice a level of self-disclosure.

In the example of Sophie, and the one of Jenny which follows, the social workers explain clearly what is happening and identify the anxieties and difficulties the parents have. They are able to speak of their own role and the concerns that belong to it. In the next scenario (Jenny) trust was an issue and to enable the work to go ahead the worker used immediacy to say, 'I understand that it is hard for you to trust me because of your worries about social workers taking children away from their families. I can't promise that will never happen, but I would prefer to find ways of us working together to support you to bring up your children at home'. This identified the realities of the situation, did not make false promises and offered a genuine reason for the parents to co-operate with the assessment by giving them the information that they could influence the outcome.

## Managing strong feelings

In this kind of situation there are strong feelings either apparent or under the surface. The situations social workers engage with daily involve loss, distress, fear, anger, guilt and many other emotions. The role of the social worker (whatever they are feeling themselves) is to focus on the needs of the other(s). Staying calm is crucial and the ability to do so comes through acknowledging your own feelings and understanding what the work provokes within the self. Part of preparing for emotionally charged work is to identify what it may trigger in you and to explore that with someone else. This can pave the way for being able to listen while someone else offloads their upset, anger, or feelings about loss of control. Often when such feelings are discharged and received this leads to constructive work on the relevant issues. Social workers need support, supervision and consultants as needed to do this well and these are often not as available as they should be

Assessment roles with children and adults can only be undertaken by a professional who is legally competent, has empowering attitudes, and interpersonal skills in gathering information, weighing it and agreeing plans with service users and other professionals. Judgements have to be made in personal areas about parenting, and the abilities of family members to sustain and provide for each other with or without external intervention. Human development-based understandings of people together with verbal abilities, which derive from psychological counselling approaches, remain essential, as the next practice example shows.

This social worker is undertaking an assessment for the agency which is responding to concerns that Jenny is not safe with her parents, that her development is being impeded and that she is likely to be harmed or maltreated. While the assessment is about safeguarding her from harm, the empowering approach of the worker is maintained alongside her use of the authority of her role. The Department of Health recommend that at the beginning of an assessment there is a dialogue between the social worker and the parents to confirm there is a shared understanding. Parents need to be aware of processes and potential outcomes. They need to know what will happen to information they give and on what basis judgements and decisions might be made. This requires knowledge and confidence from the worker as well as skills in *clarity of communication* and *an ability to convey information with both empathy and authority*. Jenny's social worker had to use some verbal and interpersonal skills to work with the resistance and defensiveness of the adults concerned.

---

### Practice example: Jenny

An injury to Jenny, aged 3, could not be explained. The local authority was unsure what harm might come to her if she stayed in the care of her parents. She had experienced a potentially serious injury but there had been no police investigation. The immediate concern was to ensure Jenny's safety and welfare. Inevitably there were also concerns about Jenny's two younger sisters (twins aged 1).

  The social worker decided that the most empowering approach was to be frank. Using the skill of *immediacy* it was openly acknowledged that in the assessment process the parents would be asked to talk about hitherto private areas of their lives and that this might feel intrusive and difficult. This approach led to the couple sharing their feelings of fear and anxiety (*open-ended questions, ventilation of feelings*) about aspects of their current involvement with child protection agencies (the close monitoring of their physical care of their child by health visitors). This *immediacy* on the part of the worker led to a relationship which was more akin to the partnership approach promoted in the Children Act. The worker's *empathy* to feelings, even though the close monitoring had to continue (and she could make no promises about the outcome) opened up the way for an honesty about feelings and process that would enhance the future of the assessment.

  After some discussion, managers in the agency decided to accept the lack of evidence about how the injury occurred so that the social workers could move on to assessing the needs, strengths and positive factors within the family, as well as identifying problems and concerns. A plan would then be drawn up for future action. To explore the parenting capacity and abilities of the mother and father one social worker conducted individual interviews with the mother and another with the father. Meanwhile the children's development was assessed by the family centre.

  The worker with the father considered it important to be an *empathic listener to* facilitate the process. For example, when the father shared some of the difficulties he had experienced during his adolescence, the practitioner *reflected back* that this could be understood and used to consider his own parenting style. The provision of a therapeutic understanding, while remaining in the role of assessor, made the worker acutely conscious of gender dynamics and the need to resolve power issues. Each worker endeavoured to enable the parents to consider the close monitoring of physical care of the child as a way of demonstrating their abilities so that close scrutiny could later be reduced.

The key worker continued to balance the assessment of risk factors, such as the parents' personal histories and current socio-economic position, with the responsibility to protect Jenny from harm while, if possible, maintaining her in the family home. The social workers endeavoured to keep open relationships, without colluding or compromising their concerns. This involved considering the difficulties posed by:

- the mother's history of care and her history of depression and anxiety;
- the father's use of alcohol from time to time;
- the stress caused by financial hardship;
- the presence of some arguments and violence between the parents;
- the pressures of professional surveillance;
- the presence of two younger children pressuring the mother's time;
- the isolation of the family within the community;
- the developmental stages of all three children, which the parents found challenging.

Practical measures, obtaining grants for furniture and day nursery places for the two younger children, were offered alongside personal support for the parents. The impact of identified risk factors on current parenting within the family was considered. The decision was taken to maintain Jenny at home with support and continued monitoring. The role of assessor gave the workers considerable power both to intervene in a supportive way and also to take action to remove Jenny if needed. The practitioner concluded:

> The dilemmas faced whilst working with this family illustrate the difficulty workers can experience in attempting to rationalize the use of power within an approach which aspires to partnership with parents.

All social workers have to make sure that children and adults are safe and protected from potential harm as far as they can. However, it is possible to use counselling skills to facilitate the process without compromising role or authority. These workers used their abilities to build a partnership approach which helped to assess the child's safety and work with the adults on their parenting abilities. This is made easier by using an assessment framework based on an ecological and strengths approach, providing the social workers remained alert to any factors which suggested they needed to take immediate action to safeguard from harm.

### Assessment in services for adults

The NHS and Community Care Act (1990) resulted in a major shift of emphasis in services for vulnerable adults. The practice guidelines set out for the first time a model consistent with social work processes of the collation, collection and analysis of information. The guidelines made clear that the emphasis was on needs-led assessment, not fitting people to services. Guidance from government said that Local Authorities had a duty to 'assess people's needs holistically in relation to a wide range of possible service options, rather than having separate service-led assessments' (Department of Health 1991a). The assessment principles specified in the practitioner's guide were to: 'negotiate the scope of assessment; choose the setting; clarify expectations; promote participation; establish a relationship of trust; assess need; determine eligibility; set priorities; agree objectives; record the assessment' (Department of Health 1991b). The implementation of this has produced some tensions and contradictions for practitioners.

**The debate about need** There has been continuous debate about what is needs-led. For example, is need disadvantage or the right to a minimum level of provision? (Doyal and Gough 1991). Alternatively, need has been understood to encompass all the dimensions in Bradshaw's taxonomy (1972): normative needs; felt needs; expressed needs; comparative needs. The literature is pre-occupied with questions such as: what is need and who defines it? To what extent is the system needs-led? It is also suggested that unmet needs are seldom well collated and that the link between population needs and individual needs is not well documented (Percy-Smith 1996).

**Differential approaches to assessment** Differential approaches to assessment have been taken by various stakeholders. Managers identify assessment as an important area of practice that should lead to more effective use of limited resources. Practitioners may see assessment as a way of responding to expressed need. Service users and carers may be unclear about the function of assessment and will have their own expectations. There is some confusion around the concept that assessments should match needs and resources, while not being led by existing resource provision. Concern is expressed that assessment becomes a tool for rationing (Powell and Goddard 1996). However as Parker and Bradley (2003: 28) emphasize, the legal duty is to assess where 'there is an appearance of need' which is 'not the same as assessment on request'.

**Centrally or locally defined models?** In the absence of centrally determined models that specify needs in relation to particular policy areas and set out optimum or minimum standards of provision, equity between geographical areas is difficult to achieve (Percy-Smith 1996: 64). Although some local authorities took the view 'that there was no substitute for authorities devising solutions in the light of their own particular circumstances and experiences' and that 'recognizing the need to develop local approaches was very important' (Beardshaw 1991) a balance had to be sought between central policy directives and local autonomy.

### Single assessment

The boundary between social care and health care remained contentious (Browne 1996) with implications for the effectiveness of interdisciplinary work. The identification of the involvement of different disciplines has not necessarily lead to an integrated service. Thus the social worker undertaking an assessment has had to consider the relationships between legal framework, procedural guidelines, eligibility criteria, local resources and social work approaches to helping. To address this, the NHS plan (Department of Health 2000d) and the National Service Framework for older people (Department of Health 2001c) propose the development of a Single Assessment Process (SAP) to be implemented by 2004. The aim is to make sure that older people obtain an assessment appropriate to their level of need, but which avoids the duplication of assessment by different professionals. This new assessment culture for older people is summarized below from Parker and Bradley (2003: 29–30):

1. Local agencies are to agree the outcome and purpose of SAP by consulting widely and focusing on potential benefits such as minimizing duplication of effort amongst a range of professionals and reducing paperwork by providing a single assessment summary — the collecting and sharing of information to be based on the informed consent of the older person.
2. Agree shared values between agencies [. . .]
3. Agencies to agree terminology and reach a common language [. . .]
4. Map the care processes [. . .]
5. Agencies to estimate the types and numbers of people needing assessment.
6. Agencies to agree the stages of assessment (for proposed details see Parker and Bradley 2003: 30).
7. Agree the link between medical diagnosis and assessment.
8. Agree the domains and sub domains of assessment [. . .]
9. Agree common assessment approaches, tools and scales [. . .]
10. Agree joint working arrangements [. . .]
11. Agree a single assessment summary [. . .]
12. Implement a joint staff development strategy.

This is intended to simplify and improve health and social care assessments for older people. However, some areas will be at the very beginning of the processes of learning to communicate and work together, others will be able to move to single assessments more easily. It will take time and resources to implement fully. However, many believe that the cultural change will have a positive impact on practice and lead to a more person-centred process (Hunter 2003: 30, 31).

### Counselling skills and assessment in services for adults

Whatever the frameworks, social workers can use counselling skills to listen carefully to service users and verbal skills to advocate the most apt service. It may be argued that service-led provision is both costly and time consuming. However, if people are carefully informed about possibilities they will not be found to be abandoning services they agreed to because they felt unable to say no or felt pressured into accepting. If hasty plans are made as a result of failure to interview carefully the time taken up by complaints, renegotiation and wastage will be more expensive than the extra time taken to listen carefully and provide a needs-led response in the first place.

Social workers in adult services say that they can use their interpersonal skills effectively to balance the needs and resources equation which the government policy has created for local authorities. They also meet families in times of crisis in their lives, which means counselling skills are often needed to facilitate the work. However good the guidelines for practice, human situations are often more complicated than guidance can outline. This means practitioners must take a flexible and holistic approach. The narrative which follows comes from an experienced practitioner who works with older people and carers.

### Practice example: Joan

We cannot divorce people and their significant relationships from the task in hand. They are interrelated. A tangled relationship will very often impede the way to a useful outcome to an assessment. A healthy relationship will more often than not facilitate the process. In all work I found myself using some counselling skills. With some relationships the use of a wide range of counselling skills was needed to facilitate the moving forward of the assessment.

There were occasions, when I would start the assessment with a carer to begin to gather facts, when the carer's experience of stress, loss, frustration and anger would overwhelm them. At this point I would set down the fact finding task and give time, using *counselling skills* to allow *expression of feeling* and offloading. I would very often find that in validating the experience in this way some trust was built and the task of assessment could proceed (*ventilation of feelings, acceptance, attentive listening, minimal prompts, clarifying, removing blocks, understanding defences, and reactions to loss*).

I would offer carers a separate interview. Sometimes people would take this up with the specific purpose of exploring their role as carers. This was very often a kind of counselling session, and change would come about as a result of it. For example by the end of these meetings one person decided to stop responding to the 'games' she felt were being played by the service user and decided that she would learn to say no sometimes, to release herself from twenty-four-hour caring, and to look after herself more.

This narrative is a reminder that social workers who undertake assessments with older people and those with disabilities or illness need the skills of listening and attending to the grief and other psychological reactions of people to loss, death, dying, dementia, separation from partners and children. People need understanding of the worries which accompany the onset of dependency on others or becoming a carer.

Henderson and Forbat (2003) add another perspective by describing how relationships are central to informal care. They argue that it matters to recognize the interpersonal dynamics in caring relationships. Those cared for are 'active' in their relationships with their carer and Henderson and Forbat say they found a 'resistance to the polarization of carer and cared for'. The emotional aspect of caring relationships and the existence of the people's other roles, such as partner or daughter, is something that professionals sometimes fail to recognize.

## Counselling skills and compulsion

Practitioners have questioned the relevance of social work approaches to situations where the assessment role has a strong element of compulsion (in courts, prisons, secure and psychiatric units). They might ask, 'Is it still social work? Does a social work approach to interviewing still apply?' It can be argued that there is nothing different except a shift in focus. Protection and control are integral to all social work and not exclusive to particular agencies. Child protection workers and approved mental health social workers also grapple with these issues. However, for social workers employed in criminal justice settings it may be that the explicit element of punishment sits less comfortably with a social work ethos. It may be more a matter of authority being made explicit rather than masked. It could be argued that this clarity is helpful in enabling the worker to be fully open about their authority and power.

Some assessments for courts have to take into account: motivation and contributory factors to antisocial behaviours; the type and level of risk posed; motivation and capacity to change; suitability for particular approaches and interventions. Assessment interviews then need to be highly focused, and require the challenging and testing of someone's beliefs and attitudes. They incorporate a high level of motivational interviewing (Rollnick 1996).

None of this however indicates a shift of technique but rather one of purpose. *Listening, reflecting, open and focusing questions, confronting, summarizing, exploring options* remain relevant tools for practice. Nor does it necessarily present a fundamental shift from a humanistic/holistic approach. For example, a wide view of an offender's situation is needed to help establish what are the significant elements in their offending and how best to address them. The *'what works'* paradigm recognizes that there are many layers to offending. It does not preclude meeting criminological and social welfare needs, it is rather a means of targeting scarce resources to specific interventions, and then working in partnerships and through community resources to meet these other layers of need (McGuire 1995).

Victim perspective and risk management are about emphasizing the offender's social responsibilities. To enable the offender to take this on board the worker needs to offer more than simplistic information, but instead should provide a space for *reflective process* and *challenge*, which enable the offender to develop awareness and motivation to change. *Confrontation* and *challenge* are key skills in this work.

Can counselling skills be used in the service of punishment? This may seem a difficult area, but the focus on this dimension in criminal justice settings highlights the ethical dimensions of the uses of any skill or technique. It is vital to be open and explicit about the framework of statutory requirements and responsibility in which the interviewing takes place. Empowerment is not impossible, it is a matter of being clear about boundaries, accountabilities, the scope and limitation of choice and options. It is possible to take account of disadvantage and discrimination when seeking explanations for people's offending behaviour while working to engage them in reducing it in future. Counselling skills can be part of this (Williams 1996).

Practitioners endeavour to use their skills to help their clients and to meet agency requirements. In this example a practitioner is able to demonstrate the use of counselling skills in a criminal justice setting. First the client is assessed and then a programme of work is planned and undertaken.

---

### Practice example: Jeff

Jeff was to be sentenced for an offence of taking and driving away a car. The initial interview for the court report used *listening skills* and *focused questions* to obtain precise and accurate information. The worker assessed Jeff's awareness of his actions and his motivation to change. She used *open and closed questions* and *challenging* to test his view of the offence. As an outcome, and in line with procedural guidelines, she was able to recommend a community sentence. A programme of work was planned for Jeff, together with his co-defendant Rob, with the objective of reducing the risk to the public of them repeating the offending. A cognitive approach was chosen because research demonstrates that this can produce motivational, attitudinal and behavioural change in offenders. The first session of work was planned with a series of *progressive questions* designed to approach specific aspects of the offending behaviour where change was sought. This was intended as a *focusing* method with the *responses* to each question *reflected back* and *clarified* before the next one was asked. *Summaries* were to be used to draw the participants into examining their attitudes, behaviours and the impact their car theft had on others. The worker planned to expect an amount of *silence*. Previous experience in a counselling context had demonstrated to her how this enables clients to collect their thoughts and/or contemplate new ideas and information. The practitioner trusted the idea that *allowing spaces and pauses* was a useful part of her repertoire of skills for asking offenders to consider their actions, motivations and the impact these had on others. Thus an intensive short programme of work used counselling skills to underpin a focused and cognitive approach to *challenging* the clients to change and plan a different future lifestyle.

### Preparation for assessment

Social work is a profession which requires an active approach to communicating, often in urgent situations and with difficult issues. Wherever possible careful preparation is needed before meetings or interviews take place. First this is best practice; second when there is time, good preparation builds the skills for the times that a practitioner has to respond quickly. The experience of more prepared work will inform the social worker's actions. While undertaking qualifying training, practitioners will have considered their values, knowledge and skills and how they relate to working with individuals, families, carers, groups and communities. This should have included work to examine the practitioner's self awareness, prejudices and motivations for being a 'helper'.

Each piece of work needs specific preparation as the practitioner brings themselves to the meeting with each individual 'other' and their situation. Practitioners must be clear about the reason for the contact, the legal context, the information they need and why, the range of possible resources, the way they will carry out their task, how the person's views will be ascertained and how decisions will be recorded afterwards.

Preparation also involves checking in advance wherever possible that communication can take place effectively. If the service user is an adult are they able to get to the office? Is it accessible to them? Does the service user have a specific impairment that means assistance will be needed? What is the person's first language and is an interpreter needed? Language barriers can cause disadvantage. Chand (2000) writing about black families draws attention to sensitivity and confidentiality issues and the need for skilled interpretation. The interpreter must have linguistic skills for the complex concepts that social work agencies handle. Chand suggests that interpreters should be offered specialist training by local authorities and social workers should be trained as to how the presence of an interpreter affects the dynamics of the meeting. Interpreters should be taken to assessment meetings with all black families, where there are doubts about the family's abilities to speak English, even if they have to wait outside (in case they are needed) or not used (2000: 75). Similarly black elders can be disadvantaged by lack of detailed attention to linguistic communication and relevant interpreters should be found.

## Key points

- Assessment and planning in all social work practice requires practitioners who are able to use their interpersonal skills in complex and sensitive work.
- Assessment frameworks alone are tools to collect information. They cannot balance, weigh risk and formulate plans.
- Professional judgement based on knowledge and skill is required in at least equal measure to well researched assessment tools.
- Assessment tasks require a reflective practitioner whose personal skills include the ability to engage with users to assess their motivation and capacity to change.
- An understanding of defensiveness, blocks and resistance, and the ability to enable users to abandon such strategies and engage openly in task is helpful.
- Advanced counselling skills are valuable to make assessment more person-centred.
- Counselling skills can underpin assessments in situations where the element of compulsion is strong.

## Questions and activities: for self development or discussion groups

1 Think of a time when you were assessed (for example an exam, driving test, or an assessment in a health or care setting). What was it like? How did you feel? What would have helped it to be better? What kind of skills and qualities did you look for in the assessor?

2 Choose one of the practice examples in this chapter and imagine that you are one of the service users. What skills and qualities would you have wanted the assessor to have?

3 Think of a time when communication between yourself and someone at work was blocked. What was contributing to the impasse (for example, strong feelings; defensiveness)? What could have been done to open the channels of communication?

# Chapter 4

## Planning, acting and providing a service: relevant counselling skills

Chapter 3 discussed assessment and the associated counselling skills and this chapter explores the way that counselling skills continue to be valuable, as social workers meet with service users, to plan actions and interventions to meet needs. Like assessments, actions and plans are subject to review in dialogue with the service user(s) and others involved. Also at fixed points formal reviews take place and are recorded by the practitioner(s), service user(s) and people from partner agencies (Everitt and Hardiker 1996). The aims of all actions should be to 'enhance the wellbeing' of the service user(s) as far as this is compatible with the safety and wellbeing of others. The aim of reviews is to check how actions are contributing to this and to modify them if necessary. A further evaluation of the whole process follows: usually when the work is complete.

All social work actions have boundaries in time and place, but while some practitioners intervene very briefly others are involved in long term situations. Some care for people on a day-by-day basis, perhaps in groups; some work in response to a crisis and others work in response to chronic and continuous need. The Academic Standards for Social Work set out the knowledge that social workers need to start working with service users (Topps 2003c: 3.1.1) and outline the conceptual boundaries within which social workers will 'plan carry out review and evaluate social work practice with individuals, families carers, groups and communities and other professionals' (Key Role 2, Standard 2 Scotland).

Social workers are expected to understand people in the context of their environments and discuss any planned actions with them. The 'do-gooder', 'interfering' image of social work which some people hold is based on fears and concerns about some highly publicized interventions, often where the legal powers of social workers have been used or withheld with perceived adverse outcomes. Actions should be capable of scrutiny and evaluation, and be underpinned by ethical principles, as described in the academic standards:

- recognize and work with the powerful links between intra-personal and

inter-personal factors and the wider, social, legal, economic, political and cultural context of people's lives;

- understand the impact of injustice, social inequalities and oppressive social
relations;
- challenge constructively individual, institutional and structural discrimination;
- practise in ways that maximize safety and effectiveness in situations of
uncertainty and incomplete information;
- help people to gain, regain or maintain control of their own affairs, insofar as
this is compatible with their own or others' safety, wellbeing and rights.

(2003: 2, 4)

Social workers offer or commission services in kind. This providing aspect of social
work intervention derives from its philanthropic origins, and the close link
between statutory functions and welfare provision in legislation and policy. A
group of social workers, asked to draw up a list of actions they might take, provided
a response which included:

- ***Methods***: assessment, care management, advocacy, counselling, advice giving,
groupwork;
- ***Tasks***: court reports, benefits advice, hostel work, liaison work, legal action,
supervision of court orders, referral;
- ***Service provision***: placement provision (in residential homes, day-care,
foster care, respite care), childcare provision, day nursery places, advice about
childminding, education packages.

This list is not exhaustive, but shows how social work intervention is wide ranging.
In some settings the emphasis is on commissioning services. Workers have to
become skilled in handling this powerful role and acknowledge that one task is to
ensure that the most suitable people receive the scarce resources available. They
also intervene directly using counselling and interpersonal skills together with
problem-solving methods. In summary, social work actions include:

- the use of social work theories and methods to plan interventions to achieve
change;
- the use of the practitioner's personal skills in intervention;
- referral to provider agencies;
- purchase of services from provider agencies;
- direct provision in cash or kind;
- advocacy to obtain services from another agency.

Often these elements are combined and counselling skills can be integrated with
theory and methods to achieve change. The practitioner's counselling skills are
significant in influencing the way services are offered, and so make a fundamental
difference to the way actions are experienced and evaluated by service users. Therefore, having set the context for actions, this chapter now considers the use of

counselling skills in relation to theories, methods and the use of self in carrying out social work tasks.

## Starting with yourself

Everyone has some communication and interpersonal skills learned in the family and community where they grew up. Skills for communicating and relating are inbuilt capacities in everyone but the way in which each individual communicates is shaped by experiences, learning, choices made and cultural environments. People develop throughout childhood and continue to learn throughout their adult lives, so communicating and relating skills can be developed and refined.

Rutter and Hay (1996) show how children learn their styles of communicating, ways of relating to others, cultural and social behaviours from their earliest and subsequent carers. This happens naturally as children discover what is effective and what is considered acceptable within the bounds of their families and their wider social and cultural experiences. Social workers begin their careers with their own unique ways of talking and relating. However, as professional practitioners they become accountable for their work and their interpersonal interactions in new ways. They learn and use theories and methods for practice which they need to be able to make explicit and communicate to others. They also have to be able to explain the reasons for their actions and the way they carried them out to those to whom they are accountable.

## Social work theories for action

All social work activity is underpinned by theory:

> to practice without theory is to sail an uncharted sea; theory without practice is not to sail at all.
>
> > (Susser quoted in Hardiker and Barker 1991: 87)

Theoretical approaches are derived from a knowledge base which is multi faceted. Hardiker and Barker (1991: 87) suggest that social work:

> requires a breadth of discipline knowledge (e.g. law, psychiatry and philosophy). Furthermore, social workers need to be sufficiently familiar with them to make informed choices, keep up to date with advances and to discard redundant theories.

Some of the underpinning psychological theories for intervention in social work practice are considered next together with some derivative methods, showing how the application of counselling skills can underpin interventions using a range of theories and methods.

### An eclectic approach to theory

To fulfil their tasks, social workers have drawn from other disciplines including sociology (to understand the social construction of problems in society), psychology (to understand individual and group functioning) and social policy (to understand the structural factors which affect individuals). It can be argued that social work has been unnecessarily apologetic about this, because the strength of social work's eclectic history has made for versatile response to the requirement to operate in diverse legal and bureaucratic frameworks. The advantages of the thoughtful eclectic approach are:

- the merging of theories for the benefit of the service user, thus meeting individual need;
- avoidance of the narrow dogmatism which can accompany a single theory approach;
- the ability to be flexible and adapt to changing social policy and social conditions;
- the ability to work with other professionals from overlapping theory bases.

No new grand theories have emerged to underpin social work practice but the known theories have been developed through practice as they are used in new contexts for practice. Those approaches which are commonly recognized in core texts (Howe 1987; Compton and Galaway 1989; Coulshed 1991; Lishman 1991 and forthcoming; Payne, 1992; Trevithick 2000) have been subjected to new evaluations as social attitudes, values and beliefs change. They have been examined in particular for usefulness in relation to changes in the legislation and policy which guide practice (Adams et al. 2002). Social workers have proved resilient in adapting their tried methods to new legislative expectations (Hardiker and Barker 1994 and 1996; Marsh and Triseliotis 1996; Seden 2001).

### Three key approaches

Having set the context for an eclectic approach to theory, there are some key psychological theories that deserve closer attention.

#### Psychodynamic theory

Psychodynamic practice was integrated into social work in Britain from America and became established in the 1950s, 60s and 70s (Brearley 1991). The ideas about how personality is formed and developed derive from Freudian psychoanalysis. Social work uses psychodynamic insights for: ways of understanding relationships, such as self and significant others; the link between past and present; and inner and outer experience. It is sometimes wrongly confused with the psychosocial approach. The psychosocial model derives concepts from psychodynamic theory and ego psychology, but combines the personal, social and practical into a more holistic framework (social casework). A narrow psychodynamic approach as practised in some counselling settings only considers the external world from the client's view. It is only rarely that such a narrow psychodynamic approach is used by social workers, but it has been highly influential in providing them with ways of understanding people. Furthermore, the important idea of the use of the relationship as an agent of change, which permeates social work practice, is essentially a psychodynamic one.

Psychodynamic ideas are particularly relevant in social work because of their influence in studies of human development (Fairbairn 1952; Erikson 1965; Winnicott 1986; Bowlby 1988; Rutter et al. 1994; Jacobs 1998; Aldgate et al. 2005). The place of psychodynamic thinking in social work is explored in a number of texts (Yelloly 1980; Pearson et al. 1988; Brearley 1991; Trevithick 2000; Lishman 1991 and forthcoming). At a very fundamental level it underpins both past and current research and practice in relation to children, families, older people and mental health. Psychodynamic ideas have also been applied in the literature on professional supervision (Kadushin 1995; Hawkins and Shohet 2000).

There is a particular facet of psychodynamic theory, the unconscious, which many practitioners find relevant when thinking about the use of themselves in transactions with others (Bird 1997). A psychodynamic approach to understanding people takes account of the significance of unconscious thoughts, perceptions and feelings. These may be met negatively as hostility, resistance and defensiveness, or positively as expectation and attachment, as significant feelings from the past appear in current relationships and situations. The technical term for this is 'transference'. If this relationship develops from the worker to the service user this is known as 'counter-transference'. This unconscious repetition of earlier experience into a current relationship is viewed as useful to the therapeutic work in psychodynamic counselling. It is a 'way of seeing old relationships come to life in the present' and might be a 'vital clue to insight and to reworking what has gone wrong in the past' (Jacobs 1988: 94–111, 1999).

While social workers would not enter into a psychotherapeutic relationship with people they work with, Kovel (1976) has argued that transference can occur in any relationship where a difference in power is involved. This is because situations of becoming dependent or relating to authority may awaken long buried feelings. Understanding transference offers a way to analyse the way people in relationships unconsciously withhold, give or demand power from one another. Cairns (1994) and Rogers (1992) give very accessible accounts of transference process in counselling and everyday relationships. What matters for social workers is to understand that:

- transference is an unconscious psychological process which can occur in everyday as well as therapeutic relationships (e.g. feeling over anxious at your child's school parent's evening, because of your own school experience);
- transference is often present when relationships involve unequal power;

- transference is occurring when someone treats another person *as if* they were a significant figure from the past and behave towards them *as if* they were that person;
- transference produces feelings which are stronger than might be expected for the nature of the relationship;
- counter-transference is the name for transference from a social worker to a service user and may distort the way the practitioner relates to them;
- there is a form of transference where a practitioner internalizes the feelings of another (feels frightened, depressed, anxious after being with someone).

The ability to work with transference relationships is at the heart of psychodynamic counselling and requires training and regular supervision to explore the processes involved. Social workers and other professionals can find this theory provides an understanding of complex and sometimes difficult work, although they should never make clumsy interpretations about the behaviour of others, or use their power as social workers to make judgements on the basis of untested feelings. However, an understanding that transference might be present could lead them to:

- be aware of the transference elements in the relationship, recognize the extent to which this is distorting interactions and manage this while maintaining a focus on what is immediate, accessible and most relevant to the social work task;
- learn about the way the person relates to others, or understand the fear or depression of someone who is vulnerable to abuse. Such understanding can inform actions to protect or monitor and needs to be discussed with a manager or supervisor. For example, social workers who visit children and leave frightened by the adults (even if there was no overt hostility) or visit an older person and leave feeling worried or depressed (although the care seemed alright on the surface) need to reflect on the relationship of their own feelings to the vulnerability and possible unexpressed feelings of their service user, and use it to carefully check out what might be happening;
- understand that the hostility or resistance that is impeding the working relationship (especially in long term work) may belong to old experiences impacting on the present, then tentatively use immediacy to draw attention to what is happening, always phrasing it in a way that invites the view and perspective of the other;
- consider whether more therapeutically skilled intervention should be available.

At the very least, it is likely that as a new professional in a situation you might inherit expectations and attitudes towards you that are based on the person's previous experiences or stereotypes of other helpers and social workers.

*Learning theory*

Behavioural social work, behavioural therapy and behaviour modification derive from learning theory. Learning theories form a body of knowledge about how behaviour changes as a result of experience and how behaviour is learned, maintained and unlearned (Hudson 1991: 123). It is based on scientific experiment and is modified on the basis of new findings. It originated from classical experiments on animals, for example the work by Pavlov and Skinner, and work with children by Watson and Rayner. Behavioural social work begins with an assessment to establish a base line from which to plan goals for change. Behaviours are analysed and social learning methods are used as the tools for intervention. Evaluation of outcome is made against the initial base line.

There are full discussions in several texts (Sheldon 1982, 1995; Hudson and MacDonald 1986; Howe 1987; Coulshed 1991; Parker and Randall 1997; Payne 1997). Hudson and MacDonald (1986) outline a range of possible applications, including: anger control and child management with parents who abuse; helping foster carers manage children's behaviour; work with adults in day centres and social skills training. Behavioural interventions are undertaken in psychiatric units to address obsessional behaviours and other issues of personal functioning. In the 1970s and 80s social learning theorists, particularly Argyle (1969; 1988; 1991) built an understanding of how social skills develop and can be modified through learning new behaviours.

Brechin and Seden (2004) suggest that a behavioural approach to learning skills is useful for health and social care practitioners. In order to build on a natural propensity to learn, adults can remain open to noticing their own and others' skills and be prepared to find new ways of doing things, by learning from what is observed. Emergent skills will depend on learning by noting and reflecting on what seems to work well between people in all kinds of settings, cultures and walks of life. The next example shows how even in a brief moment of intervention, the skills of the care worker mean it is carried out in a way which enhances the service user's wellbeing and that of those who observe what is happening.

---

**Practice example: Janice and a 'moment in time'**

It is time for a cup of tea in the lounge of a residential care home for people with dementia. About twelve people share this part of the home and six are in the lounge at this moment. Janice is sleeping on an armchair and wakes to hear her neighbour being offered a cup of tea.

'Cup of tea for you, Dora?'

'Where's my tea, then? Why am I not getting any tea?' Janice demands. Janice angers quickly and seems to see the world as set against her. Her instant response is angry and complaining and is very characteristic. I look round (visiting my father at the other side of the room) feeling for the staff and feeling in myself the slightly irritated desire to rebuke her for her petulance. 'Here is your tea,

Janice,' I instinctively want to say. 'Why do you think we would have forgotten you? You were asleep!'

Instead the male volunteer carer, Jim, who is nearest to her, responds with delight to her waking. 'Hello, Janice,' he says warmly. 'Have you woken up now?' He crouches down by her chair, smiling at her.

'Hello', she says. 'Have you had a nice sleep? How are you feeling?' All said warmly with a smile of greeting and relaxed eye-contact.

'Hello' — she smiles and reaches out towards him — 'Give us a kiss!'

She kisses his cheek — once and then again. 'Ooh you're nice' and she laughs in delight.

'Would you like a cup of tea, Janice?'

'Ooh, yes please.'

(Source: Ann Brechin, The Open University, Communication and Relationships in Health and Social Care).

Observing such ordinary or special 'moments in time' helps to mark out what is a skilful communication within social work actions; in this case in group care. The way interventions are carried through can be skilful, helpful and facilitative, or conversely, negative and disempowering, or a mixture. Practice placements provide beginning social workers with many opportunities to both observe and practice such skills. Many such behaviours and 'moments in time' are public and observable and the response of the service user will show what is effective. A behavioural approach would suggest that good processes can be observed and learned, through training in practice. Opportunities such as this one can be noted, reflected on and the good practice points learned and integrated into future work.

### Eco-systems theory

The ecological perspective is well-established in the social sciences (Siporin 1975; Maluccio 1981; Garbarino 1982). It has emerged as the most comprehensive unifying framework, drawing from ethology, ecological psychology and ethnology. Ecological frameworks are based on a cluster of key ideas:

- the person-environment relationship is continuous;
- person, behaviour and environment are mutually inter-dependent;
- systems theory is useful to analyse the ecology of the person if the situation behaviour is site specific;
- assessment and evaluation are through direct observation of the person-environment system;
- behaviour is the outcome of transactions between the person and the environment;

- behavioural science should seek to understand and analyse these interactions.
(Allen-Meares and Lane 1987).

The ecological approach takes a holistic view of the person in their environment and has the capacity for embracing other approaches (Seden 2005). Actions therefore give equal emphasis to person and environment. A systems approach reminds the practitioner that several areas of influence may need to be understood in relation to a person's situation. Actions are planned on the understanding that intervention in one area of a person's life can impact on other areas. Considering the consequences of change using an ecological framework produces a more all round picture of possible outcomes.

These three key approaches coupled with service provision and advocacy are frequently used by social workers. However, all three approaches rely heavily on the ability of the practitioner to make them operative through the use of interpersonal skills. Further, if an empowerment ideology is to underpin practice, the practitioner must be able to communicate their theoretical understandings to the person with whom they are working and achieve meaningful consent to plans.

The next example shows the value of counselling skills combined with other ways of helping. These are giving advice, providing information, direct action; teaching, and systems change. There are psychodynamic, behavioural and ecological understandings informing the work. Formal counselling proved to be an important part of the contact with this family, though the use of counselling skills underpinned all the strategies used.

### Practice example: David

David (21) lived at home with his parents. He had no specific diagnosed impairment but attended a school for children with moderate learning difficulties until 16, then transferring to an establishment for people with severe learning difficulties. It was not apparent that he had a disability until he did not learn to speak. Subsequently, his behaviour became hard to manage and his mother found it difficult to cope. She felt intensely attached to him and this seemed allied to a hope that he did not have a disability. Little help was forthcoming, either in practical terms or counselling until he was 16, when he was excluded from a special needs further education course.

The family was not receiving welfare benefits to which they were entitled. David's mother Pat felt she had no right to such benefits, which was partly due to the years she had coped unaided. However, a successful claim opened her up to accepting the extent of her son's special needs and vindicated her right to help. Information on services, behaviour management, and parent groups was vital in breaking down isolation and helped prioritize family needs. For example, the immediate problem was the absence of suitable daytime activities for David. A range of options were looked at and a further school placement identified. Pat continued to be very anxious, but over time this diminished as she began to trust the people working with David. A cognitive approach was useful here, which addressed and validated the feelings and experiences she had. For example, the worker acknowledged that the way teachers had treated David in the past was unhelpful but enabled Pat to think that it could be different in future.

The setting up of a local parents and carers group introduced Pat to other people coping in similar circumstances, enabling her to share her feelings and concerns. This group could be seen in terms of systems change as it recognized that many people in the locality were undergoing similar pressures which could be addressed in a group setting. Members themselves chose to use the group as a social support system rather than a campaigning body, and this choice was important. More formal counselling was introduced quite late in the social work with David's family. Pat had identified that David was now more settled, the pressures on her had eased, and the family had access to adequate support systems. However, she was diagnosed with nervous asthma and sometimes felt anxious and depressed. Her mother, with whom she had a difficult and strained relationship died. Individual counselling might help to get to the root of her anxiety. A psychodynamic approach enabled her to examine her childhood, marriage and life since David had been born. She described the process as like opening a secret and frightening box and then being able to sort through it, keeping or discarding whatever she wanted. A particular issue was guilt about a brief extra marital affair she had many years ago. A more cognitive approach enabled Pat to absolve herself of the gnawing guilt when the affair was placed in the context of her lonely struggle to parent a child she loved but with whom it was so difficult to cope. After only three sessions, Pat's asthma was much improved and she had a more balanced overall perspective on her life.

Much work was achieved in a short time because the social worker and Pat were well acquainted and trust was established. The social worker's experience in the field of learning difficulties had shown her that formal counselling had a useful role to play, but only alongside adequate practical support systems. The use of counselling skills such as *giving undivided time, listening attentively, being non-judgemental, warm and accepting* are paramount at all stages of working with parents with a son or daughter with learning difficulties, from the initial assessment through to leaving home and afterwards. Regular support to alleviate isolation needs to be coupled with practical assistance, specialist knowledge of the child's condition, contact with other people in similar situations, coordination with other agencies such as health and education and planning for the future. Although not every family needs help all the time, it helps if easy access to a known, skilled, professional helper is there when needed. Parents benefit from routine support and the prevention of crisis rather than response to crisis alone.

The social worker commented on the usefulness of combining a psychodynamic understanding and brief counselling support with practical assistance:

Neither one nor the other is particularly useful in isolation, but both types of approach, offered to parents from earliest stage possible, can enable families to help their learning disabled children to develop in a more rounded, healthy and positive way to achieve more of their potential.

The social worker used a combination of approaches with another parent, where issues around separation affected both parent and child.

**Practice example: Jane**

Jane, a single parent, with an eight-year-old boy who had severe learning difficulties and behavioural problems, had not had an unbroken night of sleep since his birth. A behavioural programme was set up to manage Alexander's bed time routine. After a successful start this stuck as he would go to bed, stay there and go to sleep, but only as long as his mother was still in the room with him. Jane seemed unable to take the next step and sit outside the room. By talking about and, working on, her feelings towards him she was able to see him less as a vulnerable, dependent baby and more as a growing child who could become more independent from her. Following this change of perspective Alexander coped better with going to sleep alone. Shortly after this, Jane moved out of her parents' home for the first time (she was in her 30s). This indicated the resolution of some issues about her separation from her own parents, though this was not addressed directly in the counselling.

These accounts show how psychodynamic and cognitive behavioural understandings informed the actions taken and were used to provide services which were empowering and in line with legislative thinking. The worker's continued attention to the wider environment shows that an integrated theoretical approach can be mobilized in the interests of families.

### Social work methods

Social work methods drawn from the main theories are considered next. Both these methods require underpinning counselling skills to make them effective. Life events, transition, change and crisis are part of the everyday experiences of the people social workers meet. Understanding theories of attachment, loss and transition are therefore essential parts of the knowledge base of practitioners (Seden and Katz 2003; Skye et al. 2003). Crisis intervention which is now discussed, provides a framework for action and planning.

### Crisis intervention

Crisis intervention is based on psychodynamic theory and arose from work to provide a focused, brief form of psychotherapy. The 'brief therapy' concept adds a cognitive element and matched social workers' aspirations to focus their own work more precisely. It was adopted in social work literature in the 60s and has remained relevant (Caplan 1964; Pittman 1966; Golan 1981; O'Hagan 1986; Roberts 1991, 1995). People who seek social work attention are often in a state of distress. Caplan (1964) describes this 'crisis' as a temporary period of upset and disequilibrium, sometimes provoked by a transition or a traumatic event, where the person's usual abilities to manage are temporarily immobilized. It is the person's perception of events which defines crisis. Writers such as Golan (1981) and Roberts and Nee (1971) describe a crisis as having identifiable phases:

- the precipitating event and perception;
- the upset;
- inability to use previously tried coping methods and disequilibrium;
- the potential for hope;
- the intervention which links current difficulties to past coping strategies;
- resolution or homeostasis restored within a few weeks (4–6).

This framework for acting on a developmental understanding of human responses to loss and change has been helpful to social workers. The next example shows a worker undertaking crisis intervention using counselling skills to facilitate her approach. The setting is a children and families team, but a major focus of the work is the mental health of the adult carer for the children. The worker felt strongly that it was the supportive relationship built on counselling skills that made progress possible in spite of the monitoring role that was her legal duty. The improvements for the mother and children were a positive outcome, showing the possibilities of acting in a decisive and authoritative way to meet legal duties while still offering support. The social worker's understanding of the temporary nature of crisis and her counselling abilities contributed to the progress achieved.

### Practice example: Penny

Penny (43) had three children 11, 9 and 5. Her husband died from cancer when the youngest was 1. Since then she had suffered from episodes of severe mental ill health which from time to time resulted in self harm. A crisis occurred when Penny threatened to take an overdose and 'take them with me'. Social workers became involved and the children's names were placed on a child protection register because of the perceived risk of physical harm. There were mixed feelings amongst the staff about this because Penny had never hit or threatened her children, yet clearly she might harm them. Penny became angry and hostile towards social services as a result. The allocated social worker had misgivings about the monitoring role she had to undertake, but said 'counselling skills saw me through'.

*Attention* was offered through *actively listening*. *Empathy* was employed to assess Penny's concerns. Most crucially *non critical acceptance* was shown because Penny had very low self esteem which could be exacerbated by the monitoring. Penny then revealed that she was sexually abused in childhood by her grandfather. She had never been able to discuss this with any of the therapists she had known over a period of five years. Her husband had been her main support and his loss had triggered severe depression.

The social worker persisted in the supportive monitoring role utilizing counselling skills throughout, while remaining clear about the child protection worker's role and open about Penny's view of the intervention. At the same time she made it clear she was not going away and cared about Penny's progress as a person and parent. After a few weeks, the situation stabilized and after six months deregistration was recommended. Despite a further episode of self harm, the verbal threats to the children ceased. It was considered appropriate to build on the practitioner's work and a specialist child and family counsellor became involved.

Penny had changed her outlook and accepted some responsibility for the effect of her actions on her children. She began to develop a better relationship with her psychiatrist. After twelve months the case was closed, leaving the children and family counsellor involved and some supportive mental health provision in place. Penny's reaction to the practitioner's final visit affirmed that she had valued the supportive approach combined with the monitoring functions. She even asked if she could get in touch if she needed to. She paid close attention to the worker's affirmation of the progress she had made.

### Task-centred practice

Task-centred social work is a framework for practice, developed from ego psychology. It is a focused way of supporting someone to resolve identified difficulties in their lives. The origins of the method can be found in American literature in the 60s and 70s (Reid 1963; Reid and Epstein 1972, 1976). Task-centred practice became established in social work to avoid unfocused long-term interventions which encouraged unnecessary dependency (Doel and Marsh 1992). Reid and Shyne (1969) suggested that brief work could produce equally good results as long term intervention. The tasks selected need to be achievable and a structured plan made. The task-centred approach offers a problem-solving framework requiring:

- client agreement;
- an open agenda about client and worker activities;
- specificity about concrete goals and tasks;

- allocation of tasks;
- time limits;
- review and evaluation;
- reciprocal accountability (both worker and client taking responsibility for outcomes).

The next example describes a social worker planning task-centred actions with a young man with a serious mental health difficulty. The achievement of the task-centred goals depends on good communication and counselling skills.

### Practice example: Mikesh

Mikesh (39) was referred to a residential hostel by field social workers. He found living alone in the community impossible. He had no social or recreational life, was depressed, drinking and frequently admitted to hospital. The hostel stay was to help him start structuring his time, become involved with people, reduce his alcohol intake, sort out his previous accommodation and debts and move back into the community on a better basis. He was out of touch with his relatives as a result of his drinking. At the time of his admission he was too depressed to consider living alone.

The relationship-building phase began with an allocated key worker who used *listening skills, paraphrasing and reflecting back*. There was no attempt to ask questions or delve into his background (there was enough on file already). The practitioner worked to understand Mikesh's view of his present situation. He said that depression, anger and frustration built up to a point where drinking got him through the day. He had not worked since his schizophrenia diagnosis. He had few friends. He hoped the hostel would somehow 'get him out of the rut' and give him some confidence to have a better life.

The social worker *listened* carefully, encouraging Mikesh to tell his story. He used *empathy* to think himself into Mikesh's position. His conclusion was that Mikesh believed he was powerless to do anything to change his isolation. He *checked this interpretation* of powerlessness with Mikesh by *summarizing and paraphrasing* Mikesh's own words but adding the term powerlessness. Mikesh said he could not see things getting better. There seemed no point in anything. Everything he had tried failed. In any case if he was so sick what was the point? This lack of motivation clarified how no amount of encouragement to do things had helped, especially as his illness contributed to his self perception. The social worker now had to try to support and enable without controlling or pushing Mikesh into activity which seemed pointless.

At the next session the key worker *explored* the way Mikesh experienced problems. Mikesh said he panicked and felt overwhelmed. The worker offered to support Mikesh if he could just list what panicked him. The list included: the mess his flat was in; the rent, water, gas, electric arrears; anxiety that the courses and voluntary work offered were too much for him; fears of leaving the hostel. Mikesh said he felt better for saying all this. They made a verbal agreement to work together on one thing at once. Using *listening skills, accurate responding and empathy* the social worker enabled Mikesh to make a viable plan. They agreed on four months to do the work. They began with a visit to the flat. Mikesh gave up the tenancy but they made arrangements to settle bills and planned for a future tenancy. This eased some pressure. Next some drink reduction work was undertaken and then Mikesh began to do some voluntary work in a community centre with Asian elders. The social worker felt a good start had been made.

## The practitioner's use of self in intervention

The positive or negative valuations placed on social work actions by service users often reflect on the practitioner's interpersonal style rather than the theories or methods. People are often most concerned with whether the practitioner was respectful in providing what was needed or helping with a difficulty. Interventions in social work are about roles and tasks, agency function, theories and methods together with the use of self in carrying these through. At all times the manner and skills of the worker are highly significant in the process of intervention. The worker's presence and their counselling, brokering and negotiating abilities might prove to be the significant factor in the effectiveness of the work. In the next example the worker acted with no specialized resources immediately available.

### Practice example: Zoë

Zoë (15) disclosed that her father had sexually abused her since she was seven. Her mother became aware of this when the abuse stopped, but the offences were not yet reported to the police. Zoë moved out of home to stay with some close friends of her parents before she spoke to anyone about her father. She remained there and the friends were approved as private foster parents. Her father was subsequently arrested and remanded on bail. Zoë's two sisters continued to live with her mother. Her father moved out. The practitioner identified several areas for action. These were: individual support to Zoë, her sisters and her mother, support for the foster carers, relationship work between Zoë; and her mother (feelings were running high), mediation work between the foster carers, the mother and Zoë.

The social worker used counselling skills in personal work with Zoë. The first step was sitting with her in the park (Zoë's choice of venue) near the foster carers and *listening*. She ensured that this *listening* was very *attentive*, to try to understand what Zoë felt about what had happened to her. *Linking* was used to make sense of Zoë's experiences, to hold them together. After this, in more formal sessions, Zoë was asked to write her feelings on a shield with four parts. This exercise showed how worthless she felt. At this point the practitioner focused verbal interventions on *reflecting back and summarizing* what was said. This was important because sometimes Zoë became very upset and the reflection back of her feelings was supportive.

The social worker explained that the counselling approach was different from an ordinary conversation. This seemed to give Zoë the security that the practitioner was really trying to understand her. It was also important because her mother often reinterpreted and gave a completely different version of events, so it was vital to validate her own experiences. Zoë was referred to a therapeutic counselling service but the worker had supported everyone through a difficult time until other services were available and she was subsequently able to make good use of the specialized therapeutic help.

### Social worker qualities

The *Statement of Expectations* from people who use services (Topss 2003b) shows that people want social workers like Zoë's who explain, inform, give information, are honest, listen actively, offer respect, choice and relationship. They expect involvement at all stages, good time-keeping, recognition of their own strengths, sustained contact as appropriate, advocacy, and much more. Social workers therefore need a combination of qualities and skills in their intervening and providing actions. Compton and Galaway (1989: 306) suggest qualities that are useful in people who are in helping professions: maturing and developing the self; creativity; intellectual openness; receptivity; holding most solutions to the problems of life as tentative; capacity to observe self; desire to help; courage. They also identify six sets of essential elements: concern for others for their own sake; commitment and obligation; acceptance and expectation; empathy; authority and power; genuineness and congruence.

This is in contrast to Keith-Lucas's (1972) list of people who are experienced as unhelpful. These are:

- those interested in knowing about people rather than in serving them;
- those impelled by strong personal needs to control, to feel superior, to be liked;
- those who have solved problems similar to the problems of people in need of help but have forgotten what it cost them to do so;
- those primarily interested in retributive justice and moralizing.

Personal qualities, values and attitudes overlap with skills, but skills can be distinguished as the abilities or techniques which are used to communicate the essential values of respect and understanding (Browne 1993). The personal qualities of the worker are applied through their skills. Understanding others requires empathy.

### Empathy

Empathy is important for working in a way that understands the life space of the other person. Empathy is often mistakenly confused with sympathy (an outpouring of our own identification with the other, showing pity and concern in a way which perhaps fails to understand the other because it comes from our own concern). Empathy is a capacity for a more objective concern. Empathy is often thought of as a personal quality and many people simply develop their capacity to enter another's world through their family interactions and experiences of life. There is evidence that the capacity for empathy is something that good parents have and communicate to their children (Rosenstein 1995). The accurate empathy needed for social work practice is a skill, built from the personal qualities with which each of us starts, and developed through supervised practice.

Empathy is the capacity to enter into the feelings and experiences of another; to understand what the other is experiencing as if you were the other; to stand back from your own self and identity in the process. There is an emotional (or feeling) content and an intellectual (or cognitive) element to the skilled exercise of empathy. Learning to be empathic requires knowledge (for example examination of the stereotypes we may hold about others, and the acquisition of cultural and structural understandings about society). It also requires the ability to feel with someone else, while observing the boundaries of what is your own feeling. This is particularly important with shared experiences. A worker's own experiences of loss might give some clues as to how others experience loss but, without the capacity for empathy, they might simply project their personal experiences on to someone whose reaction is quite different from their own.

For example, bereaved people feel a range of feelings, such as rage, sadness, regret, guilt, relief and many others. How grief is experienced and what is felt depends on personality, previous experiences, religious outlook and the relationship with the deceased. Practitioners need to be aware of the diversity of human responses that can exist in any particular situation, especially where loss is involved. It is suggested that in the face of terminal illness some fight, some deny, some are angry, and some despair. All such reactions and others are valid for the individuals concerned. Empathic understanding enables workers to accept and enter the world of the other irrespective of their own personal and cultural baggage. This is important because, if the necessary step of understanding another's world is not taken, actions and service provision may be inappropriate.

It is sometimes suggested that empathy implies agreement with, or support for, the other's actions, thoughts or feelings and that it is difficult or wrong to empathize with people who have, perhaps, killed or abused someone. However, empathy is not sympathy or approval, in an important way it is value free; it does not prescribe or collude with actions. Empathy can simply be used in understanding others and then planning actions. The practitioner remains free to be clear about society's or the agency's stance on the person's values and actions. Empathy identifies and works with difference constructively.

As a skill, empathy can be refined and developed from the personal qualities of concern for others to understand a range of values. Empathizing involves the professional use of self in intervention in the lives of others. Fitting people to services is ultimately a time wasting and costly exercise. Plans which undermine someone's wishes and needs usually break down. Empathy is the ability to see the world from the other's point of view, and to stay alongside them to plan appropriately. Colloquially, it is said that empathy is 'the ability to walk a mile in another's shoes'.

## Understanding life stages

Empathy can enable practitioners to understand a different life stage from their own. For example, older people who find they need services may have strong views about becoming dependent. For many previously active socially productive people a change of role profoundly affects their sense of self. Without an understanding of what this means for each individual, including understanding their background, culture, previous employment and lifestyle, it is easy to be well meaning and prescribe a raft of services which are rejected; and then to describe this reaction as uncooperative. It may be that fewer, more appropriate and agreed services are more effective. For example the loss of social stimulation might be more important to one person than their inability to cook a hot meal. There is no point in offering domiciliary meals to someone who would like a day out or conversely group activity to someone who is happy with their own company but is tired of living on sandwiches. Neither meals nor day care are of any use if they are offered in a way which takes no account of cultural preferences, vegetarian diets or the usefulness of the service for the particular person.

This may seem elementary, but sometimes the energy expended in labelling could be better spent taking time to intervene appropriately. The place of counselling skills here is listening and responding, so the service offered fits the needs of the consumer as far as possible. Such skills assist the practitioner to clarify roles, agree courses of action, use the appropriate working methods, support and sustain people through transition and change, negotiate packages of care and become involved in active evaluation.

The next example shows a worker acting to provide a service for Gemma and her grandparents. It includes explicit use of social work theory, methods and counselling skills to underpin the actions. The social worker uses empathy to understand the life space of a young person and her carers.

### Practice example: Gemma

Gemma (14) was brought up in her grandparent's home. Her mother lived nearby with her husband, his son from a previous relationship (12) and their two daughters (7) and (5). Gemma had a boyfriend, Steve (19). Gemma was not attending school and after court proceedings was referred for a social work assessment. Gemma was known to the department as her grandparents had previously requested help to handle Gemma's involvement with older men. In the past, support from a social worker had resulted in Gemma's return to school and re-unification with her grandparents.

Gemma was not co-operative at first. She described the involvement of the courts and the police as punishing. She thought no-one was concerned with her or what she wanted, only with school attendance (*active listening; minimal prompts*). The worker suggested that Gemma made a self assessment as she surmised (*empathy*) that loss of control about her life mattered. This approach (*avoiding questions*) and using an eco-map to talk with Gemma about her family and wider world helped to build a constructive relationship.

The social worker thought that a court order would alienate Gemma further and her grandparents agreed, describing Gemma as 'anti everything'. By building a relationship to work with Gemma to make sense of what was happening, the practitioner was in a position to recommend work on a voluntary basis for six months to the court. Use of counselling skills enabled her to achieve a plan congruent with the principles of the Children Act 1989 (welfare of the child, parental partnership, avoidance of court orders, least intrusive intervention, incorporating the wishes and feelings of the young person).

The action which followed was a combination of counselling and active task-centred support. Gemma identified: issues about school; her grandparents' objection to her boyfriend; feelings about not being in her mother's new family; the circumstances around her birth and upbringing. Verbal agreements were made, facilitated by *listening, responding, clarifying and goal setting*. Careful *listening* to Gemma established that formal written plans had previously put her off social work as she did not like written agreements. This was *respected throughout*, and although necessary agency records were kept, written work was minimized, although the task-centred approach continued.

A counselling aim was adopted 'to give Gemma an opportunity to explore, discover and clarify ways of living more resourcefully and towards greater wellbeing'. They explored Gemma's beliefs about herself which guided her feelings and behaviour. Her perception of being misjudged about her boyfriend, by grandparents and professionals conditioned her thoughts and actions. The worker's *acceptance* meant that Gemma talked for the first time about herself, leading into a phase of *exploration* of her view of her situation.

The practitioner then *confronted and challenged* her beliefs, while still accepting that Gemma's perception remained valid. This led to discussing what might help her return to school and the issues about her place in the family. It emerged that Gemma believed she had nothing to contribute in school or the family, but that she felt valued with Steve. The practitioner stayed *person-centred* in this stage of the work enabling Gemma to consider dimensions of her world for herself.

There were crises at various times, including threats towards the grandparents. When Gemma decided to end her relationship with Steve, the police had to be called to persuade him to leave the grandparents' home. Work was done with school to help Gemma to return, although the worker was as frustrated as Gemma at times by slow responses from other agencies. Opportunities were provided for Gemma to evaluate and plan her future with social workers, the education department and her grandparents. The social worker valued Gemma as a person which resulted in others seeing her as an individual and not just as a 'truant'. This person-centred approach, underpinned by counselling skills, created some changes in Gemma's self perception and the system with which she was in conflict. It was time consuming but it met agency goals and avoided more intrusive and expensive interventions such as a supervision order or even a residential placement.

### Endings

Ending contact and working with people towards completing work has been an area of weakness in social work practice whereas counsellors consider it essential to consider the way contact will end and discuss the meaning of the ending with people. An understanding of attachment theory and human growth and development suggests that where relationships are built and attachments occur the way the relationship ends is important (Trevithick 2000: 107–113). Gemma's social worker took care to tell Gemma well in advance of ending their meetings and spent time reviewing and agreeing what they achieved together and arranged their last meeting in a café to celebrate. Penny's, Zoë's and Mikesh's social workers were equally careful to disengage respectfully and end the work well. In Zoë's and Penny's situations they were enabled to transfer to specialist counsellors.

Endings are important and Huntley (2002) says:

> Inadequate knowledge and understanding of up to date attachment theory suggests a lack of awareness on the part of practitioners on the impact on the client of the ending of the social worker-client relationship. This may result in the reinforcement of previous negative separation experiences for the client and may undo much of the positive work that has been achieved.

Taking care with the way a contact ends consolidates what has been achieved. While many social work actions are 'one off' activities or brief meetings, others involve a longer relationship where someone is expected to share a great deal of personal information and to relate closely to a social worker. In these situations it seems essential that a profession that seeks to respect others and to promote their wellbeing makes the time to fully face and discuss the endings of work, making time to introduce new workers or as Gemma's worker did to celebrate their joint achievements.

**Key points:**

- Actions in social work depend upon legislation, policy and procedural frameworks. They are informed by social work theories and methods and services may be provided.
- The process is implemented and co-ordinated by individuals whose abilities, judgements and choices uniquely affect the quality of the service user's experience.
- A counselling skills approach to underpin actions can lead to an authoritative, ethical, holistic approach to a range of practice tasks and methods of work.
- Ending contact with service users appropriately is important.

**Questions and activities: for self development or discussion groups**

1 Think of some 'moments in time', where you think someone else's verbal actions made a positive difference. Analyse what was helpful. What can you learn from your observations and what can transfer into your own practice?

2 What personal qualities/communication styles do you bring from your own family and cultural background that make you a good helper? Conversely, what personal qualities/communication styles do you bring from your own family and cultural background that might hinder your work?

3 To what extent are you able to use empathy to understand and act in circumstances that are new to you? How could you develop your ability to be empathic?

4 Do you end your contacts service users well? Are people always informed about the progress of actions, whether future visits are planned, if referrals are made? Are they given clear information about what will happen or given time for a planned ending to the work or interview?

# Chapter 5

# Supporting service user choice and advocacy: relevant counselling skills

Social work practice is distinguished by a focus on the views of the people who use services. This includes, but is more than, facilitating service users' coping mechanisms and strengths to solve difficulties. It includes activity to enable people to say what kind of service they want and how they perceive their situation. It contrasts with notions of 'helping' that are framed in ways that make people unnecessarily dependent or passive. Social workers seek to understand and analyse the ways in which structural barriers reduce the participation of people in society. They endeavour to work in the least stigmatizing and most enabling way available. This approach is found in three main strands of social work literature, the strengths perspective, empowerment and advocacy and can be summarized as 'support individuals to represent their needs views and circumstances' (Key Role 3, Standard 6, Scotland).

Most people, at some time in their lives, will need a health or care service and when that time comes will expect to have a 'voice' about what they receive and how they receive it. It is crucial to recognize that each person is an 'actor' in their own lives whether or not social disadvantage or exclusion leads to people requiring support to reach their potential. Services are not just the way that powerful people help poor people but a tool for combating disadvantage and promoting citizenship and social inclusion (Department of Health 1998a, 2000 a, b). The emphasis in providing services therefore is on consultation, participation and partnerships between agencies, workers and the people who use the services.

This kind of underpinning philosophy for service provision and social worker activity has inherent tensions within it which provide challenges and dilemmas for practitioners. Making consultation real and service users active in the management of what is provided requires a real shift in the way services are managed and careful judgements about whose views are collected, heard and responded to (Sang and O'Neill 2002; Beresford and Croft 2003). Ascertaining what service users want from services is a complex undertaking but some messages are consistent. Consultation with some people with experience of adult services showed that they wanted:

- to be treated with respect as individuals;
- a voice in decisions about the range of services;
- recognition that while services may be an important or even essential part of their lives, services are not all of their lives;
- acknowledgement that they are reasonable people who understand about resources and other constraints but who think that is a reason for more attention to be paid to their views not less;
- to see signs that the time spent in giving their views has influenced decisions.

(Connelly and Seden 2003: 33–4)

These findings and others from research and policy documents give unambiguous messages to social workers and illustrate that there has been a tendency for social workers to view people through the lens of agency needs and their own practitioner concerns rather than as people who can participate in shaping their own solutions to needs. To hear these messages means practising in a way that helps people forward in their own life choices wherever possible and supports them actively to reach their potential, or a desired outcome, through having the resources and authority to do so. The ideology is one of identifying and working with service users' strengths and capacities to meet their own identified goals and objectives and secure their rights. This chapter considers the place in practice of the strengths perspective, empowerment and advocacy and shows through examples how counselling skills are part of such approaches.

### The strengths perspective

In a key text, *The Strengths Perspective in Social Work*, Saleebey writes:

> The strengths perspective is not a theory — although developments in that direction become bolder (Rapp, 1996). It is a way of thinking about what you do and with whom you do it. It provides a distinctive lens for examining the world of practice. Any approach to practice, in the end, is based on interpretation of the experiences of practitioners and clients and is composed of assumptions, rhetoric, ethics and a set of methods. The importance and usefulness of any practice orientation lies not in some independent measure of truth, but in how well it serves us in our work with people, how it fortifies our values, and how it generates opportunities for clients in a particular environment to change in the direction of their hopes and aspirations.
>
> (1997: 17)

The strengths perspective takes an ecological systems approach to problem solving, considering social, political and cultural, as well as individual, accounts of human predicaments and possibilities, focusing not on deficits but on the resourcefulness of others. The key terms relevant to the approach are:

- empowerment;
- membership;
- resilience;
- healing and wholeness;
- dialogue and collaboration;
- suspension of disbelief.

(1997: 8–11)

The principles are:

- Every individual, group family and community has strengths.
- Trauma and abuse, illness and struggle may be injurious but they may also be sources of challenge and opportunity.
- Assume that you do not know the upper limits of capacity to grow and change and take individual, group and community aspirations seriously.
- We best serve clients by collaborating with them.
- Every environment is full of resources.

(1997: 12–15)

This perspective fits well with empowerment philosophies and also with a person-centred approach to people as described by Rogers (1961). Counselling skills are often employed in working with people to identify their strengths and their opportunities for development and therefore can combine with this way of conceptualizing social work. Many social workers however, while committed to the idea of service user choice and enabling people to fulfil their own goals and building on identified strengths, also have to take account of their statutory roles. Sometimes they have to take a stance about someone's situation in actions such as compulsory admission to hospital under the relevant Mental Health Act, the removal of someone's children into care or other legal intervention into someone's life and freedoms. They need to be skilled enough to reconcile this and in the next practice example a social worker speaks about how she integrates the Rogerian concepts of 'genuineness' and 'worth' in a person-centred and strength-building way in childcare practice.

> **Practice example: Carole**
>
> I find *genuineness* to be an attitude of mind, achieved as you grow in confidence and personal maturity, through training and experience. Inherent in this is the idea of *acceptance* and non-judgementalism. This is experienced by the client as *unconditional positive regard*. This communicates to the client a feeling of self worth which hopefully will facilitate a process of self acceptance and growth. This does not mean the client's every behaviour is accepted.

Many of the people I meet in childcare work are experiencing low self esteem, often because of difficulties in their parenting of their children. Sometimes this was the outcome of the inadequate parenting that they themselves had experienced. Appreciating this, however, is not the whole story in social work, because the social worker has many roles to play in the job. More and more she has to be an instrument of government and of the legal system, in other words attempting to enforce solutions according to pre-stated procedures. There is still an advisory and advocacy role, and she is also involved in practical work for her clients. Thus she is forced at times to be both 'with' her client and 'against them'.

Younger people may have been rejected by a parent, accept no controls and show a very challenging behavioural style to their social worker. The *unconditional positive regard* of the worker can provide a contrast to the alienation and rejection experienced elsewhere. Social workers are sometimes misunderstood when they take this approach, as if they are approving the client's actions.

There are opportunities for counselling that arise within the job, perhaps around a trauma; or specific issues that need resolution; or a programme to build self confidence. The goals will be set but a counselling approach to achieving them can be taken. There is also opportunity for *empathic listening* and support. For example I had one client who was self-referred for causing a minor injury to a child, for whom I was able to demonstrate unconditional positive regard. She was able to sense my genuineness and was helped by that to come to a decision to tackle her low self esteem through psychotherapy. By accepting her worth as a fellow human being and not being afraid of her revelations of self-abuse, I saw her determination to sort out her life strength, though I had not the skill to take it further or the permission of the agency to do so. I saw her move on as my role ended because the children were not considered to be at risk.

Thus a person-centred approach is complex because, as in Carole's work, people may come to the attention of social workers through hitting, injuring or neglecting their children. They are often 'reluctant' or 'defensive' in their interactions with workers. However, it is still possible to be prepared *to attend* to and *listen* to them and build a working partnership. Thus the social worker accepts that each person has worth even when society is asking them to address what is viewed as unacceptable behaviour. Carole was able to describe how she would accept the person and build on their strengths in a person-centred way without compromising the authority, role or tasks required by the agency.

This can be misunderstood as agreeing with everything. The social worker who comforted the mother of one of the boys who was convicted of the sad death of James Bulger received adverse publicity. After sentence was passed the practitioner involved was able to feel compassion for a woman whom she came to know while preparing court reports, a woman criticized by society as a parent and whose son was convicted of murder and sentenced to custody. This mother obviously remained a human being who experienced distress and needed support from social workers. The social worker's understanding of this did not mean that she condoned what happened to James.

### Empowerment

The concept of empowerment came into social work through writers like Solomon (1976) writing on black communities in the USA. Empowerment has become a dominant theme in modern practice, reflecting a concern with the social inequalities and social exclusion faced by many of the groups with whom practitioners work (Cochrane 1989; Hooks 1991; Braye and Preston-Shoot 1995; Humphries 1996). Empowerment in practice is complex because it encompasses values, ideology, methods and outcomes and because each individual has more or less power in different circumstances, in the same culture, at different times. Social workers therefore need to be critical and analytical in their approach to acting in an empowering way. It has been argued that an 'empowerment strategy requires commitment to both maintenance and improvement of effective equal services and also confrontation of pervasive negative valuations' (Payne 1992: 229). The aims of empowerment are to help people to view themselves as:

• causal agents in finding solutions to their problems;
• social workers as having knowledge and skills that clients can use;
• social workers as peers and partners in solving problems;
• the power structure as complex and partly open to influence.

(1992: 230)

This leads to a model of practice, similar to the strengths perspective, which enables individuals to see themselves as having some control over their situation. The social work role becomes that of 'resources consultant, sensitiser and trainer' (1992: 230).

This role needs to be taken by social workers, because at times communities and individuals internalize 'negative valuations' of themselves that have accrued through experiences of oppression and disadvantage. A culture of 'power absence' rather than 'power failure' means people do not attempt to change the system. Social workers may collude with this if they concentrate change efforts on the individual rather than the structures which perpetuate disadvantage. Consciousness raising and radical and political advocacy approaches are needed to be effective. Seligman's (1975) work on learned helplessness is relevant here. He argues that if people constantly experience ineffectiveness as an outcome of their actions, then they will come to the view that there is no usefulness in their actions and their ability to be motivated and solve problems will be impaired. There are also times when social workers' empowerment strategies focus on working alongside individuals, who themselves advocate for their own rights.

Social workers need to be clear as to what they mean when they talk about empowerment because their work is often within agencies that control resources, liberty or the right to bring up children. There can be confusion between a rhetorical expression of empowerment ideology and radical empowering practices in action. An uncritical approach to 'empowerment' may not be very different from 'laissez faire' or the 'get on your bike' approach that believes that any individual can achieve their own solution unaided. It is therefore essential that empowerment aspirations are linked to service user consultation, advocacy practices and a clear understanding of rights. The next practice example is an account of an empowerment and advocacy approach to service provision. Antenna is a voluntary organization which has provided counselling services for disabled people. It is a project managed and staffed by disabled people.

### Practice example: Antenna, providing counselling services for disabled people

The majority of services for disabled people have been, and still are provided by non disabled professionals. Due to lack of disability awareness and lack of personal experience of disability from non disabled professionals, many disabled people have found these services to be delivered in a way which is patronising, disempowering and inappropriate to their needs. Counselling is no exception.

Through the growth of the disability movement, disabled people have identified a need for services provided and controlled by disabled people themselves, which not only increase the chances of being valued and understood as disabled people but also give credit to skills and experience that disabled people have themselves. This challenges the concept of disabled people only having a place as service users and brings to the fore the place for disabled people as professionals.

Within the voluntary sector projects where services are provided by disabled people have gradually emerged, though in terms of counselling services there are still very few organizations across the country providing these within projects staffed and managed by disabled people.

Some years ago, a group of disabled people identified a need for counselling services for disabled people provided by disabled people. They felt, through their own experiences and those of other disabled people they came into contact with, that there was a great need for disabled people to have access to counselling services. They also believed that counselling services provided by non disabled professionals were often experienced as unhelpful because of a lack of attention to access needs and poor understanding of what it means to be disabled. Further, the view of disability from non disabled professionals generally fell into the medical model rather than the social model of disability.

The social model of disability stresses the ways that disabled people are limited by the environment and by the barriers within society that prevent them from equal participation:

- lack of provision for access needs;
- lack of disability awareness;
- prevailing attitudes which mean disabled people are put down, disempowered and treated unequally;
- lack of equal access to social, educational and employment opportunities.

If these issues are not taken into account and clearly acknowledged in providing counselling services, then counselling puts the onus back on disabled people and the 'problem' becomes wholly personal rather than social. There is an important balance to be achieved in counselling where both social and personal aspects of disability are recognized. This means that neither the social aspects such as lack of access and disability awareness, nor the personal aspects such as sexuality, pain and loss are ignored.

(Liz Mackenzie, Antenna Coordinator 1998)

### Empowerment and social work with adults

The tensions between empowerment philosophy and the practice of social work are seen clearly in the delivery of services for adults. The dichotomy between resource shortfall and the concept of needs-led assessment and intervention have been a constant theme of discussion. Browne (1996) specifies the shortfalls: the extent to which service users are informed and included in the process; deficits in recording agreements in writing; and administrative procedures being difficult for service users to comprehend. Deakin (1996) agrees that the empowerment focus has been undermined by: under resourcing (with delays undercutting principles of user choice); problems of definition and procedural obstacles (whose needs are to be met, user or carer? What if these conflict?); service user choice (how can someone have choice when contracts are awarded in a quasi-market controlled by managers?). Deakin concludes that 'the user is not at the centre of the picture in community care practice'. The new single assessment process (Department of Health 2002) is meant to help agencies to simplify assessments for older people. Shortage of cash and local bureaucracy will make implementation patchy. The cultural change of working together on assessment across agencies will also require common understandings of assessment and communication.

In this climate of complexity in the implementation of what appears to be a positive policy development social workers are once more, speaking cynically, almost reduced to using their personal communication skills to, as one practitioner put it, 'say no nicely'. This would be unethical and need not be so. Workers need their interpersonal communication skills not only to enable people they meet to express their own agenda but also to use verbal skills in challenge and advocacy in order to obtain a needed resource and to make policy changes effective on the ground. As the interviewees in Henderson's (2003) consultation said they are reasonable people who can accept an honest explanation. Social workers can work with service users to identify what services are needed and then work to bring then about.

## Counselling skills for empowerment

The belief that self-directed solutions to individual problems are best achieved by service users with a supporter is as central to empowering social work practice as it is to counselling practice. Social workers operate within the overt and covert power structures that agencies embody. There is a creative, challenging and stressful interaction between agency roles, public expectation and service user voice. Counsellors mislead themselves if they think that without a powerful bureaucracy around them, they are not themselves powerful. The counsellor is often perceived as an 'expert' and in possession of knowledge and resources, such as the power to give or withhold help, offer long or short contracts and to make referrals. The nature of their training and accreditation also invests them with the power of the 'professionals'.

In any helping interaction, awareness of the dynamics of actual and perceived power is necessary. Failure to recognize the subtle and explicit dimensions of power is potentially detrimental to the service user. Within social work agencies practitioners can use interpersonal skills to build relationships and practice in a way which promotes and enables service users' agendas as far as is possible within the limitations of the agency's remit. It is also possible to use skills of advocacy and challenge to work patiently and persistently to build up people's self-esteem and achieve their aims within their family systems and communities. In addition to personal work with individuals social workers are able to intervene and broker resources in support of people's endeavours to achieve their goals.

The next practice example shows a practitioner using counselling, advocacy and other skills to support Jean to achieve her and her family's goal, that she begin to take an active role in the community beyond the immediate family. The social worker's actions are aimed at increasing the life experience and social opportunities of an adult with learning disabilities and maximizing her opportunities for growth and development.

### Practice example: Jean

The practitioner was responding to a referral from a GP. Jean Harris had previously been referred with a view to a social worker obtaining some daytime activities for her. The family's attempts to obtain contact with someone had not been followed up and the system blocked access to resources which offered opportunities to Jean.

The family had engaged the advocacy and influence of their GP who insisted that their second request for help was allocated to a practitioner. The social worker identified how Jean, in requesting services, had met delay and prejudiced beliefs about her abilities. This led to low expectations, opportunity deprivation, and negative and diminished experience, more delay and therefore negative self-evaluation and expectations. In other words, she experienced disempowerment and learned helplessness, as identified by Solomon (1976) and Seligman (1975).

The practitioner decided to use ecological theory as a framework for understanding Jean's situation, but also considered: models of disability, transitions theory, empowerment principles and ego psychology. Her main aim was to promote Jean's right to the choice of a service which met her needs and enabled her to participate in society in a way which was satisfying for her, building on her strengths and interests. The practitioner therefore began an assessment of Jean's needs and circumstances to find ways to enable her to achieve the desired outcome.

She began the first interview with the conscious exercise of *empathy* to discover how Jean viewed herself and her environment. Initially, this meant *listening to* the anger of Ida Harris, Jean's mother, who was annoyed at the way the previous request for day care had resulted in unhelpful advice and no service provision. Faced with a general complaint the practitioner *summarized to reflect back at a feeling level* the dejection and frustration this had produced in the family. She gave some time to the *ventilation* of *feelings* and *actively listened* to make *accurate responses*, with *summaries* that showed *accurate empathy*. She followed this by clarifying the reasons for the agency's past response (service review) but also made it clear that a complaint could be made and how this could be done.

A relationship was built which led to an introduction to the extended family which consisted of six people. At this stage Jean was quiet (*attention to body language*) and did not reply when gently addressed. The practitioner *listened attentively* to the expressed thoughts and feelings of the family who said that Jean was supported within a close and loving family, but had little experience to develop outside of it. She had been to school independently, but now the parents chose to provide transport everywhere she went. She had a brief spell of work experience but this was supervised by a sister. Jean had never attended a college and did not go anywhere alone. The family had been encouraged by their GP to think about the future and to enable their daughter to socialize outside of the family system. The practitioner, having *listened*, supported this view. By the end of the interview she had managed through the mother to gather that Jean enjoyed dancing and cooking.

Jean had no recent experience outside her family network and had expressed to the family her concerns about being 'different from other people'. The practitioner had established some rapport with Ida Harris but wanted to establish communication with Jean to *check out* her view of her situation. She also thought it possible that Jean had a negative self-valuation, and aimed to enable her to find her equal rights as an adult person. This meant support and self-image building and checking what she wanted for herself. The worker therefore tried to encourage Jean to speak for herself within interviews. This also meant both *challenge* to the family members and much use of *encouraging body language* and *minimal prompts*.

Once communication with Jean herself was achieved, the practitioner learnt how a previous attempt to visit a day centre had been unhappy and that the consequences were not worked through, thus blocking Jean's willingness to consider it again. The practitioner therefore stated and re-stated to Jean that she would be able to say no to anything she did not want to do, *advocating* within the family for her right to choose. She used *jargon-free language* such as '*you need only have a look to see if you like it*' and '*you will decide if you want to go*'.

The worker researched community resources and found a drop-in facility with a relaxed group atmosphere, based in a local bungalow, attended by a few others. From there opportunities arose to branch out to local courses and activities. Jean turned this down and the worker accepted her right to choose. The focus turned to her interests in cooking and dancing. There was a cookery course at a local college, but a series of delays and administrative blocks, that considerably engaged the practitioner's advocacy skills, made it difficult to make arrangements for a trial visit. Meanwhile a visit by bus to the college was made with Jean so that she could see what it was like. Contact was maintained by brief visits to the family home.

During her direct conversations with Jean the practitioner used *open ended questions and paraphrasing to check meanings and maintain the relationship, and accepted pauses and silence*. Jean shared her interest in cooking at home with the worker. Eventually a place on the cookery course for people with special needs was available and Jean attended on her own. She enjoyed it and expressed the wish to continue. This was a huge step, as it was her first social activity outside the family since leaving school. A second planned step was to attend a creative arts group in a small college within walking distance of the family home.

The social worker invested considerable time, using *empathy and linking* to gain understanding and to frame communications to Jean and her family. The practitioner surmised that Jean felt labelled and that both she and her family perceived her in a disabling way. Jean expressed her dissatisfaction and frustration by refusing to speak to family members, often for long periods. The worker had to use *empathy* and *communication skills* to build trust to talk directly to learn Jean's genuine needs and feelings.

Berne's model of parent-adult-child interactions (1961) was used to try and change the interactions between Jean and her family from parent-child to a more adult-adult model. A major part of this was *modelling* through practitioner interactions in an adult-adult style focusing on Jean's strengths and rights. An understanding of *defences helped the practitioner to clarify* that Jean was anxious about visiting new places because of a previous bad experience where she had not been told she was only 'going for a look' and believed she was going to be 'left there'. This information only emerged when the worker took time *listen* to Jean's anxiety and to gently *explore* it through *open questions*. In her work to support and promote choice the practitioner gave constant attention to *affirming Jean's communications* and encouraging her to assert her views. This was only possible through the understanding and partnership built with the family, who after the initial hostility became positive about the service received and derived benefit from the *ventilation of and acceptance of* some of their frustrations.

This example shows how skilled personal interactions build trust to promote choice and enable Jean to take crucial steps towards fulfilling her goals and lessening her frustrations. Jean was also able to build on her strengths. Through careful, planned interventions, using counselling skills, it was possible to work with conflict and ambivalence to promote the rights of Jean and her family. Through the worker's activity resolutions were found that a previous bureaucratic response had failed to provide.

Empowerment and advocacy in social work are enabled through counselling skills. Neville (1996) developed a model for social work process in empowerment. It is designed as a working tool for practitioners and provides a 'framework for analysing how a piece of work is done'. It cannot be an objective test of the achievement of empowering practice because the service user is 'is the only person who can determine that themselves'. The framework is reproduced in full at the end of this chapter and identifies four areas for analysis:

- areas of clients' lives where they wish to acquire power;
- the areas of access that social workers need to offer in order to enable the person to acquire power in these identified areas;
- the support that needs to be offered by agencies or workers for the access to become effective;
- the social work skills that are required to offer effective support to clients, in order to acquire power over areas of their lives. These include *listening; empathy; advocacy; respect; counselling; anti-oppressive practice; user involvement; negotiation and conciliation.*

In the practice example of Jean the worker used a very broad range of skills to support Jean and promote her choices. She also had to be prepared to challenge others and remain assertive about the agreed goals. The empowerment and strengths perspectives discussed so far show the need for enabling counselling skills. However, social workers wanting to employ empowerment strategies will also find they need to be assertive and challenging, sometimes within a service user's family or environment, sometimes with their own or other social work agencies.

## Challenge

Facing up to conflict and learning to challenge is part of social work experience. Exchanges between people can become heated, angry and hostile at times and it is difficult to avoid this when people find professionals taking actions when they do not agree. There are inevitably times when feelings are running high and service users are quite understandably upset. In social work, handling the tensions and confronting the issues that arise as you go along is part of the work. It is also necessary to become more skilled at handling and accepting other people's anger and distress without being unnecessarily confrontational. It is also possible to learn to present challenge to another person's point of view in a constructive way. It is important to avoid becoming insensitive to the powerful emotions and feelings that are often present and to respond by working to become more skilful at handling challenging situations. Often a simple acknowledgement that you understand what is difficult for the other person in their position (even if you are unable to agree or change your own professional view/duties) can defuse a situation to the point where difference can be openly and reasonably calmly discussed. Allowing the other person space to express their perspective is also useful provided that they are not given the impression that this will change something that cannot be changed.

If you need to confront a service user, manager or other professional while maintaining the relationship there are some key factors that help:

* Choose the time and place carefully, if you can.
* Try to ensure there is time and space for effective communication and discussion.
* Assess how you think the communication will be received and whether it is appropriate to be alone. Could someone else be helpful?
* Think about clarification that might be needed and be as well informed as you can.
* Be clear and specific about what you need to say and be sure that you really must say it.
* Reflect on your own feelings about the situation and talk them over with a colleague or supervisor.
* Think through how to say what is necessary and phrase it as constructively as possible.
* Listen carefully to responses, acknowledge them and be as affirmative as you can.
* Try to avoid being interrupted by others or prevented from saying what you must.
* Avoid being side-tracked or losing focus.
* Check carefully that the other person has understood the content of the communication;
* End by summarizing what has been said.

Heron, in *Helping the Client*, provides a useful chapter on 'Confronting Interventions'. He suggests that practitioners should:

- know what their warrant (authority) for confronting is;
- know what are the conditions for effective confrontation;
- judge the timing of the intervention;
- know the depth to which the discussion needs to go;
- be clear on the agenda;
- be aware of the process.

(1997: 43–56)

The chapter is very detailed in examining issues, agendas and techniques and is useful reading for social workers.

### Assertiveness

Assertiveness is another useful set of skills for facing conflict, or giving unpleasant news or information that it will be difficult for someone to accept. The first element is learning to understand and manage your own feelings so that you can be calm and thoughtful. The counselling skills of avoiding blame, moralizing, judging or placating which avoids the issues, distorts the communication and leaves the other person feeling put down are also helpful. Assertiveness is not aggressive, it means staying comfortable with your own position and view while at the same time remaining open to listening to the other person.

Assertiveness training involves learning a range of specific techniques, for example: 'broken record technique' making your point clearly and unambiguously several times if needed; learning how to 'receive criticism'; learning to 'buy time' to think how to respond; using 'I' statements. Assertiveness training involves learning a set of behaviours and responses through a group training programme. Assertive behaviour by social workers, often simply means having the ability, as Jean's social worker did, to hold your ground and be calmly persistent about achieving what the service user wants. It is also useful for advocacy roles.

Working with the strengths of individuals in an empowering way is harder to achieve when social workers need to act to protect someone from harm or danger, either from themselves or others. The next example shows the dilemmas of ethical practice, but shows the worker's counselling skills and personal approach were still in evidence, at the same time as using legal powers to protect the children. This is a situation where the interests of the different parties conflicted and the social workers had to be careful to come to a balanced view.

### Practice example: Megan

Megan had left her two children aged 3 and 5 in the care of her elderly parents and apparently disappeared for several months. Prior to this the social workers had aimed to support both parents to care for the children in their own rented accommodation. The children's father had recently received a prison sentence for offences related to drugs and was therefore unable to care for them. Monitoring the impact of the parent's substance use and lifestyle on the children had previously been an intermittent concern.

The grandparents contacted social services because they were no longer in good health, and were finding the responsibility of the two small children more than they could really manage. The father apparently had no relatives who might help care for the children. Megan then returned, took the children and left her parents' home. She moved with them from friend to friend, as she and her partner had been evicted from their former house.

Megan finally returned to her parents, clearly without income or a home, and probably using substances, but left the children again after a week's stay. After another week the grandparents asked social services to accommodate the children. Support services were offered, but to no avail. The children were therefore placed with short-term foster carers. After a few weeks Megan returned, resumed contact, and then removed the children from foster care (as was her right since they were voluntarily accommodated).

She began moving from friend to friend again, until the police found her by the roadside late one night, with no money or food, possibly using substances and with the children in a neglected condition. The children were returned to the foster carers, but this time emergency protection orders were obtained. Subsequently, a decision was made to promote the rights and welfare of the children by applying for care orders and assessing their long-term future. It was considered increasingly important to ensure some stability for them. They were old enough for day nursery and school and were showing behavioural signs of distress, as well as experiencing physical neglect and developmental delay.

At this stage, another relative, the mother's sister (previously unknown to social workers) came forward to offer care. She had her own home, older children and was willing to help. She and her family were assessed and the children were placed with her with the back up of orders and social work supervision, although the grandparents were very ambivalent about this development. At this stage Megan's whereabouts were not known but the father, who was in custody, was agreeable to the arrangement. The parent's right to contact was maintained but when Megan returned she was angry about the removal of the children and the existence of the court orders.

In this situation efforts were made, unsuccessfully, by social workers to support Megan to establish a permanent base for her children. While they seemed resilient, their former lifestyle had affected them. They needed continued stability of care at home and school. They appeared to have settled happily in the extended family and were beginning to catch upon their development. They remained in touch with their grandparents and their mother on an occasional basis. This was a situation where several people had views and judgements had to be made, about what to support and whose choices were to be respected. In the end the children's developmental needs came first.

The skills needed to establish their right to a safe upbringing were many. Legal and administrative knowledge were essential, as was a sound knowledge of the needs, views and rights of parents, grandparents and children. Work in this framework of statutory functions also required a high order of counselling skill. Firstly the social workers had the task of *attentive listening* to all the adults involved, without compromising the child-centred approach. The Children Act requires social workers to work in partnership with parents and other kin as far as possible, while promoting the welfare of children. Secondly the skills of *paraphrasing responses* to the adults were needed, which included the communication of some contested decisions. Here they used *reflecting back* and *immediacy* to check that each party was clear about the reasons for the actions of the social workers.

The task of collecting information to make an assessment needed skills in *questioning* with the use of *alternatives to questions* to explore options. The skills of *confronting and challenging* Megan about the children's needs in such a way that partnership and contact were retained were essential. In this situation, despite the efforts of social workers to maintain partnership with the mother and grandmother, the mother was angry because of the care orders. The grandmother also became alienated by the legal action despite the fact that she had initially requested assistance. The grandmother needed help in accepting that she was unable through illness to care for her grandchildren, and decisive action was needed to secure a safer lifestyle for the children.

Skills in *working with and containing strong feelings*, allowing some *ventilation*, were used. The father was involved and his views sought. He was *facilitated to express* his concerns. Throughout this work the practitioners chose to take a person-centred approach, without compromising the child-centred focus of practice, by *understanding* that each person in this family had worth in themselves and could interpret their own lives in ways that were valid and worthwhile. However they also acknowledged that the agency view, of the mother's incapacity to care for the children consistently, *challenged* this. Thus in making a clear decision to promote the children's right to a settled life, education and freedom from harm, at least two of the adults experienced distress and disempowerment.

This example shows many of the complexities when counselling skills are employed in social work practice. Care has to be taken not to use skills to manipulate or persuade or to give false assurances. At all stages there must be honesty about events and intended actions with areas of disagreement or conflict as clearly identified as possible. Careful and ethical use of counselling skills can facilitate interactions and make the negotiations clear and unambiguous.

In this work acceptance of the person and a non-judgemental approach to the difficulties the parents were experiencing was important. Difficult decisions had to be made to provide alternate care for the children until their parents were in a better position to bring them up. It was important to keep the possibility of the parents resuming care alive in the minds of the workers, children and extended family. A placement within the extended family was thought to be less likely to cause permanent loss of attachment to their origins for the children than foster care outside the extended family.

Skills such as *the ability to be empathic, to tolerate strong and hostile feelings, to communicate honestly and clearly, paraphrasing, summarizing and checking meanings, understanding defences, splitting and projection* were all in evidence. Responding to the anger and distress of parents when difficult decisions have to be made is a very skilled process. The principles of the Children Act 1989 are that whenever children are separated from parents, social workers have to be involved in maintaining positive contact and supporting parents to regain care of their children, wherever this can be achieved, without significantly harming the children's health and development. Sometimes decisive action to separate children from parents who are harming them has to be taken and the reasons communicated unambiguously.

Similar constraints surround the concept of empowerment and advocacy in mental health and criminal justice settings, where skills are harnessed to the primary tasks of ensuring the safety of and supporting people with mental illness and tackling offending behaviour and its consequences, respectively. Voluntary and community agencies are often better placed to use counselling skills in empowerment and for advocacy purposes. Agencies are often set up and funded precisely to ensure that advocacy services are available to those affected by the legal intervention of the state. Counselling skills can also be used in community activity to facilitate change as the next example shows. Social workers can be involved in gathering community views and advocating for new services.

### Practice example

Gandhi writing in *Professional Social Work* describes an 'innovative open space forum where older people could express their needs without being intimidated by professionals'. Working from an empowerment philosophy, Liverpool social services set up a consultation forum for older people in an ethnic minority community to be able to express their views about the services they wanted. Using the mechanism of small groups working on an 'open' participation system, people were able to express their views and so be *listened to*. Gandhi concludes that the main messages she understood from this work were:

- if we want partnership in the true sense then we must go out and find ways to communicate with service users, carers and representatives;
- even with so much research and written literature devoted to improving services for ethnic minority groups, they are still struggling to receive help for their basic needs;
- we can empower service users only when we listen to them and integrate their wishes in future policy and planning. Anything else is lip service;
- even if nothing comes out of this forum, it made service users and professionals aware of their needs and of the gaps in our present system.

(1996: 13)

## Advocacy

Advocacy is an activity which may follow an understanding of the client's wishes in order to achieve their fulfilment. Advocacy may be used to help someone obtain something from another person or institution with more power. Forbat and Atkinson (2005) suggest that in essence advocacy consists of 'speaking up' whether it is for the self (self-advocacy) or with others through a collective process. Social workers may act 'as advocates' and may use their own power and influence in the interest of the real expressed wishes of another. Bateman describes advocacy as a 'sequential activity based on learned skills'. Social workers frequently undertake advocacy activities for clients to ensure that other agencies meet their responsibilities. Bateman offers six principles for social work advocacy:

- act in the client's best interests;
- act in accordance with the client's wishes and instructions;
- keep the client properly informed;
- carry out instructions with diligence and competence;
- act impartially and offer frank, independent advice;
- maintain the rule of confidentiality.

(1995: 25–41)

However, advocates do not always act 'in the best interests of services users' but rather 'to their direction'. Advocates are often independent and to be effective may need to be free of other interests. If they are, for example, employed by an agency, their advocacy may need to challenge or criticize it and this can set up an unhelpful conflict of interest. Forbat and Atkinson's research shows that advocacy as a service is 'a helpful and beneficial strategy for many people'. However, the availability and funding for advocacy services can be stretched or unavailable. Social workers find themselves:

- *referring people* to advocacy schemes;
- *whistle-blowing* on behalf of clients, speaking up about neglect/abuse;
- *supporting* people to speak up for themselves;
- *representing the* wishes and views of clients (as distinct from acting in their best interest).

(Forbat and Atkinson 2005)

The role of the social worker and acts of advocacy are not always the same thing so that while social workers take on advocacy roles, often because they are available to do so, they need to be aware that independent and professionally based advocacy workers may be better placed to challenge professionals and speak up for those who are oppressed or disempowered. This is especially so where the oppression comes from the employing organizational system. As the delivery of care becomes inter-agency and 'joined up' it will become harder for social workers to be seen as independent of any of the agencies and their actions. It might be preferable to support individuals and to represent their needs, views and circumstances accurately and effectively in the first place.

In all activity the practitioner will find it useful to use their listening and responding and linked counselling skills before moving to enactment. Failure to use these counselling skills in the processes of social work may contribute to mismatches between service request and outcome, and the gap between the aspirations to empowerment and the failure to achieve it. Accurate support of choice is based on competent interpersonal skills, including the ability to challenge and be assertive and to advocate.

## Key points

- Social workers can use counselling skills to hear and respond to what people say they need.
- Strengths perspective and empowerment strategies can be underpinned by counselling skills.
- Person-centred approaches to people who use services can be combined with the authority in the social work role.
- Empowerment strategies should be linked to service user consultation and advocacy.
- Social workers need to be able to constructively and assertively challenge when necessary to achieve empowerment strategies or to advocate.

## Questions and activities: for self development or discussion groups

1 Study Neville's framework for empowerment in social work. Write the four headings on a piece of paper. Choose a practice situation where you think an empowerment strategy could achieve change for yourself or a service user. Analyse what skills you will need to mobilize to achieve change and draw up an action plan.

2 Think of a situation where you needed to say something difficult to someone else and did not manage to do so constructively. It might have required challenge and/or confrontation. It could be a situation that became heated and confrontational or one where the needed communication was avoided. Use the guidelines below to help you to work out how the situation might have been handled better. This exercise works particularly well in a group, where people can benefit from each others ideas and experiences.

Follow these steps, making a note of your responses as you go along.

1. Say what you really want to say just to yourself and hold nothing back.
2. Analyse what it is that you must communicate.
3. Disentangle your own feelings.

4.  Compose a way of putting the message across. Think about how to phrase it so that the other person can hear and accept it. Don't soften the message by asking a question. Keep the central message clear and direct. Be sure that you are communicating in line with your role and responsibilities.

(Adapted from Jacobs 1991: 40).

**3** Use the same guidelines to prepare for a future situation where you need to communicate something difficult or challenge effectively.

**Table 5.1** Skills for empowerment in social work

| Power to be acquired over | Social work activity — access | Social work activity — support | Social work skills required for activity |
|---|---|---|---|
| 1 *Resources* — e.g. Income, Housing, Support Services, Transport. | Enabling influence over current and future services by access to decision makers. Allowing advocates to act on behalf of clients. | *Developing themes* — Assisting users to make a link between personal and social issues. For example, poor housing (social issue) and family functioning (personal issue). | Listening, empathy, advocacy |
| 2 *Relationships* — Relationships with professional staff who provide services. | Offering clients choices about the services they use. Offering clients methods and support in making complaints about the service. | *Evaluating self-image* — Assisting users to revive self-confidence and self respect. *Defining and selecting problems* — Helping users to define their own problems and avoid definitions made for them by professionals. | Empathy, respect, counselling, negotiation, advocacy, empathy, respect, counselling |
| 3 *Information* — Giving information about services and their standards. | Giving information to clients about service offered. Setting standards for services so clients know what to expect. | *Becoming aware of policies* — Assisting users to become aware of the services and resources that exist and assisting as part of an educational and political process. | Anti-oppressive practice, advocacy |
| 4 *Decision making* — The way decisions are made and by whom and in what settings. | Offering places to clients on decision-making bodies. Enabling influence over current and future services by access to decision makers. | *Developing and using choices* — Helping users recognize that choice is available and recognize what might be possible. | User involvement in negotiation |

| | |
|---|---|
| *Experiencing solidarity with others* — Bringing users together to share and develop confidence, trust and solidarity. | Empathy and respect |
| *Acquiring and using language* — Helping users develop language that allows them to make connections between one context of power and another. | Advocacy |
| *Resisting a return to a state of powerlessness* — Helping clients not to return to familiar positions of powerlessness (i.e. a return to an institution or a situation of domestic violence). | Counselling, anti-oppressive practice |
| *Developing interactive and political skills* — Helping clients to learn through action and reflection on action towards achieving specific objectives. | Negotiation and conciliation |
| *Evaluation* — Helping users examine the objectives of empowerment and where necessary to redefine the objectives and strategies to achieve them. | Advocacy, listening |

(Neville 1996)

*Chapter 6*

# Managing risk and working together: relevant counselling skills

This chapter considers some relevant communication and counselling skills in relation to two areas: managing risk and working together. It shows that partnership is not entirely dependent on systems and structures, although those matter, but depends significantly on the quality of practitioners' interpersonal work within and across organizational boundaries. Risk assessment has already been explored in Chapter 3 and the organizational frameworks for social work will be discussed in Chapter 7.

When social workers are managing risk to individuals, families, carers and groups (Key Role 4, Standard 3 Scotland) partnership working is crucial and several inquiries have evidenced a failure to get even the basics right, for example, in the events surrounding Victoria Climbié (Laming 2003). For social workers with older people and other adults there are also challenges to co-ordinate service provision well. Those working in residential and day services also have to plan in partnership. The term collaborative work embraces a range of diverse experiences (Leathard 1994, 2001, 2003).

Terms, such as 'working together', 'collaboration' and 'joined-up services' permeate health and social care policy documents. While inter-agency collaboration is expected by government (Department of Health 1998a, b; Balloch and Taylor 2001) it remains difficult to achieve in actuality. For the worker, acting alone can seem simpler, quicker and less complex but the evidence is that service users often get a better service when agencies collaborate to meet their circumstances according to their needs. In 2000, the government issued guidance called '*No Secrets*' about protecting vulnerable adults (Department of Health 2000b). A research study into implementation (Foskett 2004) identifies partnership as one of the most problematic areas, with inadequate partnership frameworks and processes impeding best practice for service users: none-the-less the 'benefits of combining knowledge, expertise, influence and resources in as a unified approach to the issues are plainly evident'.

There is also protection for the services user from abuse in care settings, if when professionals work together, they check and evaluate each other's practice as they discuss who is providing what, how, when and where. Unfortunately, what passes as 'working together' is often a series of unplanned, unco-ordinated events carried out by individuals from different agencies in parallel. This may be loosely co-ordinated by a record of events but falls short of being an actively co-ordinated response to individual need. It is essential that it is clear who will carry out the function of key co-ordinator and actively check that each part of the plan is in place, initiate review and organize evaluation.

Individuals often require inputs from a range of services. The rationale for this, in relation to children, is expressed clearly by Aldgate and Colman:

> Because children's development is multi-faceted, for the first time the Children Act introduced the idea of a range of co-ordinated local authority services being used to promote children's health and development, not just those provided by social services departments. Guidance and regulations emphasise the need for co-operation: sections 17(5), 27, and 30 provide duties and powers in relation to co-operation between and consultation with different authorities including social services, education departments and housing authorities, health authorities and independent organisations. The introduction of Children's Services Plans was designed to enable local authorities to engage in corporate planning of services for children and their families.
>
> (1999: 31)

Proposals for Children's Trusts (DfES 2003a, b, 2004) suggest new structures for the delivery of services. The introduction of a developmental model for common assessment within the Integrated Children's System offers a framework for professionals from health, social care and education to work in partnership. Each brings their unique perspective to build the whole picture and assess what is needed to promote the child's wellbeing and safeguard them from harm.

Managing risk involves protecting individuals from perceived harm, protecting society from the risks posed to them by others and protecting people from harming themselves. It is necessary in practice to balance the rights and responsibilities of the different people concerned. To understand risk it is also necessary to understand vulnerability. Theories of human growth and development are essential for this understanding as 'harm' usually means that someone's health, development, wellbeing and quality of life is being impaired. It is necessary to be able to identify what is happening in order to respond effectively. Professionals from different backgrounds will need to find ways of sharing their perceptions of harm, vulnerability and how they conceptualize protection.

For example, will being accommodated in a secure unit better protect a young person from offending behaviour then a supervised support package at home? People living near the young person might think so, but a community programme working on the behaviour might better protect everyone in the long run. When Mrs Holmes, aged 86, who has been living at home supported by paid carers, falls and breaks her wrist is it better if she is discharged home quickly so that the support package continues unbroken and her confidence in arrangements at home are maintained or should she have a few nights in hospital? Will a stay in hospital restore her wellbeing or is it confusing and disabling, making her feel less able to return home? There are different risks in both situations from each option. Probably in the first example, professionals and/or the courts will decide. Mrs Holmes, if asked, may be able to say what she prefers herself.

Decisions about risks and likely harm are contextual and made by a range of people. Social work literature is pre-occupied by concerns about vulnerability and abuse which are often narrowly defined to specific incidents. However, many very real 'risks' to all individuals are daily accepted by society. Statistically, the risks to children of being injured on the road remain higher than those of meeting someone who might abduct them while walking to school, despite the media panic about the latter possibility. Piachaud (2001) describes how a range of social factors, especially poverty, operate to harm many children, while cases of maltreatment may be more acute, but fewer numerically.

Social workers have legal responsibilities that focus on defined maltreatment, physical, emotional, sexual abuse and neglect, but they are also responsible for assessing needs and promoting welfare. Older people and disabled people are also made vulnerable by societal attitudes, poverty and other contextual factors. Social workers are concerned to address these inequalities and are also concerned about specific abusive incidents. Social policy points to the value of interventions at a range of levels as conceptualized by Hardiker et al. (2002: 50). These are:

(1) measures to protect whole populations;
(2) measures to protect vulnerable groups within communities;
(3) interventions to support people with early stresses;
(4) measures to support people with severe stresses;
(5) responses to social breakdown (for example, 'in care').

These five levels describe a continuum of stages in the development of social problems in models of welfare.

Brown, with Seden, writing of vulnerable adults identifies a range of risks (2003: 244). The four main areas are: predatory and hate crimes where a vulnerable person is targeted and groomed for abuse; risks which arise out of service relationships and paid for relationships; risks arising out of situations created by impairment and having challenging needs; risks arising out of discriminatory or inadequate service provision or failure to access health care, benefits, legal remedies, housing and so on. There are still the 'ordinary' risks of life and the exposure to personal or familial violence or ill treatment.

This chapter considers some skills needed for protection and the management of risks through a case study (Ms Baker) where intervention through all Hardiker et al.'s levels can be seen. Some of the risks outlined by Brown and Seden are also present. Risks were assessed and balanced against each other at every stage of the intervention. However, first there is a consideration of inter-agency collaboration as relevant to the practice example.

### Inter-agency and inter-professional collaboration

Professionals are expected to work collaboratively, as appropriate, throughout all their assessment, planning and actions. Research in children's services shows that the failure to achieve a holistic assessment and plan undermines opportunities for positive outcomes in children's lives (Parker et al. 1991; Birchall and Hallett 1995; Hallett and Birchall 1995; Sinclair et al. 1995). Co-operation between agencies seems to work well at the early stages of assessment and at that stage most professionals seemed to have an understanding of each other's perspectives and roles (Birchall and Hallett 1995).

Birchall and Hallett (1995) also found that after the initial assessment phases, social workers took a lead in case-management roles in child protection cases and a crucial issue in managing risk and working together was maintaining the early liaison through the later stages of the protection plan. Reder, Duncan and Gray (1993) suggest that issues of responsibility and accountability in respect of children at risk make relationships between disciplines less co-operative. This finding is supported by Birchall and Hallett (1995) who say (in summary) that in 'child protection' cases:

- inter-disciplinary training is not in place or sufficient;
- different perspectives are taken by paediatricians and social workers;
- role confusion and uncertainty about who should act is apparent;
- political factors and resourcing issues lead to territorial disputes;
- professional training most clearly affects the way an issue in a case scenario is viewed by a worker.

Valente writes from a practitioner perspective:

> Smooth inter-agency working does not always come naturally. It can be fraught with pressure and conflict, especially in the field of child protection where difficult, contentious decisions abound. Inter-disciplinary collaboration is not a choice . . . there is much to be gained by investing in positive inter-agency working. The mutual support, cross-fertilisation of ideas and pooled resources which result serve to enhance the universally agreed aim of protecting vulnerable children from harm.
>
> (1998: 42–3)

Cleaver et al. (2004: 251) reporting on the outcome of a study into the implementation of *The Framework for the Assessment of Children in Need and their Families* found that where it was thought that collaboration was increased relevant factors were:

- the structured way information was recorded;
- a more holistic understanding of the child's needs and circumstances;
- a greater clarity over the roles and responsibilities of the agencies;
- a greater willingness to share information.

Factors that hampered collaboration included:

- a lack of agreement over the definition of children in need;
- poor social work practice and particularly the failure of social workers to communicate with other professionals;
- unavailability of resources identified as necessary by the assessment;
- increased paperwork through having to record the assessment in a structured and systematic way (without the benefit of an adequate electronic recording system);
- general difficulties related to introducing a new system.

Although practitioners have different professional backgrounds, there are considerable overlaps in knowledge and overall aims, which can be pooled in the interests of children and their families and in the interests of adults living in the community needing support, if the professionals take care to communicate well. The next practice example shows the detail of skilled work, using relationship and basic counselling skills at all stages to assess risk, meet need and work collaboratively. Ms Baker is a woman with mental health and other issues and meeting her needs is balanced with concerns about harm that might occur to her child. A range of professionals and community support are mobilized in a long-term piece of work co-ordinated by social workers.

As you read the narrative notice how the basic counselling skills of listening, responding, paraphrasing, summarizing, asking questions and checking meanings in all the communications permeate the field social worker's active involvement in holding the work together. There were also times when the social workers provided support for others who were involved and took on counselling roles (for example with the foster carers). This narrative summarizes years of sensitive, painstaking and authoritative interpersonal work by social workers, health visitors, family centre, day care workers, foster carers, health visitors, doctors and others, and a great deal of work by a service user struggling to combat disadvantage and a history of conflict in relationships, working to agreed, but renegotiated according to circumstances and crises, plans. Noticing the way skills are used by others is a key way to develop your own.

**Practice example: Ms Baker**

**Part 1**

Ms Baker was 39 when she became pregnant for the third time. She had two other children who had been adopted. At that time she had a violent male partner who used substances. Eventually the situation broke down and she became depressed. Subsequently, the children were removed from her care permanently and this was a source of much regret. Ms Baker was supported by alcohol advisory and mental health services for many years. She had lost touch with her first two children and seemed very motivated to bring this child up herself. Ms Baker took care with her health during the pregnancy, was looking forward to the birth and made adequate preparations. She lived alone within half a mile of her parents who offered some support, although there was also some conflict. Alice was born two weeks prematurely and the birth was difficult. One paediatrician thought this was a very high risk case and that an emergency protection order should be sought. The other members of the multidisciplinary team disagreed, and arrangements were made to support mother and baby at home in consultation with field child care workers. Alice's name was placed on the child protection register and the key worker appointed.

*Social worker's co-ordinating role (1)*

When Ms Baker was first pregnant the alcohol service social worker offered *brief supportive counselling* about her options and she decided to keep the baby. Maternity services became involved and the hospital social worker was asked to make an *assessment* when Ms Baker's history of having children in care became known. A field social worker for her home area was also involved. A pre-birth case conference was held (chaired by a manager from the hospital social work team) and two consultants who had different views. Finally, *listening* to Mrs Baker's wish to keep her child, and *acknowledging differences* of professional views, it was decided that the baby's name would be on an 'at risk register' and support and monitoring at home would be co-ordinated by the field social worker, Linda. The psychiatrist and social workers in the alcohol and drug advisory service would continue to offer individual support to Ms Baker. Linda, the field social worker, began to work with Ms Baker (*listening, responding, and using open-ended questions*). She also used *communication and counselling* skills with her professional colleagues, creating an open climate for them to express their different views (*openness, immediacy, challenge, empathy, summarizing and checking, negotiation*) and engaging with them to make specific commitments to provide services. Linda also explored the issue of Ms Baker's lost contact with her other children, and together they made contact with the adoption services to register Ms Baker's willingness to be contacted.

**Part 2**

Ms Baker's home was near a health centre where a general practitioner and health visitor were easily accessible. It was found that Alice had epilepsy and a mild form of cerebral palsy, and it became important that access to the health centre was immediate when Ms Baker was worried about Alice's health or development. A specialist Health Visitor for disabled children became involved. The hospital's consultant paediatrician monitored Alice's health closely and responded helpfully when Alice needed hospital admissions. To provide further support the social worker applied for a childminding subsidy and found a placement. Ms Baker was initially reluctant to take this offer up, but it worked well. The childminder and Ms Baker built up a good relationship. Later this was repeated with another childminder when the first one was unavailable. The childminders gave Ms Baker a break from child care, helped her build her parenting skills, and crucially provided a link to community networks. Alice was deregistered when she was about 2 and the social worker stopped visiting gradually.

*Social worker's co-ordinating role (2)*

Linda, in partnership with Ms Baker, co-ordinated a complex network of professionals to promote Alice's welfare and safeguard her from harm. In agreement with Ms Baker, a core group of the midwife, health visitor and GP kept in close touch with each other (*phone calls, listening and responding to each other concerns, liaison, checking, information-sharing meetings*). Linda continued to support Ms Baker and also the childminders (*listening, responding*). With time, the situation seemed stable and Linda moved carefully to less regular contact with Ms Baker (*preparing for endings and changes*). This support package was maintained over two years despite some changes of personnel. It was particularly important that communication was kept open with information shared openly, but within an information-sharing agreement. In particular, Linda actively checked communications as received and understood, and ensured that feedback happened often, especially after public or practitioner holidays. In particular she made sure that Ms Baker was informed about any practitioner actions or views about her care of Alice.

**Part 3**

From the age of 2 Alice had a place at the combined day nursery/family centre. Ms Baker attended activities for parents. There were good relationships between the health visitor and family centre social workers, nursery and childminding staff. The fieldwork monitoring stopped and regular reviews were held at the nursery with Ms Baker to discuss Alice's place and evaluate her progress. However, when

Alice was about 3, Ms Baker's father died and she experienced a severe depressive episode (including attempts to harm herself) and was admitted to hospital. Alice was placed with foster carers by agreement but taken daily to see Ms Baker. When Ms Baker returned home Alice returned gradually but respite care with the foster carers continued. Social work, psychiatric and community health service professionals then worked together to support Ms Baker to return home and to community networks, the day centre and family centre. Alice's development was progressing well and a range of services supported this (counselling support for Ms Baker, transport to nursery, health assessments, toy library, welfare rights advice, alcohol advice, psychiatric services, adaptations to the home, welfare benefits advice). Around this time Ms Baker's older daughter made contact, wrote then visited, and took an interest in Alice. The early risks to Alice had been addressed through a support programme. Ms Baker's mental health was stable again and a more positive period followed. Ms Baker's mother recovered from losing her husband and became more involved with her daughter.

*Social worker's co-ordinating role (3)*

For a time, the field social worker, Linda, had a background role and the day nursery acted as a focus of support. Co-ordination was through the nursery place review system which Ms Baker and Linda attended. Alice's speech and motor skills were developing although she still needed nappies and her medication needed careful monitoring. However, when a crisis occurred, Linda's co-ordinating became more foreground and intensive again (*careful liaison, checking, supporting foster carers and others and keeping the communication loop working*). At this point Linda was promoted to manager and Joyce became the social worker. The change was phased in and the two workers met with Ms Baker together to make the handover comfortable for Ms Baker.

**Part 4**

When Alice was 4 she left nursery for school and was allocated a place in a specialist unit. Transport was arranged but she didn't always attend. Ms Baker was a long way from the school (by public transport) and missed the contact with other parents at the family centre/nursery. She began to go drinking with some of her former partner's friends. Then some abusive incidents began, Ms Baker would squeeze Alice too hard or pull at her hair. Medication for Alice's epilepsy was not adequately controlled and there were increasingly frequent hospital admissions, often on an emergency basis. The hospital doctors remained supportive but were concerned about the possible misuse of Alice's medication, especially at night time. Joyce monitored what was happening and together with education and health increased support was offered. However, Ms Baker did not participate in school reviews as she had with the nursery ones. Respite care was not as useful as in the past because Ms Baker wanted to see Alice at weekends when she had been at school all week, although she still found respite helpful in long school holidays.

*Social workers co-ordinating role (4)*

Joyce's role changed to more actively protecting Alice from harm and responding to concerns about her wellbeing, although she was using the same range of skills. The relationship between school and Ms Baker was poor, so Joyce attended a review with Ms Baker who felt criticized about not always having Alice ready for the school bus. Joyce found herself negotiating between the school and Ms Baker (*listening, paraphrasing, exploring, mediating, challenging*). Ms Baker felt isolated at home, so Joyce found her a role as helper to a parent's group at the family centre. This helped but Alice was too tired when she came home from school to respond well to activities with Ms Baker. The respite care arrangement, used flexibly, worked well, and Alice loved going and playing with the foster carers' children.

**Part 5**

By the time Alice was 5 concerns had increased. There was marked deterioration in Ms Baker's mental health and she started to drink heavily, coming to police attention. As Alice grew older she became more challenging, wanting her own way and having tantrums. Concerns were growing about Ms Baker's ability to look after Alice. It seemed that Alice's behaviour at the foster carers' was different from at home and the fits happened more often in her mother's care, possibly because the medication wasn't given consistently. An application for a care order was made but instead the court suggested that Alice was accommodated on a voluntary basis with a written agreement between the social workers and Ms Baker. This covered areas of concern and agreements from Ms Baker to co-operate with assessments of Alice's long term needs. These plans didn't work out and eventually, following a return to court, a care order was made. A placement with the foster carers was made to give Alice some continuity. In the meantime contact with Ms Baker was maintained. Joyce continued to try and promote the partnership between the foster carers and Ms Baker (*careful listening, summarizing, confronting and mediating*) but Ms Baker's visits were reduced as Alice's behaviour after contact became challenging. Ms Baker then began to ring up the foster carers late at night, and was sometimes drunk and abusive. The foster carers then wanted to adopt Alice, but social workers wanted to keep the relationship between Alice, her mother and the wider family, including her grandmother and stepsister intact. Another long-term foster placement with a view to some permanency for Alice was made as Ms Baker became unable to cooperate or make plans for Alice's return home.

*Social workers co-ordinating role (5)*

Joyce, while finding herself advocating for Ms Baker with others, had a difficult assessment to make, but eventually the potential for harm to Alice outweighed the aim to enable Ms Baker to raise her daughter. Even with a great deal of support the situation had become worrying and there were concerns that Alice's health and development were impaired and that she was being neglected. A series of critical incidents eventually led to a successful application for a care order. The professionals involved had worked well and a high level of skilled communication work had been maintained.

### Skills for partnership work

At an organizational level there are many models for promoting inter-agency work. Charlesworth (2003: 142) identifies that there are three levels of joint working for agencies:

### Different levels of joint working

1  Strategic planning: agencies need to plan jointly for the medium term, and share information about how they intend to use their resources towards the achievement of common goals;

2  Service commissioning: when securing services for their local populations, agencies need to have a common understanding of the needs they are jointly meeting, and the kind of provision likely to be most effective;

3  Service provision: regardless of how services are purchased or funded, the key objective is that the user receives a coherent package of care and that they, and their families, do not face the anxiety of having to navigate a labyrinthine bureaucracy.

(Department of Health, 1998a: 6)

Although there are policies to promote joint working, there will still be structural barriers to overcome (Hudson 1998; Hudson et al. 2003). Individual practitioners have to work out how to collaborate to make partnership working a positive reality for service users and not the kind of nightmare non-service where all people hear from each professional is that 'it's not my job' and 'someone else is responsible'.

Charlesworth describes an experience of this kind of practice when someone's 93-year-old mother developed leg ulcers in hospital:

> I was told very, very clearly I was in a grey area. Now the social services used that. When the social services came to see me, she said 'We didn't realise your mother's legs were that bad'. I said, 'Well I told you they were when she was in hospital.' When the district nurse comes, they say they don't do legs any longer, they're too busy, they haven't got time to wash people's legs, that's the social services' job. So they are arguing in my mother's house about who's going to do what.
>
> (2003: 139)

In *Community Care* (2004: 42) the Practice Panel present a situation where two separate sets of plans are arranged for a married couple aged 91 and 89, when the husband, who had been the wife's carer, was admitted to hospital. One worker had arranged a double room in a residential home, while another had arranged a community support package. To compound matters the workers had involved two different relatives with different ideas about what was needed. Had information been shared between the health and social care workers concerned the confusion could have been avoided. New work was required to untangle the situation, ascertain the views of the husband and wife and plan with them together.

Counselling skills are essential in the detailed work that happens if partnership at practice level is to protect service users from harm and maintain care packages effectively, avoiding arguments in front of the service users about who should be doing what or unhelpful duplication of plans. Charlesworth (2003: 161) identifies what is needed to manage partnership work. In her research a senior local authority manager said that in recruiting for partnership managers his requirements were:

> . . . [we] want people with good analytical skills . . . You need skills in dealing with the community, speaking the same language because they have a different set of language to the professionals and then you need skills of diplomacy, negotiation, empathy with partners, being able to look at the broad horizon and short term project management . . . But the interpersonal skills are probably the most important because you get people who in an organisation progress from being a professional to being a manager . . . If you're constructive and positive and you recognise that if you have a personal relationship, they're much more likely to help you and be someone you can call on if things go wrong, or if you upset them, they'll probably be prepared to live with it . . . Command and control might deliver a project by pushing people to get things done by a certain date but it's probably [more] the ability to be able to use a menu of different skills on appropriate occasions.

Interpersonal skills facilitate partnership work at practice level. The report on the death of Victoria Climbié (Laming 2003) describes how she was seen on numerous occasions by different professionals (doctors, social workers, police, pastors, nurses, child minders and voluntary sector child care workers). Sadly, they were unable through lack of training, the pressure of work and lack of communication skills to co-ordinate and bring together the whole picture in Victoria's interests. It was not the rhetoric of 'joined up working' that failed but rather the lack of a co-ordinated structure to deliver collaborative action together with many examples of poor basic practice, especially lack of communication:

> Although the front-line staff who came to deal with Victoria's case were not helped in their task by the structure within which they operated they were, in many cases, guilty of inexcusable failures to carry out basic elements of their roles competently. In Brent, as elsewhere, the social workers involved would have needed only to do the simple things properly in order to have greatly increased the chances of Victoria being properly protected.
>
> (Laming 2003: 105)

The report made recommendations which led to the green paper, *Every Child Matters* (DfES 2003a). A key message from the Laming report is that *seeing and hearing* children is essential:

> Directors of social services must ensure that no case that has been opened in response to allegations of deliberate harm to a child is closed until the following steps have been taken.
>
> • The child has been spoken to alone.
> • The child's carers have been seen and spoken to.
> • The accommodation in which the child has to live has been visited.
> • The views of all the professionals involved have been sought and considered.
> • A plan for the promotion and safeguarding of the child's welfare has been agreed.
>
> (Laming 2003: 376)

The starting point for working with other agencies and professionals is a 'non adversarial' mind set. People who want a service are very disadvantaged when they find themselves in a 'turf war' between professionals whose first concern seems to be the agency and its territory rather than their needs. Networks of agreements and relationships can be built in order to make services both holistic and accessible (Wigfall and Moss 2001; Hornby and Atkins 2003; Hudson et al. 2003). It requires an understanding of the barriers, awareness of the transactions and power relations in partnerships, trust and, at practice level, close collaboration between service users, their carers and professionals.

In the practice example, Ms Baker, the social workers used counselling skills to relate to other workers, Ms Baker, her child and relatives. Partnership skills are essentially about very careful communication, *listening, responding* and checking out by *paraphrasing, summarizing* and using *immediacy* to be clear about expectations. This will happen in a range of activities: meetings, memos, emails, telephone calls and letters. Face-to-face work will also require some understanding of groups.

Verbal interactions of a high quality are necessary. Careful listening to what is available from another organization, careful *checking* and *responding*, the ability to *question* and *challenge* and the ability to make a considered and boundaried set of effective working professional relationships are all vital. Working together within PCTs and Children's Trusts should reduce some of the boundary issues and make people more accessible to each other.

Reder, Duncan and Grey (1993) suggest that the issues of responsibility and accountability in respect of children at risk make relationships between disciplines less co-operative:

> Our own experience is that closed professional systems arise in a number of ways. For example, workers may be so conscientious that they are unable to take a step back, and instead resolutely continue with the same focus. Furthermore, the stress of child protection work can drive staff to seek allies to share their anxieties or confirm their beliefs. Some workers hold a passionate conviction that their views are right, so they become even more dogmatic when challenged by possible alternatives.
>
> (1993: 71)

This demonstrates how anxieties produce defences such as denial and projection that make it difficult to consider alternative perspectives. Enabling others to contain anxiety, lower their defences and engage in a problem-solving dialogue is very important, when difficult courses of action have to be agreed between practitioners as diverse as the police, social services, health professionals and the family practitioner. It is easy to project blame for what is not going well on to others, rather than to stand back reflectively, take responsibility appropriately and agree co-operatively about what to do. Likewise awareness of the creative tension of differing perspectives and roles and the ability to constructively challenge are needed to avoid collusion, since this can also lead to poor decision making.

Tensions can exist in adult services work between medical practitioners, social workers, relatives and service users. The personal skills of the worker are necessary in these situations to achieve the best outcome. Adults with ill health or disabilities, and those with mental health problems, need a well co-ordinated interdisciplinary approach if their needs are to be met holistically, and tragedies avoided. Children and adults are put at risk when professionals fail to communicate and work together, therefore:

- Although professionals might have different backgrounds, perspectives and responsibilities, there are considerable overlaps in bodies of knowledge, understandings and overall aims. Since counselling skills are used by a wide range of professionals they can be a unifying factor, offering a common language and approach to people and practice.

- Interdisciplinary research and training have a crucial role in developing attitudes and experiences of co-operation and the sharing of skills.
- Knowing who should be involved is only the first stage in working towards providing a seamless interdisciplinary service; an attitude of bridge building where commonalities are established by explicit linkages in knowledge, understandings, training and purposes can best mobilize resources for the consumer; counselling skills can be used to make this happen.
- Social workers have a heritage of working from a breadth of professional knowledge bases and are ideally placed to act as brokers and co-ordinators for clients; their underpinning counselling skills can assist communication and the exploration needed to make effective professional judgements.

Murphy (1993) considers the communication issues in multidisciplinary working and says that 'as practitioners, we value our interpersonal skills but do not always extend them to our colleagues'. He suggests the need for:

- listening, giving attention to colleagues;
- valuing the opinions and contributions of others;
- respect for the contributions others bring;
- recognizing stress in others and ourselves;
- willingness to ask questions;
- recognizing structural blocks to communication;
- exploring differences of opinion.

(1993: 171–9)

Harrison et al. (2003) argue that partnerships are about people and how they relate to one another and those organizations should be involved in:

- Enabling the people within the partnership to get to know each other's organization and to know the people involved both as professionals and as individuals (developing understanding through *communication*).
- Ensuring that all the partners are involved in ways that enable them to make a full and positive contribution to the work of the partnership (promoting engagement and *commitment*).
- Developing a consensual way of working which enables the partnership to develop and implement a joint strategic plan and which will be the basis for dealing with any future opportunities or threats (*building consensus*).

(2003: 29)

All this hinges on communications which enable practitioners to know each other as 'people and professionals' so that communication can be open and positive relationships built, nurtured and sustained.

Understanding different ways of communicating and different uses of language requires attention to detail. The practice of talking in agencies tends to develop according to professional identity and so convey the way each group sees the world. Joining a new team in a social work agency can be very baffling, especially when you find people talking in acronyms, for example ICT (integrated children's system), NAI (non-accidental injury), AOP and ADP (anti-oppressive and anti-discriminatory practice). These short-hand ways of speaking may help busy professionals but they exclude others. Such jargon becomes familiar within a professional group but it is difficult to decode for newcomers.

Contextual factors are important because communications have to be made taking into consideration the expectations of others. There are differences in power and status impacting on the exchange. It cannot be assumed that professionals always draw on a shared stock of expectations, understandings and beliefs. Work is needed to unpack what is meant at each level of communication. This means checking that what is transmitted is understood and decoded, and that when you receive a communication you are also clear what is being said. Regular built-in feedback points are helpful. Therefore, in multi-agency or interdisciplinary practice, meanings must be clarified. A helpful way to start is to create a climate that is open for the exchange of views: open and supportive communication behaviours which convey an attitude of willingness to collaborate are typically characterized as:

- *Descriptive*: statements tend to be informative rather than evaluative.
- *Solution-oriented*: there is a focus on problem solving.
- *Egalitarian*: communication values everyone, regardless of their role or status.
- *Forgiving*: the inevitability of error or misjudgement is recognized.
- *Feedback*: this is seen as an essential part of maintaining good relationships.

Conversely, the kind of climate that will make collaboration very difficult and undermine any structural arrangements can be characterized as:

- *Judgemental*: there is an emphasis on apportioning blame.
- *Controlling*: people are expected to conform to certain kinds of behaviour.
- *Deceptive*: messages are expressed in a manipulative way.
- *Non-caring*: communication is detached and impersonal.
- *Superior*: communication stresses differences of status, skills or understanding.
- *Hostile*: the approach places little importance on the needs of others.

(The Open University 1999)

Without using empathy and thinking 'outside the box' of agency territory it will be difficult to collaborate. If old professional allegiances are prioritized above building new open relationships based on trust, partnerships will not work. Crucial to achieving this is an understanding of the nature of boundaries within organizations and between individuals and organizations.

### Understanding and working with boundaries

An understanding of the importance of boundaries is part of counselling skills training. Counsellors consider which boundaries are relevant and the impact on practice. They work within limits, knowing when crossing a boundary is necessary or effective. Counsellors manage boundaries between the self, others and the outside world. Boundaries in counselling are in relation to issues of time, place, touch, setting, confidentiality, supervision, fees, recordkeeping, frequency of contact, endings of work, personal disclosure and contract. Trainee counsellors discuss these and to what degree flexibility is appropriate. This kind of thinking can be useful in understanding inter-professional work.

Some of the counsellor's concern with boundaries is to maintain the safety of the relationship. Social workers equally need to be mindful of possible harm that may come to themselves or others through the carrying out of their roles. Clarity about the boundaries of meetings, who will be present, what the agenda is, when the meeting will end, helps to create a climate of safety. Equally, maintaining boundaries about self disclosure, touch, and where meetings happen in a thoughtful way contributes to safer practice. Using assertiveness and counselling approaches can often defuse and contain hostility and strong feelings.

Boundaries in social work are essential to form ethical relationships which do not use the social worker's personal resources or impose on the life of the service user inappropriately. Boundaries are needed for professional and ethical reasons and also because, thoughtfully observed, they keep both the counsellor/social worker and the person they are engaging with safe. The contract is clear and the terms of the relationship are spelled out. These kinds of ground rules, established early, give both parties something to go back to if later there are issues. It puts them in a more (if not completely) equal position if these things are discussed and mutually agreed. There is no quick way to do this effectively; it requires detailed, sustained work with special attention to information sharing.

Boundaries, then, are helpful in delineating where something begins or ends, the roles and responsibilities that go with a role or the area of discretion each practitioner has. However, they also set up barriers, territories and differences which can make working across them difficult. Wherever a worker is based, the service user needs them to have the capacity to build a 'community of practice' around the service user's identified needs. For example workers may be based in different offices but cover a similar geographical area. This is a complex challenge for practitioners. It is puzzling and often frustrating for service users that the boundaries for different functions of welfare may not be co-terminous.

Practitioners have to develop the skills for recognizing this complexity and finding ways to act together as necessary across the administrative and attitudinal boundaries that create barriers. They also need structures and line management that supports their efforts. Thus practitioners are actively involved in setting up and maintaining the networks which deliver the best service to a particular individual. Each individual's network is a 'community of practice' relevant to their need, evaluated, co-ordinated and managed, either by social workers, other professionals or by the service user and/or relatives as relevant for each situation. This is illustrated by the next example.

---

### Practice example: Mrs Briggs

Mrs Briggs is 90 and lives alone. She has heart problems, mobility problems and pernicious anaemia. Support includes the area warden, agency carers in the morning and evenings to help with getting up and going to bed, a weekly shopper, an emergency alarm system and meals on wheels (all commissioned/ part funded by social services). A district nurse visits to give injections. Mrs Briggs pays directly for a cleaner, a gardener and a washing service. Her renal condition is monitored by the hospital and a medicar takes her to clinics. The local library delivers large print books as her sight is failing. Neighbours and relatives take her to the bank or other appointments. Without these arrangements Mrs Briggs could not manage to live alone and would be a bit lonely and depressed. From time to time she falls or needs urgent hospital treatment. The care package, set up by a hospital social worker some five years ago, has been maintained with minor variations ever since. Mrs Briggs is a bit forgetful at times but can manage to co-ordinate it herself, supported by relatives who live 50 miles away. She telephones them if she cannot manage something herself and they discuss any issues for her with the professionals concerned.

Mrs Briggs recently took part in an evaluation of her services at the request of the commissioning authority. She said that she values those professionals who 'talk to me as if I am in charge of what happens', who 'listen to what I need and don't try and force me to do things I don't like — like going to that day centre — I keep on telling them I don't like card games and bingo'. She was very upset when admitted to hospital after a fall, because a member of hospital staff talked to relatives in front of her saying 'it'll have to be residential care now'. This was a frightening and distressing experience about which her relatives complained. Mrs Briggs likes her home and neighbourhood and although she is in poor health and feels 'fragile' wants to stay there.

---

Collaboration may involve legal, financial, and decision-making activities, and a range of people. While this may be reasonably manageable at the level of commissioning services, detailed conversations need to happen to clarify how the care package/arrangements will work, be maintained and evaluated. In the case of Ms Baker the social workers were skilled at building, creating and maintaining supportive networks by frequent and clear communicating, checking and listening. They used the review system to co-ordinate and evaluate plans and agreements. In the case of Alice, without this careful work the network would not have supported Ms Baker and safeguarded Alice. The lack of flexibility in educational provision (in contrast to liaison between health and the various parts of social services) perhaps contributed to the later difficulties. If Alice had attended her local school with individual support this might have made a difference. Ms Baker might have been better, if she were involved in the school as much as in the nursery. However, it could also be argued that Alice had a right to benefit from relating to other adults and children in the school setting independently.

Mrs Briggs (with relatives) co-ordinates her own services, there is no allocated social worker, but says if it were left to the professionals sometimes she would come out of hospital to 'no services or worse'. Her biggest worry is being admitted to hospital and being discharged without her services 'back on'. Once the care workers asked the police to break in because they did not know she was in hospital and she returned to find the door needed repairing. Mrs Briggs has found a range of counselling and communication skills in the workers she meets and she likes them to check out with her how she likes to be addressed.

Her situation raises a number of issues about talking with older people. She was pleased when the manager of the home-care agency, on the first assessment visit, sat opposite her and then said, 'Now what would you like me and my staff to call you, Mrs Briggs or Dorothy?' This immediate acknowledgement of her right to decide to be Mrs Briggs was very reassuring. She had been worried enough to ask a neighbour to sit in with her. However, she was quite upset when the same agency, without warning, sent a new male carer one evening instead of the usual female carer. She was anxious about the possibility of this happening when she would be undressed and had a long talk with her relatives about it.

Valios (2004: 33) suggests that 'speaking disrespectfully to an older person should be treated by an organisation as a minor disciplinary offence'. This comment is in the context of a discussion about the use of words like 'duck' 'love' or 'darling'. The codes of practice (2000) for social care workers state that they must:

- communicate in an appropriate, open, accurate and straightforward way;
- treat each person as an individual;
- respect and maintain the dignity and privacy of service users;
- take service users' and carers' complaints seriously and respond to them.

Using counselling skills flexibly can enable workers do this, especially if they keep to the maxim to 'listen more than you speak'. It is only by listening very carefully that they will learn service users' individual needs and cultural preferences. It is a challenge to practitioners to use their skills in a flexible and natural way. It would be a shame if spontaneity were lost. Mrs Briggs has lived in a village all her life where everyone calls everyone else 'love'. It is a cultural practice with no belittling overtones, in her world, but to someone else that might be different. Overuse of endearments can seem patronizing especially when people are upset or vulnerable through temporarily losing control of events in their lives.

This is another area where understanding the context and the person is the key. Older people, like everyone else, like to chat, especially if they are alone for long periods. Hinds (2003: 40) discusses research which highlights the extent to which older people enjoy sharing their memories and passing on their stories. The implication here for care workers is to spend time listening rather than talking and to make space to do so. 'Just chatting' is a useful part of what care workers do when delivering meals, attending to baths and other activities in residential homes and in peoples' own homes. Hinds also explore the way organizations can formally promote 'reminiscence activities'.

Some critical issues that arise for working together have been summed up for childcare work (and can equally be applied to work with adults):

- the use of language in all processes of the work with a child;
- agreeing a common process and timetable for action;
- obtaining consent and the sharing of information;
- agreeing how information is recorded and how this record is shared with children and families;
- the exchange of information across agencies;
- the aggregation of information and its use for strategic management and overview and scrutiny.

(Department of Health 2004)

Working together to safeguard from harm needs structural partnerships between agencies but also depends heavily on a high quality of interpersonal and counselling communication skills at practice level between individuals, groups and teams. Effective working relationships have to be constructed on trust, mutual understandings, openness and skilled interactions. This remains elusive in practice because it takes time and a high level of commitment, honesty and respect for others at a time when practitioners may be preoccupied with keeping up with the pace of change and feel overloaded and unsupported by the structures in which they work. However, it is essential that service users can depend on a 'community of practice' which responds sensitively to their needs in a timely way. Effective communication and relationships are the key to success.

## Key Points

- Partnership work depends on good systems and skilled interpersonal work in practice to be effective.
- Inter-agency collaboration is essential to manage risks to service users and protect them from harm.
- Effective collaboration requires the identification of a key co-ordinator who can initiate, actively sustain and evaluate the work.
- Communication and counselling skills permeate and underpin collaborative work.

**Questions and activities: for self development or discussion groups.**

1 Identify an example of when you needed to work collaboratively then:

   a. Evaluate how effective it was on a scale of 1–5 where 1 is not very effective and 5 is very effective.
   b. Identify the factors that helped and/or hindered the effectiveness of the work.
   c. Plan a strategy for more effective collaboration in the same or similar future situation.

2 If you are in health or social care or other work, consider the way you communicate with other agencies. Can you write down the roles and tasks of other professionals with whom you collaborate? When do you meet and talk to share perspectives and each others concerns and priorities? Is there, or could you start, a multi-agency forum in your area? What could you contribute to building communities of practice in your area of work to benefit local service users?

3 If you are a health or social care practitioner, to what extent do you check that interventions you make into people's lives are co-ordinated with the activities of others? Always, sometimes or rarely? How does this affect the people you work with? What the benefits of better coordination for people who use services?

# Chapter 7

# Practice within organizations: relevant counselling skills

Social workers need to understand the opportunities and constraints of the organizations where they work. This involves understanding the nature of organizations, formal, informal, bureaucratic, hierarchical (Smith 1991; Handy 1993) and possessing appropriate interpersonal skills to operate effectively within them. Qualifying social workers must be able to, 'manage and be accountable, with supervision and support, for your own social work practice within your organization' (Key Role 5, Standard 5, Scotland). This chapter discusses the organizations within which and from which social workers operate, and considers further the challenges of inter-disciplinary and multi professional work, including identity, confidentiality and accountabilities. Supervision and support are discussed in Chapter 8.

The relationship between the social worker and the employing agency is one where it is essential to maintain the appropriate personal and professional boundaries. Counselling skills used within the organization are therefore subject to agency expectations and purposes. Standards of practice and legal requirements are to be met and records maintained. Workers are expected to take responsibility for their ability to practice and to seek relevant assistance where needed. There is also a responsibility to work openly and co-operatively with others, treating them with respect. In frameworks for partnership working this applies both within the employing agency and across networks that are developed in order to provide services.

## Accountability

The first and most immediate accountability social workers have is to service users. Organizations also have layers of accountability, such as senior managers, boards of trustees, elected members, inspection and registration, all the way through to central government. Social workers are also accountable to practice in a way that is consistent with the guidelines provided by professional bodies. So, accountability and individual responsibility go together (Clarke and Asquith 1985).

Eby (2000: 187) points out that 'it's not easy to be accountable in contexts where practitioners feel under pressure, and face diminishing resources and increasing workloads'. She adds that there may well be contradictory challenges to be accountable coming from people who use services, employers and professional bodies, partner agencies and the public who will have different priorities and views about what they want to happen. The 'joined up' structures for arranging care services mean that accountabilities are becoming more complex and may need to be mapped, as it is easy for each party to think the 'others are accountable'. Each individual therefore has their part to play in checking that they can account for their activities both to service users and anyone else who has a reason to ask for an explanation of their practice.

### The role of the social worker

In the past, the role of the social work professional has been defined through the boundaries with other professions such as law, medicine and teaching, but over the years there has been more clarity about a distinctive social work role. However, there has also been a tendency to public and internal doubt about the legitimate professional territory of social work, as well as a debate about the knowledge, skills and value systems that equip social workers for their tasks. The establishment of a system for registration with the General Social Care Council together with a clear set of National Occupational Standards for Social Work clearly delineates the role at the beginning of the twenty-first century.

Traditionally social work brought personal and helping skills to other professional settings such as hospitals and courts. The first social workers were in charity organizations. The work done by volunteers with prisoners, destitute children, the mentally ill, older and 'infirm' adults, was formalized into the welfare state during the twentieth century. The new professional social workers of the 1940s found roles in the penal system, children's services, education, mental health and hospital services, as well as remaining a substantial presence in charitable and voluntary sector caring services.

The social work presence in some of the more controlling aspects of public welfare was an important contributor in keeping public services humane and caring. This reflected the contribution of religious and other philanthropic concerns in society, as well as the recognition in political ideology and social policies that individual misfortune or deprivation is not simply about personal deficits, but also about the way individual life experience is affected by structural social inequalities. Social workers were employed to humanize and mitigate the effects of state intervention in the lives of its citizens. They quickly developed a role in challenging the inequalities they perceived in host organizations.

Health and social care provision has grown piecemeal over the decades but the establishment of social services departments in 1971 for the first time gave the profession a clear separate organizational identity. The old divisions between almoners, children's officers and mental health department social workers were eroded as new generic services were created. This continued until local authority reorganization and a spate of legislation affecting social work tasks in the late 1980s and early 1990s meant social workers were regrouped in specialist teams, while still employed mainly in local authority social services departments.

By the beginning of the twenty-first century the pattern had shifted again. The probation service merged with the prison service, social workers for older people, people with learning disabilities and the physically or mentally ill became employed in multidisciplinary teams within Primary Care Trusts (PCTs). New groupings were created to support children and their families (Sure Start, Connexions, Youth Offending Teams). The creation of Primary Care and Children's Trusts reshaped the organizational structures where social workers are employed and further organizational change is likely.

This means that individuals may move out of organizations which specialize in social work practice into multi disciplinary groupings where they might struggle to maintain a sense of professional identity. In these circumstances it becomes essential to be able to communicate what is unique to the social work roles, what areas of expertise and what particular contribution a social worker can make to the needs of the service users. The social work degree (2004) together with post qualifying training identifies the general and specialist bodies of knowledge that social workers are expected to have. However, inevitably there are concerns that maintaining a clear sense of professional identity may be more difficult.

Primary Care Trusts are combinations of the NHS, local authorities, voluntary and private sector agencies, depending on local arrangements. Each PCT works jointly with local government and local communities in a Local Strategic Partnership. The partnership assesses local needs and draws up plans in line with the National Service Frameworks for groups of people. From these detailed local plans are made. Patterns of health and social care within trusts vary from one area to another depending on history and circumstances.

Plans to create Children's Trusts were published in 2004 (DfES 2004). These integrate local education, social care and some health services for children and young people. By 2006 most local authorities will have a children's trust which will have three core features:

- clear short- and long-term objectives covering the five green paper (DfES 2003b) outcome areas of enjoying and achieving, staying safe, being healthy, making a positive contribution and economic wellbeing;
- a Director of Children's Services in overall charge of delivering these outcomes and responsible for services within the Trust and coordination of services outside the organization;
- a single planning and commissioning function supported by pooled budgets. This would involve developing an overall picture of children's needs within an area, and developing provision through public, private, voluntary and community providers to respond to those needs. The Trust should involve children

and families in putting together the picture of their needs and in designing the services to meet those needs.

(DfES 2004)

The key characteristics of a trust are described as:

- co-located services such as Children's Centres and extended schools;
- multi-disciplinary teams and a key worker system;
- common assessment framework across services;
- information sharing systems across services so that warning signs are aggregated, and children's outcomes are measured across time;
- joint training with some identical modules so that staff have a single message about key policies and procedures such as child protection and can learn about each other's roles and responsibilities;
- effective arrangements for safeguarding children;
- arrangements for addressing interface issues with other services such as services to parents with mental health problems.

(2004: 1)

It is within these frameworks, with their many local variations, that social workers practice and work out their roles and responsibilities to children and adults in partnership with service users and other professionals. This chapter therefore considers the way in which being part of an organization affects the professional use of helping skills as well as the concept of relationships built with service users and other practitioners. These frameworks include large bureaucratic structures for managing and making strategic decisions, small teams at local level delivering services and loosely connected networks of agencies in localities to meet particular needs. Understanding organizations and how to make relationships within them therefore becomes an essential professional skill for social workers.

### Organizations and organizational climate

There has been a debate about what kinds of organizations are best for delivering social care services (Seden 2003). Organizations are complex and involve structures (formal arrangements to define roles and responsibilities) and cultures (the informal ways people operate within the structure). It is very important to understand the relationship between your own organization (or part of it) and external factors. In this chapter the focus is on the importance of relationships for co-operative working, whatever structure professionals are employed in. Usually social workers are working with a complex network of service users, carers, other professionals, managers, regulators and communities.

A key factor in service delivery is organizational climate. Glisson and Hemmelgarn (1998) found that a positive organizational climate (low conflict, co-operation, role clarity, and personalization) produced the better service outcomes in the services they studied. Where there is a mixed economy of welfare with commissioning and contracting relationships, Petrie and Wilson (1999) argue that contracting needs to be 'relational' (based on shared values, trust, open and extensive communication, good working relationships and problem solving) if the model is to provide welfare services that work for children. Working in partnership within teams and across organizations needs the personal skills that effective counsellors have in conveying (putting across to the other) respect, understanding and genuineness to create a positive climate and a relationship between agencies.

## Some aspects of human services organizations

Hasenfield (1983) analyses how large bureaucratic service organizations are a product of the growth of the welfare state, designed to manage and promote the personal welfare of citizens, and establish mechanisms whereby eligibility for services is assessed, so that resources are shared out equitably. In order to do this organizations use formal rules, procedures and systems of accountability. The core activities of these service organizations are 'relations between staff and clients'. Mechanisms are established that regulate issues of intake, who makes decisions about the activities and mandates of others, and who has authority over resources. Within these large organizations, both clients and front line workers may lack power, because the organization of the agency mediates the 'series of transactions by which resources and services are exchanged' (1983: 178) and 'the power advantage of human service organizations enables them to exercise considerable control over the lives of recipients of their services' (1983: 180). It also provides a buffer for the professionals within it from their concerns about the less pleasant roles they have to undertake, as the organizational rules take responsibility for rationing or lack of provision away from them as individuals.

The structure usually contains complaint mechanisms to challenge decisions, but sometimes these may seem so bureaucratic that workers lose confidence in their effectiveness. Sometimes informal networks of consensus between workers and clients may arise which subvert or sidestep formal procedures with informal ones. Lipsky (1980: x) describes social workers in large public agencies as 'street-level bureaucrats' and writes:

> the decisions of street-level bureaucrats, the routines they establish, and the devices they invent to cope with uncertainties and work pressures, effectively become the public policies they carry out. I argue that public policy is not best understood as made in the legislatures or top floor suites of high ranking administrators, because in important ways it is actually made in the crowded offices and daily encounters of street-level workers. I point out that policy conflict is not only expressed as the contention of interest groups but is also located in the struggles between individual workers and citizens who challenge or submit to client processing . . . At best street-level bureaucrats respond by inventing benign modes of mass processing that more or less

permit them to deal with the public fairly appropriately and successfully, at worst they give in to favouritism, stereotyping and routinizing, all of which serve private or agency purposes.

Lipsky concludes that 'we must have people making decisions and treating other people in the public services' and that these agencies can 'reinforce the relationships between citizens, both clients and workers, and the state. Many of the criticisms . . . focus on the extent to which people fail to receive, appropriate, equitable or respectful encounters' (1980: 193). Good practices are described as: clear communication; advocacy; guides to rights; summaries of transactions; routine reviews; investigation and accountability (1980: 185). Discretion is identified as another significant element that needs monitoring (1980: 196). Managers need to be:

- encouraging client autonomy and influence over policy;
- improving current street-level practice;
- helping street-level bureaucrats become more effective proponents of change.

(1980: 193).

Lipsky's ideas have been influential. Ellis, Davis and Rummery (1999) examine the tension between care management systems and 'bottom up' decision making by social workers, as described by Lipsky. They noticed that this was played out in different ways by the different teams they observed. Some workers would use rationing to protect their time and resources, while others still saw discretion and autonomy and the promotion of service user defined need as a valued part of their professional identity.

## Social work territory

The boundary of social work territory and the nature of social work tasks have been much debated (Lhullier and Martin 1994; Abbott 1995). Abbott, writing from an American perspective, concludes that:

- social workers should not be disturbed about changing structures of professionalism. Most professions undergo transition and change;
- social work as a discipline of connections across boundaries is related to changes in other professions;
- public assistance is an area where social work holds the territory;
- the public perception of social workers is still that 'they help people'. Social work is unusual in having retained a public image based on a character trait.

However, it could be argued that in the UK the public perception of social work is tarnished through lack of resources, inflexibility in deploying them, managerialist practices and a preoccupation with control functions. The concept of a more emancipatory kind of practice coming through a coalition of service users and practitioners is put forward by Beresford and Croft (2004) who argue for closer links and alliances between professionals, service users and their organizations and movements. Jordan (2004: 17) argues that social workers will need to manage their identity and expertise through organizational change which has the potential for fragmentation of their role. Jordan suggests (2004: 17) that 'this distinctive identity and expertise lies in its emphasis on the social aspects of problems and their resolution'.

The analysis of the role of social workers in their organizations is important because it identifies the extent to which social work is about social relations. It contextualizes the arena in which counselling skills can be used, as they are inevitably part of facilitating encounters within bureaucracies and other kinds of organization. Care needs to be taken that this is ethical; and that counselling skills are not being used in the service of pacifying those whose legitimate requests are being denied. It should rather broker entitlements, advocate and facilitate appeals or complaints as needed, support and convey the values of social work and enable movement towards the emancipatory paradigm and new coalitions need to emerge (Abbott 1995). Indeed, as welfare services in the four countries of the UK move forward into the twenty-first century, new kinds of organizations and groups of agencies for delivering services are already being created.

Counselling and relationship skills remain as a set of abilities which can assist social workers negotiate boundaries between individuals and welfare services in the interests of the public. Counselling skills are used to represent users accurately to managers, and vice versa, and to support individuals though turbulence and change. Counselling skills are used to negotiate the interface between social inclusion and exclusion. Values of respect, understanding and genuineness have to be conveyed by skills (Browne 1993).

Genuineness and understanding are conveyed in organizational matters by: care and consideration in all communication, paying attention to the other, sharing appropriately about your own role and remit, paying attention to confidentiality and discussing differences openly. Respect is shown through active listening, attentive posture, respectful telephone manner, avoiding judgements or blame, accepting difference, remembering what has been said, maintaining boundaries (e.g. being on time for meetings, making sure venues for meetings are comfortable and accessible, avoiding interruptions and careful and accurate shared record keeping). Such attention to details and the communication process requires use of the self and skills. The 'emotional labour' involved in this has been recognized as a key component of work in health and social care (Rogers 2001).

### Information technology and confidentiality

Counselling has always had codes of confidentiality and so has social work. Counsellors have been able to keep confidentiality between their client, themselves and their supervisor (except where disclosure is needed to protect from harm or danger). The ethical framework for psychotherapists and counsellors states:

> Respecting client confidentiality is a fundamental requirement for keeping trust. The professional management of confidentiality concerns the protection of personally identifiable and sensitive information from unauthorised disclosure. Disclosure may be authorised by client consent or the law. Any disclosures should be undertaken in ways that best protect clients' trust. Practitioners should be willing to be accountable to their clients and to their profession for their management of confidentiality in general and particularly for any disclosures made without their client's consent.
>
> (BACP 2004: 7).

Managing confidentiality in social work organizations has become more complex, because of the numbers of people involved, the nature of the information held and the number of agencies who might input to the electronic databases which are used. The legal framework is set out by the Data Protection Act 1998 and there are two key principles:

1. The right of access: the right to know what is held about you and to check that it is accurate and fair.
2. The right to confidentiality: the right to expect that others shouldn't have unwarranted access to information held about you.

In practice this has proved very difficult. For example, concerns about confidentiality have been used (mistakenly) to withhold data generally. However, there are restrictions on what may be shared and with whom. As Winchester (2004) writes, 'social care has more problems with this piece of legislation than most. Much of the information accessed by social care professionals is sensitive, yet sharing it quickly and appropriately can save lives'. There are additional concerns around the use of shared data bases between agencies, for example as in the Information, Referral and Tracking System introduced in 2004 to improve child protection. The principle should be that, 'you should only collect the information you absolutely need on people, only those who have a real need for the information should be able to access it, and it should be destroyed immediately when no longer needed' (Bingham in Winchester 2003: 39). However, who defines 'need' and on what criteria? It will be crucial for practitioners to 'keep talking' with service users and each other as the nuances of guidance are worked out in practice situations (Sone 1996).

Social workers are employed in new coalitions with health, housing, education, juvenile justice and others with the aim of creating accessible and better services that are more responsive to local need. However, as Eaton (1998) writes, 'it comes down to the same thing; it is not the structure, but the staff and the attitude they and their managers have, that matter most'. Social workers will want to work (whatever the shape of the organization) in ways which respond humanely to service users in an accountably autonomous way characterized not only by technical rationality but also by reflection in action (Schon 1983) in which the use of counselling skills to facilitate practice will remain ethically viable. Changes of philosophy about social policy and approaches to welfare inevitably affect social workers at the interface with the public, but it remains possible to maintain a relationship to consumers within practice, and to use counselling skills to facilitate 'choice' and 'voice' without being manipulative.

The next practice example shows counselling skills used within the framework of an assessment process with a couple needing residential care. The social worker is working from an older people's team and liaising with residential care homes. It is a 'routine' piece of work, yet the needs of the people are both joint, individual and critical.

### Practice example: Mr and Mrs Davis

Mrs Davis needed an emergency residential placement because her husband and carer Mr Davis suffered a heart attack. Mrs Davis was physically very fragile and diagnosed with dementia. A short-term emergency bed in a local psychiatric unit was provided, but after Mr Davis was discharged from hospital there were concerns about him caring for his wife. Mr Davis felt his main need was to be with her. He was visited at home and his needs assessed. He needed minimal assistance with personal tasks, but much assistance with domestic tasks (caused by lack of mobility, wheeziness and advice from the hospital to relax because of his heart condition). Mrs Davis had been assessed separately and the two assessments identified different needs in terms of the physical and mental aspects. It was clear that the overriding concern was the couple's wish to be together. Mr Davis could not relax when apart from Mrs Davis and she fretted for him.

A joint placement was sought, but it had to be one that could meet Mrs Davis's mental health needs as well as Mr Davis's physical care. The organization of homes (according to the person's identified condition) meant that when somewhere possible for Mrs Davis was found, most residents except Mr Davis had a cognitive impairment. The couple moved into a shared room, on a trial basis, with a four weekly review arranged. Mr Davis however began to find the demands of his wife and living with so many confused people very tiring. Nonetheless he felt that he would miss his wife if he returned home. He was also worried about losing his accommodation. It was agreed that he would stay the month on a trial basis. He would have a separate room and the staff would link him to some of the less confused residents so that he had some social support within the establishment. The social worker would visit him weekly.

These visits were important as they gave Mr Davis the opportunity to share his concerns with someone he could trust. The practitioner *listened* to his comments about the establishment which were *fed back* to staff for action, especially as planned introductions to less confused residents weren't made. The limitations of the placement were talked through and Mr Davis was able to reflect on what he would say at the forthcoming review. He shared concerns about the future, worry that relatives were not visiting and some of his feelings about Mrs Davis. There were also practical issues, such as making a will and sorting out financial arrangements (*attentive listening, exploratory questions, clarifying, summaries, ventilation of feelings, empathy*). Unfortunately Mr Davis suffered a further heart attack and returned to hospital just before the next review date.

This example shows a social worker competently completing assessments, enabling the purchase of appropriate care and reviewing progress within organizational structures which do not really fit Mr and Mrs Davis's joint needs. She also works closely with the social care staff in the residential settings. Within the procedural framework, the practitioner built a relationship with Mr Davis, and other signifi-cant work is achieved as counselling skills are used to help him to express his views and exercise his choice as much as possible. The practitioner's work was based on Scrutton (1989) who writes that, 'at its simplest, counselling is no more and no less than the development of a warm, empathetic and understanding relationship with those who are experiencing emotional and social stress, giving them time, listening to their troubles and responding to them' (1989: 6–7).

In the four weekly sessions between assessment and review, the practitioner made good use of personal skills in the service of effective social work practice. The worker reflected that *unconditional positive regard, empathic understanding and genu-ineness* were offered, but that *empathic understanding* did not mean denying prob-lems. She reflected that perhaps opportunities to open up difficult subjects and *allow the expression of fears and worries* were not taken enough. At times the social work role meant giving advice about what might be most useful, but it was also possible to *listen* to Mr Davis's wishes. The worker could *attend to feelings about the loss* of social role, friends, home and the loss a lifelong companion through a degenerative illness.

Initially Mr Davis said that his emotional need to be with his wife was more important to him than any needs around his physical disabilities. When worry about her was beginning to affect him, counselling skills were used to help him talk about the unavoidable changes in circumstances. He had had, in a very short time, to cope with his partner's increased confusion, his own inability to go on caring for her, worries about moving out of his home and worries about his own deteriorating physical health. He wanted to care for his wife as long as needed, but her relatively good physical health compared with his own ill health was changing this. He talked to his social worker about his concerns about his own death, and the fact he could no longer talk with his wife who had always been there for him. He talked about the absence of solutions, and various family concerns. In retro-spect the worker wished they had been able to talk more about his concerns about dying before Mrs Davis because Mr Davis died following a second heart attack and admission to hospital.

Counselling skills were used to facilitate choices despite organizational and resource constraints. An entirely administrative approach to the social work task would have been disempowering and potentially ageist. Older service users face a substantial loss of status and identity as illness and disability affect their usual coping methods. This is compounded by the illness and death of peers and partners and the realization of the nearness of their own death. As these limitations increase, workers' respect of their ability to exercise as much control as possible is crucial. A positive choice can be made to practice in a person-centred way from a developmental perspective.

## Voluntary and independent sector agencies

PCTs and Children's Trust can be organized to include voluntary, charitable and private organizations who often take key roles in leading developments and representing service users even though they have no statutory obligations. As services which are often seen as more accessible and approachable by service users they also retain key roles as service providers and will (depending on local arrangements) have representatives on Trust Boards. These organizations employ many qualified social workers, train social workers and provide direct services to the public (for example, National Children's Homes, The Children's Society, NSPCC, MIND, MENCAP and Age Concern). Social workers are also employed in housing services, alcohol and drugs advisory services, family centres, residential care services for children and adults, advice centres and advocacy services.

Many of these agencies offer therapeutic services which require a high level of counselling skills, and workers engage in direct counselling work. It is therefore important to have the personal skills to work in both large and small organizations in an accountable and effective way. Smaller organizations or those with less hierarchical structures often give practitioners the opportunity for different kinds of practice. For example Family Service Unit, a large national organization, is characterized by small units that operate at local level responding to local need, enabling a variety of practice, including community work, group work and intensive individual family support, using therapeutic techniques based on counselling approaches. There is evidence that consumers respond well to accessible, informal mechanisms for helping. These give workers scope for creativity in their methods and interventions. A family centre social worker was able to offer counselling, based on feminist approaches and a cognitive model, to a young parent in a way that would not have been possible in a different setting.

### Practice example: Louise

Louise requested individual counselling because of her depression. The centre's open door policy made this possible and she was offered counselling through a structured weekly meeting. The outcome was positive. When the work was complete, Louise said that she felt able to separate out her problems and to recognize the issues she needed to work on. She had begun to see that meeting her own needs was equally important to meeting her family's needs; that although she still felt unhappy at times, she realized that this was in part due to the way she had been treated in the past. The practitioner concluded, 'for my part, what Louise told me made me realize our counselling had achieved some positive purpose'.

Another example is described in *Community Care* where a family were working with social services following the sexual abuse of a child by a relative. After monitoring and case conferences, some specified work was recommended in relation to family dynamics and the child's behaviour. The mother wrote:

> We asked if the work could be done at the family centre, not only because of the friendliness of the place but because we had built up a relationship with the staff there. We will be co-operating fully with the family centre to do this work, so we will not have to go back to the case conference. We do realise how silly we were not to admit to the injury to Kieran straight away, but we panicked, thinking the children would be taken away from us. Looking back we have received a lot of support and help from the family centre, not just with the children, but also with our marriage. We do acknowledge that social workers do not always have the time to do the long term work with families that family centres can.
>
> (23–31 July 1997).

If children and families are to work in partnership with social workers, this only truly occurs when the choices made by users are on the basis not of coercion, but recognizing need and genuinely co-operating. A climate of trust facilitates this. Fear leads to covering up and avoidance. The family strengths approach to working with families (Whalley 1994; Scott and O' Neill 1996; Turnell and Edwards 1999) uses an empowering approach based on relationship skills, without losing focus or authority.

### Working in multidisciplinary teams

Social workers in mental health have moved into multi-disciplinary teams within Primary Care Trusts. This was a relatively untried organizational structure at the time, so that as teams formed they were developing models and means of practice as they went along. They had to explore how to understand each other, develop common skills bases and approaches to service users while retaining their own professional identities. While it required some adjustments, collaboration was often improved. One worker said:

> The joint working we get now is just superb . . . It used to be so difficult to get messages to people, and there's so many things you just wouldn't bother to

say to people. Whereas now, you catch their eye while you're writing up your notes, and you just start having these sort of conversations . . . I think my manager's really crucial to making the team work effectively . . . We have regular community team meetings and through those we've developed that sense of team identity and support and we use those.

(Charlesworth 2003: 150)

Team meetings where people can talk play a crucial role. Practitioners are concerned about threats to their professional identity and whether their jobs and roles will get merged. However, despite initial worries and concerns, and time spent working out the practice implications 'for real' those who contributed to some research (Henderson 2003) were able to identify some positive changes:

. . . there was an understanding of social workers and community nurses doing very similar jobs and they could be knocked together . . . I think that what's happened is that we've become much more understanding of each other's role. We have been able to stand together with the social workers and defend our role, so the difference between social work and nursing has become amplified and more clear . . .

(The Open University 2003: manager consultations)

Another manager thought that closer joint working would lead to a better understanding of roles and benefits to service users:

I think what we're talking about is maintaining professional identity. I think people who are from the social care background need to advocate for what they believe in, that they believe social care can effect change in people, and I believe people from a health care background need to do the same. Now the issue is, why are we putting these people together? We're not doing it for the workers, we're doing it for the service users, they don't want to have two assessments, they don't want to have two organizations at each other's throats . . . it's [also] about respecting the difference, but in a way where we work together, instead of competing against each other . . .

(The Open University 2003: manager consultations)

One of the benefits of professionals working together in integrated teams seems to be the lessening of territorial allegiances, some refocusing of roles and responsibilities and an easier exchange of information and ideas. One of the common features of language between such professionals is their understanding of counselling and communication skills, which while not necessarily gained by training together can carry currency across boundaries. This was identified by a group of mental health professionals who contributed to a course on communication and relationships in health and social care (The Open University 2004). Here is a summary of what they said:

**Practice example: a multidisciplinary team speak**

Lynne (an occupational therapist) said that she uses social skills to set people at ease and then manages the time to enable service users to talk and share their view of their situation. She uses *empathy and repetition* to draw people out trying to avoid questioning. She *leaves space and stays silent* so that she *doesn't interrupt* the narrative or concerns that the other person is expressing. In the second half of the meeting she does use *questions* to obtain the information she needs to provide the service. She wants to *build rapport and trust* and thinks it is *sensitivity and empathy* that do this best. She is careful though to *listen* carefully to the feedback from the service user and to *respond* to this as she goes along. Lynne learned her social skills from her parents and work experiences but has since benefited from professional and counselling training, supervision and sharing with colleagues.

Chris (a consultant psychiatrist) talked of *influencing* people and defusing difficult situations. This is so that he can help patients and the team to manage and support mental illness. He learned his communication techniques through his medical training and experience, but is very aware that such skills need refreshing and checking out on a regular basis.

Siân (a community psychiatric nurse) also uses *verbal skills* but is very alert to *non-verbal language*. This is so that she can set people at ease and be sensitive to the non-verbal messages they may give about how they are feeling. Siân says skills of communicating are learned early in life, but that they are 'fine-tuned' on the job through training and experience.

Carly (a social worker) is very sensitive to the disadvantages that the service users experience. As well as other skills she uses *advocacy and assertiveness* to try and improve people's situations and make sure they are heard. She brings a high awareness of social inequality from her own background and has improved her skills through training. She says that '*ongoing reflection*' is very important indeed in thinking about how to develop and improve your practice.

Jean (the team clerk and receptionist) works to be calm and approachable. She uses *empathy* to reassure people when they are anxious. She treats people 'as I would like to be treated' and has a flexible approach to the different styles of others. She has learned from others 'on the job' and now feels able to help others learn. Keeping *confidentiality* is important in her role.

The Community Mental Health Team members identified many skills, but maintained a high awareness of the context and appropriateness of their actions. Many of their service users are ill or distressed so they need to be very sensitive and careful to communicate as skilfully as possible in order to enhance the service users' capacity to communicate and to tell their own stories. They are using their own skills to enable others to be heard and to respond. Their work is to assess risks and provide support working together in the team and with other agencies (e.g. housing) to benefit their service users. They use these basic counselling approaches with colleagues as well as with the people who use services as they carry out their work.

### Specialist counselling services

It has been argued that counselling skills are useful to social workers in fulfilling their tasks in their own organizations, in inter-agency work and multidisciplinary teams. This section considers the specialist roles of social workers in some organizations where more advanced skills are needed. A few key thematic areas are covered here, but there are many settings where social workers can make an effective contribution through providing brief supportive counselling. People are often best helped by immediate assistance, rather than experiencing delay before referral to expensive and distant services. It is helpful if social workers in advice and intake services can offer brief counselling input to resolve immediate difficulties. Workers in specialized agencies obviously need further advanced skills relevant to their particular area of practice.

### Adoption and fostering services

The involvement of social workers in the specialized and complex area of placing children temporarily or permanently in the care of others requires high levels of counselling skills. Adoption, foster carer assessment and post-adoption work mean helping individuals adjust to many changes and uncertainties. Specific work is often undertaken in relation to tracing or not tracing birth parents for adults who were adopted in the past and have lost touch with their origins. Social workers in this area need specific kinds of knowledge, sensitivity and advanced counselling abilities.

### Safeguarding children

All work with child protection issues needs sensitivity. Social workers need advanced and post qualifying training to work well with children who have experienced physical, emotional, sexual abuse and neglect. Some of the examples given earlier show how using counselling skills can enhance this work. Some of these practitioners have undergone training in more advanced interviewing skills, to enable them to interview children who will give evidence in court when perpetrators have been charged with offences (Wickham and West 2002). Social workers who are undertaking work towards disclosure of abuse and providing evidence for the court process have to be competent in direct work with children (Jones 2003, 2004; Aldgate and Seden 2005). Children do not always at this stage have the opportunity of specialized therapeutic help. Some social workers are employed in

voluntary agencies which offer this. There has also been an expansion in telephone counselling services for children aiming to give the young people control of
the process and choice about referral to direct services. There is similarly a need to
work with adults and older people about past abusive childhood experiences,
which requires specialist counselling expertise.

### Learning disabilities

There has been increased recognition of the need to enhance the choice and life
opportunities of adults and children described as having learning disabilities. New
ideas about communicating and understanding have taken the work forward, carefully considering ways of reducing power differentials and genuinely creating
therapeutic encounters in which the service user's voice is heard. Brandon (1989)
explores the ways in which such counselling can usefully take place, including
verbal, music and art therapies. A crucial issue for service users remains having
control of your own life, and having social workers who start from the premise that
this is what should happen (Sinason 1992).

### Hospices, death and dying

Social workers employed in health settings, alongside counsellors, occupational
therapists and medical specialists, are primarily involved in practical matters and
care planning but some have a more therapeutic, counselling role. However, this
may be an unreal distinction, because in caring for the dying or bereaved people, a
unique set of needs for emotional and practical assistance are present (Katz 2003).
Those working in these settings are often trained to a more advanced level about:
bereavement counselling; feelings and attitudes to death and dying; awareness of
their own feelings and the impact of the work on themselves. Such skills are essential to facilitate their own work along with the skill to refer to appropriate counselling services as needed. The voluntary sector and private sector provide hospices
for adults and services for parents and children who are seriously ill or dying. There
are also specialist services for parents whose babies are stillborn or die in
unexplained 'cot death'.

### Disasters and crises

Local authorities in partnership with health, police and other services have emergency planning responsibilities for incidents such as rail or air crashes or terrorist
activity. Social workers are usually designated to join the team of caring professionals who will assist the survivors and shocked relatives at the scene and afterwards. This kind of work requires warmth, compassion and the ability to simply
'be there', and knowledge of the effects of trauma and post-traumatic stress

(Hetherington 2001). There are long-term effects on people involved in shock or crisis.

Social workers are often the chosen confidantes of people struggling with difficult life events, simply because they are there and the service is visible. Sometimes social workers are already involved with a family when a violent incident or tragic accident occurs. In this capacity they will find themselves at least involved in brief counselling, for which particular skills are needed. In Madrid in 2004 when train bombs went off in the morning rush hour, social workers found themselves acting as a point of reference for families of victims, supporting families through identification and funeral arrangements, supporting those whose carer or parent was killed and arranging alternative care. This was co-ordinated by a social emergencies unit (Sale 2004).

## Globalization

The fast pace of change around the world brings new issues, for example, social workers have become involved with immigration and unaccompanied asylum seekers. While the appropriateness of some roles social workers have been asked to perform in relation to immigration is questionable (Humphries 2004) the capacity to respond flexibly to the adults and children and trying to re-establish themselves in a new and often hostile environment is important (Department of Health 2001a; The Open University et al. 2005). Social workers need to have an understanding of the impact of both previous and current experiences on adults and children alike. They may have fled hostility and violence, be uncertain about their future, miss a familiar cultural environment and relatives left behind, experience hardship, isolation and perhaps hostility in their new location. All these feelings require skilled support and help.

## Alcohol and substance use

Working with people who use substances is also central to social work practice. All social workers need a basic understanding of the issues involved in alcohol and drug usage, and when they become harmful to the individual or family in relation to mental health, parenting capacity and offending behaviour. They need to be aware of the research that has linked certain counselling styles to better outcomes. For example the use of cognitive approaches with offending behaviour has been found the most helpful. Many social workers are employed in specialist agencies which counsel and advise on problem drinking or the control of drug use. Some counselling skills training in specific approaches is needed (Unell 1996; Williams 1996).

These are only some of the areas where social workers need both general counselling skills to facilitate their work, and to be offered more advanced training in specific areas. Social workers are also involved in fertility and genetic counselling, mental health settings, termination of pregnancy, HIV and AIDS counselling. Much of the work of social workers in these areas takes place in inter-disciplinary teams where care is co-ordinated and methodologies shared. Training is necessary to know exactly which counselling styles might be most useful in each situation to avoid the unnecessary duplication of approaches: to achieve this, consumer feedback is essential. Jacobs (1996) provides a useful overview of care activities and the relevant counselling skills and resources.

## Key points:

- Organizational change to the contexts for social work practice is a continuous process.
- Organizational arrangements affect social workers' roles and define how they carry out their tasks and the way they can relate to the people who use services.
- Organizational climate is as important as organizational structure and can be influenced by interpersonal skills.
- Social workers can use counselling skills to represent service users and work for ethical practices in organizations.
- Some social work roles require advanced counselling skills and specialist knowledge.

## Questions and activities: for self development or discussion groups

1 List the organizations that you have worked in or know. How do the ways the organization is structured affect social work or other working practices? Do you think that large bureaucratic organizations make personal work and relationships with service users more difficult to achieve? (For example because they have so many layers of management making decisions.) Are smaller organizations always better places to practice social work? Or are large and formally arranged organizations more accountable and fairer in the way they share out resources?

2 What can individuals do to influence the working climate of an organization? In your current or past workplace are there specific ways counselling skills could contribute to creating and sustaining better working relationships?

3 What are the particular skills and attributes that social workers bring to working in:
   a. multidisciplinary teams
   b. networks across organizational boundaries?

*Chapter* **8**

# Developing professional competence: relevant counselling skills

It is crucial for social workers to demonstrate their ability to take responsibility for their own learning and professional development. Although many roles and tasks are created by policy and guidelines, there is still considerable scope for professional judgement. The quality of the service depends significantly on the communication and relationship skills of the individual practitioner. The variety of methods for achieving goals in intervention relies on the worker's ability to select the appropriate methods and to work with people ethically and responsibly, sharing their thinking. As adult learners, social workers contribute to their own development and practice while supported by managers and peers. Qualifying workers have to show that they can 'demonstrate their professional competence in social work practice and then take responsibility for their own continuing professional development' (Key Role 6, Standard 4, Scotland).

Commitment to professional development remains essential for social workers throughout their careers. Post Qualifying and Advanced Awards are designed to build on qualifying training and enable candidates to reappraise their abilities in relation to complex work. Additionally, all practitioners need to keep abreast of changes in the law, new research findings, and the implication of all this for practice. The fast pace of change seems constant and needs practitioners who are responsive and reflexive. Local authorities responded to fundamental changes introduced by Margaret Thatcher's governments, only to find these redefined by the New Labour initiatives of Tony Blair's governments. Both administrations put their own philosophies into practice in ways which heavily influenced both the context for social work practice and the details of what practitioners were able to do. Responding creatively to policy changes is fundamental to social work.

At the same time, social workers have to show that they are able to carry out their roles and tasks effectively and ethically (competently). The British Association of Social Work code of ethics (BASW 2004) expresses the values and principles that are integral to social work. The requirements for the degree in social work (2003) are accompanied by two codes of conduct and a Statement of Expectations from individuals, families, carers groups and communities and those who care for them (Topss 2003 a, b, c). This chapter considers the way that social workers can develop their competence using counselling skills for practice to promote a person-centred and relationship-based approach in line with BASW's ethics statement and the requirements for qualification. In summary, there are three key aspects to consider:

- promoting wellbeing:

  > Every human being has intrinsic value. All persons have a right to wellbeing to self fulfilment and to as much control over their lives as is consistent with the needs of others.
  >
  > (BASW 2004)

- building ethical working relationships:

  > Maintaining constructive relationships that don't exploit and promote development.
  >
  > (BASW 2004)

- combating disadvantage by challenging what may be:

  > not in the best interests of service users
  > unfairly discriminating
  > oppressive, disempowering or culturally inappropriate.
  >
  > (BASW 2004)

This is complex. Social workers must demonstrate that they can carry out their mandatory duties well, sometimes involving elements of compulsion. At the same time they have a professional responsibility to reflect on whether their actions contribute to the human dignity and worth of others and to social justice. If the way statutory duties are framed appears to conflict with professional ethics, then questioning, identifying conflicts of interest, and whistle blowing about what is wrong is part of ethical professional practice. This chapter now turns to some key areas where counselling skills contribute to the development of professional competence. These are: listening to services users; taking a developmental, related approach; using evidence from research; working in the team; using supervision; self care; taking responsibility for self-development. Each section ends with some questions to prompt reflection and exploration of particular situations and circumstances.

### Listening to people who use services

The necessity of learning to listen to what service users say they want from services and to their evaluations of practices is fundamental to professional competence (Connelly and Seden 2003; Topss 2003b). Beresford (1994, 1995) describes the parents of disabled children as 'active agents' and not 'passive recipients' in relation to services. The concept of the service user as actively involved and in charge of their own lives as far as possible is one which should transfer into all practioner interactions with people, provided it does not degenerate into avoiding the responsibility to provide a resource. Service users report of meetings with practitioners who are 'transmitting' but not 'receiving' communication. They say that often practitioners give opinions, impose their own ideas or cultural prejudices and assumptions. Listening skills have been discussed in Chapter 2 but the development of competence in active listening cannot be over-emphasized if the policies regarding partnership, valuing and listening to people are to become real.

Isaacs writes that the capacity to listen puts the listener in contact with the dimensions of the world and opens the door to participation in it. He also argues that it is important to listen to the self to become more aware of your own inner prejudices, stereotypes and assumptions:

> The heart of dialogue is a simple but profound capacity to listen. Listening requires we not only hear the words, but also embrace and accept, and gradually let go of our own inner clamourings. As we explore it, we discover that listening is an expansive activity. It gives us a way to perceive more directly the ways we participate in the world around us.
>
> This means listening not only to others but also to ourselves and our own reactions. Recently a manager in a program I was leading told me 'You know I have always prepared myself to speak but I have never prepared myself to listen'. This I have found is a common condition. For listening, a subject we often take for granted, is actually very hard to do, and we are rarely prepared for it.
>
> (1999: 83)

### Questions and activities: for self development and discussion groups

1 If you audited your listening skills at the end of Chapter 2, or kept a diary, return to it now and re-appraise how well you are able to actively listen. Obtain feedback from others on your listening skills and note any ideas they have for you to improve. If you are in a group, practice your listening skills in pairs by one person talking for five minutes about a recent experience and then the other having listened carefully, paraphrasing what has been said. Then reverse the process. Give each other feedback.

2 When you prepare for a meeting, a visit to someone's home or other social

work activity do you prepare to listen to the other as well as preparing what you will say? If you do not prepare to listen, plan your next activity with listening as well as talking in mind by identifying areas you think the other(s) may wish to talk about and also leave time for them to raise their concerns. Review any differences in the outcome afterwards.

## A developmental, related, approach

Anand and Sen (1994) in a philosophical paper for the United Nations Development Program argue for social justice and the unacceptability of bias and discrimination. Individuals' circumstances, they argue, depend not on individual initiative alone but on the social circumstances in which people live and the opportunities that are made available by social institutions. In particular they argue strongly for a focus on 'sustaining the quality of human life' and 'developing humans'. This emphasis on enabling the fulfilment of human potential underpins the international definition of social work which informs the requirements for the degree in social work and is consistent with the Human Rights Act 1998.

Understanding human developmental needs and working in relationship to meet them remains central to effective practice. To do this practitioners will need to understand the issues for developing children which promote or impair their development (Aldgate et al. 2005) and the sociological and psychological impact of life events on adults who need services (Seden and Katz 2003). Counsellors and counsellor training emphasize the need to learn the capacity to stay in touch with the emotional and psychological needs of others. Social workers also need to develop the capacity to understand the emotional needs and feelings of those they work with and to manage the strong feelings often involved in the work.

The professional relationship does appear to be a contradiction in terms and yet it remains the conduit for the delivery of services in social work, health care, education and other human service professions. A counselling skills approach to ethical communication provides a sound basis for a range of professional practice. In human transactions, the use of the relationship cannot be ignored and practitioners need to be able to appraise the impact of their ability or inability to relate well to others.

Most emotional, attitudinal and social growth and change for people takes place through their interactions with others. Practitioners often work with people at a time of life crisis or acute stress. Service users can be very vulnerable and exposed, challenging and hostile, very ill, socio-economically disadvantaged or oppressed. It is important to understand that this situation is not the whole of a person, or necessarily permanent. It may be a turning point or transition. Social workers will need to draw on knowledge of psychological concepts, for example, attachment and resilience, to understand how people react to and deal with events like loss and change if they are to respond competently (Rutter 1985; Rutter et al. 1994; Rutter and Hay 1996; Gilligan 1997; Jacobs 1998; Seden and Katz 2003; Skye et al. 2003; Aldgate et al. 2005).

The Department of Health in a consultancy paper, *The Obligations of Care*, said that, 'In social services more than in many other professions, personnel at all levels can have sustained one to one contacts with vulnerable clients' (1996: 4). The nature of such transactions makes it particularly important that ethical, boundaried, non-stigmatizing, enabling, yet warm, empathic and accepting relationships are offered by social care staff to people in their care or on their case loads conveyed through skills. The skills of relationship are the foundation from which other abilities are practised, so that where trainees do not meet these first requirements adequately it is difficult to contemplate how they can operate at all.

Counselling has been criticized for preciousness about 'the relationship' and so has social work. Workers involved with children who died at the hands of carers have been considered to have put relationship with the adults first to the detriment of children, a perception which changed subsequent child care practice. Social work and counselling relationships must have the right boundaries, and should only be entered into, in order to achieve an ethical and agreed purpose. Social work has been also criticized for becoming over bureaucratic and concerned with organizational aims at the expense of the wishes of consumers and workers. Brand (1997) sums up the frustrations of many practitioners:

> I finally and sadly abandoned social work when Shropshire joined London and the rest of the South East in discarding genuine personal involvement with people needing help in favour of mechanistic rituals designed to protect the organisation.

She describes the nature of the human and helping encounters of her earlier working experience:

> I had never before failed to maintain my optimism and enthusiasm despite the heart aching task I had often to perform — what could move any woman more than to hear a young mother dying of cervical cancer describe what she wants for her children when she is no longer with them. I have heard the painful revelations of a small child whose body has been abused, and I have seen that pain shared and that child helped by the social worker.
>
> (1997)

Efficient administration, easy-to-handle forms, clear guidelines and policies are an essential part of caring. They can facilitate action, ease dilemmas and save precious time. Importantly, they help to make the worker accountable, ensure more equitable service distribution, protect the service user from potentially abusive hidden actions, and avoid the misuse of individual discretion by workers. However, a reaction to the conflicts of competing demands, high caseloads and dwindling resources can be the reasons why social workers take refuge in bureaucracy. It is therefore important to question over preoccupation with agency routines at the expense of quality service to users in terms of relationship. To focus entirely on the agency agenda flies in the face of the well articulated voice of users for supportive relationships from social workers which acknowledge their feelings as well as their situation.

The challenge to social work education and practice is to integrate a personal and relationship-oriented service with accountability built in to organizational procedures and mandates. The achievement of this balance in a professional, focused, reflective and humanistic way is the key to a holistic service in which professionals, the public and policy makers may have confidence. As Dominelli (1996) argued, 'public confidence is not maintained when this aspect is neglected'. In understanding the relationship between client, society and ourselves we discover what social work is, how it should be taught and assessed. Social work's particular role focuses on:

- the promotion of people's wellbeing, using a developmental understanding;
- understanding and intervening in political and social contexts, combating disadvantage;.
- keeping the service user's expressed wishes, views and feelings central.

Social work process, based on interpersonal skills has high potential value and function for society, in managing deprivation, deviance, abuse, injustice and malfunction in the social system. This role of intermediary between the public and government is very important and requires the quality of process to be effective as it is largely (if not always) based on consent. If the public loses confidence in the ability of the profession to broker between personal needs and the state in a person-centred and process conscious way, social work practice as it is known will become marginalized. As Statham asserted:

> recovery of the importance of process in human interactions revitalises the social care process . . . managers are increasingly recognising the importance of process and style in achieving change. Similarly, service users, carers and their organizations say that it is the style of the worker, the relationship and their ability to spend time working with them which is valued.
>
> (1996)

## Questions and activities: for self development and group discussion

1 How would you characterize the relationships that you build with people you work with? What skills do you need to build honest relationships based on open clear communication?

2 Obtain and read the Statement of Expectations from individuals, families, carers groups and communities and those who care for them (Topss 2003b). Compare the views expressed in it with the practices in your work place and examine the extent to which they reflect these views. Plan any changes that are needed to meet the expectations.

### Using evidence from research

Social workers must keep up to date with research to make sure that practice remains competent and informed by relevant evidence. Knowing how to assess the reliability and relevance of research findings is also important (Gomm and Davies 2000; Shemmings and Shemmings 2003). One key factor when considering what weight to give to research findings is a steady build up of evidence confirming previous and current findings. An example of this is *Child Protection: Messages from Research* (Department of Health 1995) where an accumulation of evidence from several research studies led to proposals for a refocusing of work with children and families towards family support. There has been much research to evaluate the implementation of legislation at the point of delivery in social work agencies. While the primary focus of such research has not necessarily been counselling skills, one outcome which recurs is thematic reference to the value of counselling skills and personal support based on a helpful relationship.

Hardiker and Barker (1996) examined the implementation of the Community Care and NHS Act in a large social services area. They systematically interviewed commissioners, carers, providers and service users in relation to 24 cases of needs-led assessment and care management. The user groups included older people, disabled and learning disabled and mental health referrals. The primary aim was to examine how social workers used existing values, knowledge and skills in a time of rapid agency change and development to meet the requirements of new legislation. When the researchers examined the work methods chosen, they found that what they termed 'counselling/casework' was rated highly. For example in one not untypical situation, the social worker provided counselling including:

- listening and engaging a young man in constructing his own plan;
- helping him to manage anxiety and stress regarding job applications and interviewing;
- helping him to reconstruct his negative views of his own performance;
- helping him to build a realistic relationship with his parents.

The young man participated in all parts of the plan. His parents were impressed by the care showed by the workers, and were very satisfied with the outcome (1996: 34). In relation to the 24 cases, the researchers commented that 'social care planning, casework and counselling were central approaches to meeting need and managing the transitions the users needed to make', and that:

> Many of the service users had long-term needs, and their disabilities were often serious, with the prospect of deterioration. Some were isolated and living narrow and restricted lives (often shared by their carers). In many cases their living arrangements were at a point of change. Sometimes their support networks and interactions were at risk. These factors led to a considerable amount of stress, in both users and carers. Some were very

distressed, and needed the opportunity to express their grief and fears about the future.

(1996: 23–4).

Aldgate et al. (1997) studied the contribution of respite care (temporary planned accommodation) to family support for children in need. They were able to examine the outcome of services provided to families in several local authorities, chosen to represent divergent populations and geographical areas. The study shows the provision of respite as successful in 60 per cent of the cases and quantifies the ways in which social work processes facilitated this. One factor in achieving success for families was the use of counselling skills in casework interventions. The researchers write about the importance of social work support:

> What emerged during the study was the complex role of the family support social worker as complete case managers, integrating the activities: of social care planning and social casework. Not only did social workers organise the service but they undertook direct work with parents, identifying problems and together seeking strategies to ameliorate them. Carers were co-opted into these strategies when appropriate, for example to advise parents on improving their parenting skills or to make children feel special. Throughout the placement, the family support social worker kept in touch with parents by letter or phone to monitor the progress of the placement. In short they engaged in the classic social work processes of assessment and intervention which are best described as social casework. This professional relationship was valued and used by clients to good effect.
>
> (1997: 206)

It was also clear from this study that the counselling skills of workers were used to facilitate the classic processes of intervention, managing the transition and ending the contact positively. When needed, skills in interviewing parents, carers and children were used to facilitate this process. The use of skills to broker community networks which could exist into the future was also crucial.

Consultation also provides valuable evidence of what is needed. Reference has already been made to the consultation undertaken for the degree in social work. The *Every Child Matters* summary document (DfES 2003a: 7) sets out five outcomes which mattered most to children and young people who were consulted about their views on future services as: being healthy, staying safe, enjoying and achieving, making a positive contribution and economic wellbeing. These are the outcomes to be achieved for individuals through initiatives such as Connexions, Sure Start, CAMHS (child and adolescent mental health services), the youth justice system and extended schools. Connelly and Seden (2003: 27–47) discuss service users' views and consultation, making clear that it is critical to both listen and respond, avoiding tokenistic and mechanical responses which lack commitment.

A further area of research to consider is the relevance of the different approaches to counselling to specific situations. Trevithick (2000) suggests that five particular 'schools' of counselling are influential within social work, mainly because they 'promote personal freedom and are consistent with anti-discriminatory and anti-oppressive practice.' These are:

- client-centred counselling (sometimes called person-centred or humanistic counselling);
- feminist counselling;
- cognitive behavioural counselling;
- psychodynamic counselling;
- eclective and integrative counselling (adhering to no single 'school' but instead combining different approaches).

(2000: 135)

While each 'school' of counselling has its own underpinning knowledge base and associated practices, all tend to use the basic counselling skills outlined in this book. Social workers need further training to take on more than brief and support-ive counselling roles, but can be aware of where the benefits of certain approaches to counselling have been demonstrated to help in particular areas of work. Examples of this are the use of cognitive behavioural approaches in work with offenders and people who use substances, feminist approaches for women who have experienced abuse, or the research findings on effective interventions with sexually abused children and their families (Jones and Ramchandani 1999). Readable accounts of different approaches to therapy given from the client's per-spective can be found in Jacobs (1995a, b) and Walker (1995a, b). Corey (1997) critically examines the major theoretical strands of counselling practice, discussing some ethical and professional issues associated with each with the aim of helping readers to select from them in a relevant way.

### Questions and activities: for self development and discussion groups

1 Can you list three research studies which would provide you with evidence-informed knowledge about your work? Where can you look for the outcomes of research studies for your field of practice (university websites, professional bodies, government and research centre websites, professional journals, government publications)?
2 How could you consult the people who use your service and find out their views? If your agency has done this, to what extent has the outcome permeated the way the service is arranged and influenced what is done?

### Working in the team and groups

Social workers usually work in teams and counselling and communication skills are directly transferable to understanding groups and the way people relate in teams. It is also helpful to have an understanding of some of the complex dynamics which can operate in teams and ways to build teams (Belbin 1981, 1995; Ward 1993; Jay 1995; Syer and Connolly 1996; Payne 2000; Ward 2003). For everyday tasks open communication and the ability to collaborate are the key qualities that help to nurture a sense of team and teamwork. For example, teams work best when the members can talk easily to each other about relevant information, what is working well and where there are difficulties. It can be extremely important to be honest, especially when part of a new multidisciplinary team where the members may have different expectations brought from their particular background. For example a manager of a new Sure Start team said:

> Everybody's ideas of team meetings were different. Some have never had team meetings and that was really quite difficult at first because some people didn't think you had to come . . . and I think it was very difficult because you just made assumptions from what you'd done yourself and so we actually very early on sat down and wrote our own ground rules. And they've actually been really useful 'cos we're now sort of two years on and we still refer back to them sometimes . . . When we had two people working together they actually set themselves a co-working contract . . . how they were going to deal with things, what skills they were both bringing, what their styles were, and what would annoy them, and then at the end of each group session they would actually talk about that . . . they talked very honestly about it and they got so much out of it and, at the end of it they visibly had increased their confidence.
>
> (Charlesworth 2003: 161–2)

Members of social work/care teams seldom choose one another, as usually they are selected by the employer along with others with the aim of putting together the knowledge and skills mix needed for the particular workplace. Often teams are multidisciplinary, so that they really do have to talk to each other to understand the skills that each other brings, working styles and preferred ways of operating. This kind of open communication can create a 'climate' to work in that is enabling and supportive, especially if the team members also have the skills to offer each other honest feedback when things are not working well. Teams which have a 'climate' of grumbling and blame can be a poor experience. Seden (2004) wrote that a good team leader:

- communicates what you are expected to do, but chooses words that do not criticize or belittle, especially when your practice is less than desirable;
- is honest about your failings and offers a way to do better;
- offers encouragement and recognition for what is going well;

- leads by example — you can watch and hear ways of doing and speaking that are good practice;
- leaves space for the team members to build relationships with and support each other;
- retains a sense of humour and proportion while still keeping to work tasks;
- conveys respect, genuineness and empathy to staff within the boundaries of the work relationship;
- makes opportunities for team members to learn together and from each other.

### Questions and activities: for self development and discussion groups

1 List the communication skills that you think are needed for contributing to building a positive team climate.
2 Jot down the skills and qualities for the ideal team member to work with in your situation. Now consider how much you offer these attributes to others. Think of ways you contribute to building a sense of teamwork. Try and identify actual examples that you think work well that you could use again, or that are new but could be tried.

### Supervision

The experience of supervision and processes of induction and appraisal are central to any worker's professional development. It enables them to: check out that the work is undertaken in a way that is appropriate to the service user and the agency; be given time to discuss and explore different, new or better ways of working; receive support with any particular issues the work is raising for them; receive assistance with any issues that need to be dealt with in a different part of the agency or in another organization.

Supervision in social work has similar antecedents to supervision in counselling practice. Both have a history that includes understandings of the process from a psychodynamic perspective. The roles and functions of supervision are well established (Morrison 1988/1999; Richards, Payne and Shepperd 1990; Kadushin 1995; Hawkins and Shohet 2000) from which they can be summarized as:

- *management*: ensuring agency policies and practices are understood and adhered to; prioritizing and allocating the work; managing the workload; setting objectives and evaluating the effectiveness of what is done;
- *education*: helping staff to continue to learn and develop professionally, so that they are able both to cope with societal and organizational demands and to initiate fresh ways of approaching the work, according to changing needs;
- *support*: enabling staff to cope with the many stresses of the work;

- *mediation*: helping staff to find the relevant resources and means of carrying out their tasks.

The knowledge, skills and frameworks from which to practice are well established (Sawdon and Sawdon 1995; Morrison 1988/1999) but the extent to which there is good practice in agencies can be questioned. Pritchard (1995) writes:

> I have been very fortunate both as a student and as a practitioner always to have had regular supervision of a high standard. I know this is rare; many workers and managers do not regard supervision as important and do not make it a priority. I have seen the consequences of workers not having supervision and of situations in which colleagues have 'done their own thing'. In these times of high stress and low morale, supervision is crucial for all workers.

The gap between knowledge and practice in this area seems wide, contrasting starkly with counselling practice, where detailed and close supervision of practitioners on all levels is considered essential and it would be exceptional for it to be accorded a low priority. Marsh and Triseliotis write:

> Newly qualified staff have major problems establishing their practice. Induction courses are poor and in-service courses are rarely tailored to their needs. 25% of new staff in social services report that they have no supervision in their first year, and for many others it is unplanned and erratic.
>
> (1996: 1)

Cleaver et al. note that:

> Neither practical tools nor extra training will lead to better decision making if social workers are having to work with an infrastructure which is not supporting them. The overview published by the Department of Health (1995a) of research programmes noted the variable quality of the supervision received by social workers and the frequency with which inexperienced staff had to deal with difficult situations alone.
>
> (1998: 40)

In practice, few managers appear to receive special training in supervision skills despite the models available to them. Ability to supervise relies heavily on role and 'apprenticeship', which is just as likely to result in new supervisors passing on oppression and poor practice, as empowerment and good practice. Where practice is competent no doubt it will be modelled and transmitted, but this seems a very crucial area of managerial activity to leave to such a hit and miss approach.

Another critical issue is the extent to which workers in multi-disciplinary teams and their managers share a common approach to supervision. The literature described here belongs to social work, and in nursing clinical supervision may have a very different content. Learning to work together means that the opportunity to consult with and talk through practice issues regularly and in a structured way with an experienced manager is essential for professional development, so common understandings and practices will have to be negotiated.

There has been a tendency for supervision to become very focused only on case management. Alongside this, however, it is important to have the ability to contain and allow ventilation of the stresses and anxieties about the work. These, if left unresolved, reduce the workers' coping mechanisms and contribute to stress and sickness. This ability includes not only the basic counselling skills described for practice, but also more advanced understandings of power dynamics, the defences and resistances that affect worker performance.

Supervision in social work practice is clearly neither psychotherapy nor a personal support system for the practitioner. But given that any feeling human being is likely be affected by the nature of the work, then listening, responding, checking and empathic support from managers towards staff all remain important. Likewise, if errors are to be avoided in complex cases, some understanding seems essential of how workers may deny or distort their understandings under pressure. Whatever the model adopted, effective communication skills are needed to facilitate process. Workers need time to reflect upon and analyse decision making and the personal components of their responses.

## Questions and activities: for self development and discussion groups

1 Are you provided with the supervision and support you need to carry out your job effectively? If not what do you need to do to influence your manager/agency to provide what you need?

2 If you are receiving supervision does it educate, support, manage and mediate, while allowing you space to discuss any concerns or strong feelings you have about the impact of the work on yourself?

3 What contribution do you actively make to the supervision process? Do you prepare your agenda? Are you open about your strengths and concerns? Are you thinking about training that you need and asking to be sent on relevant courses?

### Self care

Supervisors, however well trained, cannot be experts in everything. Opportunities to use the expertise of consultants, in a non-managerial role, can be useful. Likewise, the day-to-day demands of stressful work may precipitate other personal issues. Counselling is useful in supporting people through times of crisis or personal change. This view has been challenged in the press, with writers suggesting that stress is positive, or that counselling creates a dependency culture, of which the only good outcome is more jobs for counsellors (Gordon 1995: 23). While counselling is no panacea, and unnecessary for those whose inner resilience, personal support systems or other interests sustain them, there are times when the emotional support of a professionally trained counsellor with no personal agenda is helpful.

There appears to be a culture in some social work environments whereby social workers are expected to survive with few supervision sessions, and no other accredited personal support, despite the amount of work, time pressures and the stressful nature of much of the work. It is clearly recognized in counselling literature and training that the experience of 'being helped' is part of the development of the ability to help. There is therefore no stigma attached to being a client, although this does not seem to be the case in the hierarchical approach to helping which sometimes appears in social work. It seems sad that a profession with a clear set of values, knowledge and skills for practice, does not view the ability of workers to seek assistance with complex work, or personal support, as maturing and strong but rather as a weakness. The change in emphasis in requirements for the social work degree might influence this. Certainly, the issue is discussed from time to time in the professional journals, for example, Dougan in *Community Care* says:

> As a social worker who has attended a variety of workshops over the years and is now in training as a therapist, I have been continually struck by the absence of other social workers on courses which often included teachers, nurses and other professionals. This is largely to do with the often abusive environment that is endemic in many social services departments. There appears to be a notion that seeking counselling is a sign of professional weakness. In my view the opposite is likely to be the case.
>
> (1996: 12)

It is also apparent that helping professions attract those people with personal histories that give them insights into some of the difficulties faced by others. This can be an excellent motivator, but it is not surprising if, from time to time, the human nature of much social work triggers a personal reaction in the helper. Training assists beginning practitioners to look at their personal values and the impact of the work on them, but even the most experienced worker will be emotionally affected by their work and in some situations it would be surprising if any worker were unaffected. One of the workers with the West family, dealing with the aftermath of sadism, abuse and murder wrote:

> Eventually the children were found permanent placements and the care team's task came to an end . . . The personal cost was high. All of us felt we would never be the same again. We had gone around for so long with all this information locked in our heads and we were unable to let it out. You felt you could never be normal again. We were all offered counselling and many of us are still receiving it. We have group sessions where it is a real relief to be able

to say anything you want and know that no one will be shocked or upset by it.

(West Social Worker 1996)

The nature of social work is such that stress and burn-out have become more common. There are times when counselling, separate from supervision or appraisal, can be helpful. Agencies facing escalating costs from absence and retirement due to stress and ill health in the work force need to address the human needs of their workers. Writing in *Community Care*, North quotes a manager as saying:

The pressure of caseload management means a lot of time previously available to discuss the issues of a particular case and also the effect on the social worker has been squeezed and we have lost the time to deal with personal issues . . . It came as no surprise that months after the launch of council's employee assistance programme this summer, social services staff have become its biggest users.

(1996)

Such schemes show belated recognition of the stress that social workers face, and reflect the way that supervision has become almost wholly managerial in some agencies. Workers need another service to meet the outcomes of increasingly complex work and the impact of some hostility and violence towards them. However, where such schemes are available, it has to be recognized that the agency context has an input on what is offered. Carroll and Walton (1997: 2) offer a helpful checklist for organizations considering employee counselling services including issues of the boundaries of the work contract and confidentiality.

Employees, naturally, have fears and anxieties about approaching an employment-based service with legitimate, work-related issues, in case their career progression is affected adversely. It is therefore essential that these issues, mainly around confidentiality and future employment prospects, are openly and publicly resolved at the outset. The benefits of a completely confidential service to employees along the lines of student health services in universities might be the most empowering way to assist with work stress. As Walsh suggests:

All human systems, indeed all humans, can profit from periodic reflection on their behavior with the help of the perspective of a third party. Many mental health and social service professionals spend considerable time playing just such a consulting role for others; we should accept its value for ourselves as well.

(1987: 283)

While it is important that employers provide such schemes to workers to alleviate stress by offering support and counselling services at times of personal work-related crisis, both as a matter of right and on a confidential basis, these should not be seen as a substitute for addressing working practices on a day-by-day level. Strategies such as formalizing and disseminating employee rights; respecting employee rights; ensuring that workers take their holiday entitlement each year and claw back unpaid overtime promptly; providing good information; making space for team meetings and support groups; facilitating workshops and further training all help (Cartwright and Cooper 1997; Nucho 1988; Seden and Katz 2004).

### Questions and activities: for self development

1 Identify up to three things in your work place that cause you to feel stressed, then:
   a. Reflect on what exactly worries you, concerns you, makes you feel uncomfortable or pressured (leading to stress) for each item you identified.
   b. Think about what you/or others could do to alleviate the build up of stress Could you delegate some work, take time off, find some training or support or improve the working environment?
   c. Identify what makes you relax/unwind. Plan to do more of it.
2 Do you contribute to creating stress for others in any way? (For example, creating tight deadlines, making it hard for others to ask for time off, criticizing unnecessarily.) Is this the best way to develop staff competence and commitment? What other approaches are there to your relationships with others at work?
3 Do your know what your employment rights are and what services the agency or trade union offers you?

### Taking responsibility for self development: becoming a reflective practitioner

Agencies have responsibilities for developing staff and for enabling learning throughout the organization (Pearn and Mulrooney 1995). However, practitioners move from job to job and have a personal responsibility for identifying gaps in their own competence and seeking training. In relation to communication and counselling skills, there are courses and workshops that can be helpful and also distance learning packages such as Communication and Relationships in Health and Social Care (The Open University 2004). It is also possible to learn much from noticing the skills of others in practice and by obtaining feedback from colleagues and service users.

Social work is a challenging profession and practitioners need to be engaged in emotional, reflective and practical ways with service users. Continual professional development will be everybody's responsibility, agency, worker, team, managers and service users. It is important to learn to reflect before, during and after each event in practice. This is so that practitioners can explain what they are doing when they meet with service users, and also enable them to evaluate, review and learn. As Parker and Bradley (2003: xi) write:

> Reflection is central to good social work practice but only if action results from that reflection.
>
> Reflecting about, in and on your practice is not only important during your education to become a social worker. It is considered key to continued professional development. As we move to a profession that acknowledges life-long learning as a way of keeping up to date, ensuring that research informs practice and striving continually to improve skills and values for practice, it is important to begin the process at the outset of your development. The importance of professional development is clearly shown by its inclusion in the National Occupational Standards and reflected in the General Social Care Council (GSCC) code of practice for employers.

In teaching and social work education, reflection 'in' and 'on' action is most often conceptualized from the work of Schon (1983), Kolb (1984) and Honey and Mumford (1982). Atherton (2003) provides a useful summary:

> Reflective practice is perhaps best understood as an approach which pro-motes autonomous learning that aims to develop students' understanding and critical thinking skills. Techniques such as self and peer assessment, problem-based learning, personal development planning and group work can all be used to promote a reflective approach . . . when we speak of 'reflect-ive practitioners' we usually refer to adult learners who are engaged in some kind of activity (often professional) which they can use to reflect on their strengths weaknesses and areas for development.

Reflection on activity can be embedded into the workplace and agencies which aim to be 'learning organizations' will include space for reflective analysis of prac-tice. Time for reflection can be part of induction, appraisal, supervision, team and group discussions. At the same time each individual needs to take responsibility for their own learning in practice and reflect on what is good practice while preparing for, doing and evaluating each piece of work. The skills needed to do this include:

- listening;
- responsiveness to feedback;
- awareness of the impact of self on others;
- the capacity to stand back and analyse (cognitive skills);
- the capacity to reflect on feelings and intuition.

Such reflection combines experiences, knowledge and feelings in order to examine the way the practioner handles work situations which may be uncertain and com-plex. The Open University Open Learning Programme for Social Work describes the skills for reflecting as follows:

Reflecting is an essential skill in being able to make judgements and decisions in social work. One way of looking at it is that it allows us to develop our professional knowledge through practice and through analysing experience systematically. By putting practice and experience at the forefront, it fits the way most social workers go about their work.

Theory far from being absent in reflecting, is revealed through practice. In other words, reflecting is essential in helping us to understand what is informing what we do, so that we can benefit from experience and use it in a way which improves practice. It helps us to develop our own 'theory' through what we do, to put alongside the ideas of others.

Like all skills it will be helpful if we have a way of starting our efforts to improve. The framework we use here for reflecting has been adapted from an unpublished paper by Abraham (1992):

- reflecting on what underlies our judgements;
- reflecting on theories which are implicit in a pattern of behaviour;
- reflecting on feelings, and what they imply for action;
- reflecting on the way the problem we are thinking about has been explained and what alternatives there might be;
- reflecting on how we or others see our role in relation to the problem or issue we are thinking about.

Everybody reflects to some degree, but social workers must make the most of the thoughts and ideas they have about their work, and approach reflection as an integral part of practice, requiring time and discipline to do properly.

(Dimmock et al. 2004)

Continuing professional development can only happen within an organizational climate which shows recognition of the value of reflection 'in' and 'on' action by formally building in the time for practitioners to undertake group and individual developmental activities.

The questions and activities for reflection in this book are one way, if undertaken carefully, of doing some self-development in relation to counselling and communication skills. Counselling and communication skills provide a core of techniques than can be relied on to facilitate communication and relationships. However they are never wholly 'learned'. They are new each time they are employed in a new relationship and fresh situation. They are constantly refined and reshaped by changing relationships and contexts. The skilful practioner therefore will learn techniques and practice, but through reflection 'in' and 'on' each situation will use them appropriately and as led by the expressed wishes and feelings of the service user as far as is possible.

Many have written of the need to bring the 'care' back in to the caring professions and the 'heart' back into social work practice. This lobby for a renewed attention to service user voice, a focus on human development, relatedness and wellbeing are reflected in the requirements for the social work degree (Topss 2003a, b, c). However, this will be of no avail if trainees and practitioners are not supported within their workplaces to handle the challenges, stresses, uncertainties, complexities, difficult human dilemmas and events that are a daily part of the experience of being a health or social care professional practioner.

Much has also been written of the emotional costs to practitioners (emotional labour) of undertaking work in care agencies such as hospitals, schools and social work agencies (Malone et al. 2004). The role of such practitioners in carrying the anxieties of society about death, illness, crime, child abuse and other social issues has also been discussed and analysed (Reynolds et al. 2003). The theories for understanding the impact of the work on individuals and for supporting them exist within counselling literature, however this remains underused partly for fear of 'pathologizing' individuals, and partly from concerns about losing the focus on agency tasks and mandates. This caution is, to some extent, a reasonable one and the workplace should not become a therapeutic community which loses sight of the needs of the service user group, who should come first. None-the-less there is a balancing act to achieve between using the insights and knowledge available for understanding people, and supporting them to do their tasks in a professional and boundaried way, remaining focused on the work to be done. It can be argued that if management use these 'humane' approaches with their team members, to support them and develop their skills, practice will improve and stress or sickness decrease (Seden and Katz 2003). The more 'humane' approach will also be communicated to service users. As Rogers argues such skills can be used to bridge the intersection between care and bureaucracy:

> There is a growing recognition of the costs of emotional labour in the helping professions, and the implications for nurture and caring. At the same time, the organisational world is faced with increased managerialising and bureaucratising in the interests of an audit culture and a commodity mentality. In a depersonalised, technically focused environment, the sustaining of a rich emotional climate upon which the development of relationships and care becomes increasingly difficult. There has been a call to focus on soft skills in continuing professional development, for education and training to provide avenues and support to use feelings to maintain a therapeutic connection with users, patients, clients . . . Creating and sustaining communities of care that focus on the role of emotion in education and work can offer 'continuing professional development that recognises the significance of personal development and the social world of the learner' (Gorman 2000, p.157) . . . Such communities of care move the agenda beyond skills development to exploring the intersection of nurture and bureaucracy.
>
> (2001: 190)

### Conclusion

This book began by outlining a tension between 'top down' managerial approaches to social work practice and 'bottom up' service user and practitioner-based approaches to shaping services and practices. It has been argued that communication and relationship skills drawn from counselling practice are essential tools to building partnership and participation between service users and practitioners, where they are the means of establishing what the people who use services need and a means of conveying respect. Counselling skills are also useful to practitioners for building supportive inter-agency networks and individual 'communities of practice'. They can also assist them to handle the emotional demands and challenges of caring work.

Counselling skills can underpin and permeate all key social work activities: assessing, acting, planning, advocating, working in organizations and developing competence to practice. Social work provides services *for* people delivered *by* people where the ethical use of competent counselling skills to build and enhance the relationships between the people who receive and those who offer care is a critical component of best practice.

# References

Abbott, A. (1995) Boundaries of social work or social work boundaries? *Social Services Review*, December: 546–62.

Adams, R. Dominelli, L. and Payne, M. (eds) (2002) *Social Work: Themes, Issues and Critical Debates*. Basingstoke: Palgrave.

Aldgate, J. and Colman, R. (1999) *A Conceptual Framework for the PQ Award in Child Care*. London: Department of Health.

Aldgate, J. and Simmonds, J. (1988) (eds) *Direct Work with Children*. London: Batsford.

Aldgate, J., Bradley, M. and Hawley, D. (1997) *Supporting Families through Short Term Accommodation*. London: The Stationery Office.

Aldgate, J. and Seden, J. (2005) Promoting developmental outcomes for children in J. Aldgate, D. Jones, W. Rose and C. Jeffery (eds) *The Developing World of the Child*. London: Jessica Kingsley.

Aldgate, J., Jones, D.P.H., Rose, W. and Jeffery, C. (eds) (2005) *The Developing World of the Child*. London: Jessica Kingsley.

Allen-Meares, P. and Lane, B.A. (1987) Grounding social work practice in theory: ecosystems, *Social Casework: the Journal of Contemporary Social Work*, November: 515–21.

Anand, S. and Sen, A. (1994) *Sustainable Human Development Concepts and Priorities*, http://meltingpot.fortunecity.com/lebanon/254/sen/htm: accessed 10 May 2004.

Argyle, M. (1969) *Social Interaction*. London: Methuen.

Argyle, M. (1988) *Bodily Communication*. London: Methuen.

Argyle, M. (1991) *Co-operation: the Basis of Sociability*. London: Routledge.

Argyle, M. and Cook, M. (1976) *Gaze and Mutual Gaze*. Cambridge: Cambridge University Press.

Atherton, J. (2004) *Reflections [On-line] UK*, http://www.dmu.ac.uk/jamesa/learning/critical1.htm: accessed 4 May 2004.

BACP (2004) www.bacp.co.uk, accessed 5 March 2004.

BASW (2004) *Code of Ethics in Social Work*, www.basw.co.uk, accessed 2 March 2004.

Balloch, S. and Taylor, M. (eds) (2001) *Partnership Working: Policy and Practice*. Bristol: Policy Press.

Barclay, P. (1982) *Social Workers: Their Role & Task*. London: Bedford Square Press.

Barnes, R. (1990) The fall and rise of casework, *Community Care*, July 12: 822.

Bateman, N. (1995) *Advocacy Skills*. Aldershot: Arena.

Beardshaw, V. (1991) *Implementing Assessment and Care Management*. London: Kings Fund College Paper.

Belbin, R.M. (1981) *Management Teams*. London: Heinemann.

Belbin, R.M. (1995) *Team Roles at Work*. London: Butterworth-Heinemann.

Beresford, B. (1994) *Positively Parents: Caring for a Severely Disabled Child*. York: Social Policy Research Unit.

Beresford, B. (1995) *Expert Opinions: A National Survey of Parents Caring for a Severely Disabled Child*. Bristol: Policy Press.

Beresford, P. and Croft, S. (2003) Involving service users in management: citizenship and support in J. Reynolds, J. Henderson, J. Seden and J. Charlesworth (eds) *The Managing Care Reader*. London: Routledge.

Beresford, P. and Croft, S. (2004) Service users and practitioners re-united: the key component for social work reform, *British Journal of Social Work*, 34: 53–68.

Berne, E. (1961) *Transactional Analysis in Psychotherapy*. New York: Grove Press.

Biestek, F.P. (1961) *The Casework Relationship*. London: George Allen and Unwin.

Birchall, E. and Hallett, C. (1995) *Working Together in Child Protection*. London: HMSO.

Bird, G. (1997) Letter, *Community Care*: 25 Sept–1 October.

Bowlby, J. (1988) *A Secure Base: Clinical Applications of Attachment Theory*. London: Routledge.

Bradshaw, J. (1972) The concept of need, *New Society*, 30 March: 640–3.

Brand, J. (1997) Letter, *The Independent*, 19 April.

Brandon, D. (ed.) (1989) *Mutual Respect*. Surbiton: Hexagon Publishing.

Braye, S. and Preston-Shoot, M. (1995) *Empowering Practice in Social Care*. Buckingham: Open University Press.

Breakwell, G. (1990) *Interviewing*. London, Routledge.

Brearley, J. (1991) *Counselling and Social Work*. Buckingham: Open University Press.

Brechin, A. (1998) Introduction in J. Walmsley, J. Katz and S. Peace (eds) *Care Matters*. London: Sage.

Brechin, A. and Seden, J. (2004) Communication skills in *Communication and Relationships in Health and Social Care*. Milton Keynes: The Open University.

Brown, H. with Seden, J. (2003) Managing to protect in J. Seden and J. Reynolds (eds) *Managing Care in Practice*. London: Routledge.

Browne, A. (1993) A conceptual clarification of respect, *Journal of Advanced Nursing*, 18: 211–17.

Browne, M. (1996) Needs assessment and community care in J. Percy-Smith (ed.) *Needs Assessment in Public Policy*. Buckingham: Open University Press.

Cairns, F. (1994) A beginner's guide to transference and counter-transference within counselling, *Counselling*, November: 302–3.

Caplan, G. (1964) *Principles of Preventative Psychiatry*. New York: Basic Books.

Carroll, M. and Walton, M. (eds) (1997) *Handbook of Counselling in Organisations*. London: Sage.

Cartwright, S. and Cooper, G.L. (1997) *Managing Workplace Stress*. London: Sage.

Chand, A. (2000) The overrepresentation of black children in the child protection system: possible causes consequences and solutions, *Child and Family Social Work*, 5(1): 67–77.

Charlesworth, J. (2003) Managing across professional and agency boundaries in J. Seden and J. Reynolds (eds) *Managing Care in Practice*. London: Routledge.

Clarke, C.L. and Asquith, S. (1985) *Social Work and Social Philosophy*. London: Routledge and Kegan Paul.

Cleaver, H., Wattam, C. and Cawson, C. (1998) *Assessing Risk in Child Protection*. London: The Stationery Office.

Cleaver, H., Walker, S. and Meadows, P. (2004) *Assessing Children's Needs and Circumstances*. London: Jessica Kingsley.

Cochrane, D. (1989) Power, probation and empowerment, *Probation Journal*, 36(4): 177–82.

Compton, B.R. and Galaway, B. (1989) *Social Work Processes*. Pacific Grove: Brookes Cole.

Connelly, N. and Seden, J. (2003) What service users say about services: the implications for managers in J. Henderson and D. Atkinson (eds) *Managing Care in Context*. London: Routledge.

Cooper, A. (2003) Risk and the frame work for assessment in M. Calder and S. Hackett (eds) *Assessment in Child Care*. Lyme Regis: Russell House.

Corby, B. (1996) Risk assessment in child protection in H. Kemshall and J. Pritchard *Good Practice in Risk Assessment and Risk Management*. London: Jessica Kingsley.

Corey, G. (1997) *Theory and Practice of Counselling and Psychotherapy*. California: Brookes Cole.

Cornwell, N. (1990) Who directs the power in talking with clients? *Social Work Today*, September: 28.

Coulshed, V. (1991) *Social Work Practice: an Introduction*. Basingstoke: Macmillan.

Crompton, M. (1990) *Attending to Children*. London: Arnold.

Curnock, K. and Hardiker, P. (1979) *Towards Practice Theory, Skills and Methods in Social Assessments*. London: Routledge and Kegan Paul.

Dalgleish, L.I. (1997) *Risk Assessment Approaches: The Good, the Bad and the Ugly*, paper to the Sixth Australasian Conference on Child Abuse and Neglect, 20–4 October, Adelaide, South Australia.

Dalgleish, L.I. (2003) Risks needs and consequences in M.C. Calder and S. Hackett (eds) *Assessment in Child Care*. Lyme Regis: Russell House.

Dalgleish, L.I. and Drew, E.C. (1989) The relationship of child abuse indicators to the assessment of perceived risk and to the court's decision to separate *Child Abuse and Neglect*, 13: 491–506.

Davies, D. and Neale, C. (1996) *Pink Therapy*. Buckingham: Open University Press.

Davies, M. (1985) *The Essential Social Worker*. Aldershot: Arena.

De Shazer, S. (1985) *Keys to Solution in Brief Therapy*. New York: Norton.

De Shazer, S. (1988) *Investigating Solutions in Brief Therapy*. New York: Norton.

Deakin, N. (1996) Contracting and accountability: the British experience in H.J. Schultze and W. Wirth (eds) *Who Cares: Social Service Organisations and Their Users*. London: Cassell.

Department of Health (1991a) *Assessment Systems and Community Care*. London: HMSO.

Department of Health (1991b) *Care Management and Assessment: Practitioners Guide*. London: HMSO.

Department of Health (1995) *Child Protection: Messages from Research*. London: The Stationery Office.

Department of Health (1996) *The Obligations of Care*. London: Department of Health.

Department of Health (1998a) *Modernising Social Services: Promoting Independence, Improving Protection, Raising Standards*. London: The Stationery Office.

Department of Health, DfES and Home Office (1998b) *Working Together to Safeguard Children: New Government Proposals for Inter-Agency Co-operation*. London: The Stationery Office.

Department of Health (2000a) *A Quality Strategy for Social Care*. London: The Stationery Office.

Department of Health (2000b) *No Secrets: Guidance on Developing and Implementing Multi Agency Policies and Procedures to Protect Vulnerable Adults*. London: The Stationery Office.

Department of Health (2000c) *Assessing Children in Need and their Families: Practice Guidance*. London: The Stationery Office.

Department of Health (2000d) *The NHS Plan: a Plan for Investment, a Plan for Reform*. London: The Stationery Office.

Department of Health, DfES and the Home Office (2000) *The Framework for the Assessment of Children in Need and their Families*. London: The Stationery Office.

Department of Health (2001a) *The Children Act Now*. London: The Stationery Office.

Department of Health (2001b) *Valuing People*. London: The Stationery Office.

Department of Health (2001c) *National Service Framework for Older People*. London: The Stationery Office.

Department of Health (2002) The *Single Assessment Process: Guidance for Local Implementation*, www.doh.gov.uk/scg/sap/scg/facs, accessed 31 December 2002.

Department of Health (2003) *Fair Access to Care Services: Guidance on Eligibility Criteria for Adult Social Care*, www.dogh.gov.uk/scg/facs, accessed 1 December 2003.

Department of Health (2004) www.children.doh.gov.uk/childrenstrust/faqu/htm, accessed 20 April 2004.

DfES (2003a) *Every Child Matters*. London: The Stationery Office.

DfES (2003b) *Every Child Matters: Summary Document*. London: The Stationery Office.

DfES (2004) *Every Child Matters: the Next Steps*. London: The Stationery Office.

Dickson, D. and Bamford, D. (1995) Improving the inter-personal skills of social work students: the problems of transfer of training and what to do about it *British Journal of Social Work*, 25: 85–105.

Dimmock, B., Johnson, J. and Page, M. (2004) 'Reflection' *Aids to Practice Card*. Milton Keynes: The Open University.

Doel, M. and Marsh, P. (1992) *Task-centred Social Work*. Aldershot: Arena.

Dominelli, L. (1996) *Address, NOPT Conference*. University of Leicester, 11–13 September.

Doueck, H.J., Bronson, D.E. and Levine, M. (1992) Evaluating risk assessment implementation in child protection: issues for consideration *Child Abuse and Neglect*, 16: 637–46.

Dougan, T. (1996) Counselling can add to the benefits of experience, Letter *Community Care*, 18–24 January: 12.

Dowie, J. and Elstein, A. (eds) (1988) *Professional Judgement: A Reader in Clinical Judgement Making*. Cambridge: Cambridge University Press.

Doyal, L. and Gough, I. (1991) *A Theory of Human Need*. Basingstoke: Macmillan.

East, P. (1995) *Counselling in Medical Settings*. Buckingham: Open University Press.

Eaton, L. (1998) How long have we got? *Community Care*, 4 June: 18.

Eby, M.A. (2000) The challenges of being accountable in A. Brechin, H. Brown and M.A. Eby (eds) *Critical Practice in Health and Social* Care. London: Sage.

Egan, G. (1990) *The Skilled Helper*. Pacific Grove: Brooks-Cole.

Ellis, K. Davis, A. and Rummery, K. (1999) Needs assessment, street-level bureaucracy and the new community care *Social Policy and Administration*, 33(3): 262–80.

English, D. and Pecora, P. (1994) Risk assessment as a practice in child protection services *Child Welfare*, 53: 451–73.

Epstein, L. (1988) *Helping People: The Task Centred Approach*, 2nd ed. Columbus: C.E. Merrill.

Erikson, E. (1965) *Childhood and Society*. Harmondsworth: Penguin.

Everitt, A. and Hardiker, P. (1996) *Evaluating for Good Practice*. London: BASW and Macmillan.

Fairbairn, W.R.D. (1952) *Psychoanalytic Studies of the Personality*. London: Routledge and Kegan Paul.

Forbat, E. and Atkinson, D. (forthcoming 2005) The troubled position of advocates in adult services *British Journal of Social Work*.

Forbat, L. and Nar, S. (2003) Dementia's cultural challenge *Community Care*, 25–31 September 39.

Foskett, A. (2004) No secrets in practice *Community Care*, 11–17 March: 38–9.

Frances, D. and Woodcock, M. (1982) *Fifty Activities for Self-Development*. Aldershot: Gower.

Franklin, C. and Jordan, C. (1995) Qualitative assessment: a methodological review *Families in Society*, May: 281–95.

French, S. and Swain, J. (2004) Disability and communication: listening is not enough in M. Robb, S. Barrett, C. Komaromy and A. Rogers (eds) *Communication, Relationships and Care: a Reader*. London: Routledge.

Gandhi, P. (1996) When I'm sixty four: listening to what elderly people from ethnic minorities need *Professional Social Work*, February: 12–13.

Garbarino, J. (1982) *Children and Families in the Social Environment*. New York: Aldine.

Gaudin, J.M., Shilton, P., Kilpatrick, A.C. and Polansky, N.A. (1996) Family functioning in neglectful families *Child Abuse and Neglect*, 20(4): 363–77.

Gilligan, R. (1997) Beyond permanence, the importance of resilience in child placement practice and planning *Adoption and Fostering*, 21(1): 13–19.

Glisson, C. and Hemmelgarn, A. (1998) The effects of organizational climate and inter-organizational coordination on the quality and outcomes of children's service systems *Child Abuse and Neglect*, 22(5): 401–21.

Golan, N. (1981) *Passing Through Transitions*. London: Collier-Macmillan.

Gomm, R. and Davies, C. (eds) (2000) *Using Evidence in Health and Social Care*. London: Sage.

Gordon, J. (1995) Counselling, who needs it? *You*, 22 October: 23–7.

Haines, J. (1975) *Skills and Methods in Social Work*. London: Constable.

Hallet, C. and Birchall, E. (1995) *Co-ordination and Child Protection*. Edinburgh: HMSO.

Handy, C. (1993) *Understanding Organisations*. London: Penguin.

Hardiker, P. and Barker, M. (eds) (1981) *Theories of Practice in Social Work*. London: Academic Press.

Hardiker, P. and Barker, M. (1991) Towards social theory for social work in J. Lishman (ed.) *Handbook of Theory for Practice Teachers in Social Work*. London: Jessica Kingsley.

Hardiker, P. and Barker, M. (1994) *The 1989 Children Act — Significant Harm, The Experience of Social Workers Implementing New Legislation*. Leicester: University of Leicester School of Social Work.

Hardiker, P. and Barker, M. (1996) *The NHS and Community Care Act 1990: Needs-led Assessments and Packages of Care*. Leicester: University of Leicester School of Social Work.

Hardiker, P. with Atkins, B., Barker, M., Brunton-Reed, S., Exton, K., Perry, M. and Pinnock, M. (2002) A framework for conceptualising need and its application to planning and providing services in H. Ward and W. Rose (eds) *Approaches to Needs Assessment in Children's Services*. London: Jessica Kingsley.

Harris, J. (2002) *The Social Work Business*. London: Routledge.

Harris, J. (2003) Let's talk business *Community Care*, 21–7 August: 36–7.

Harrison, R., Mann, G., Murphy, M., Taylor, A. and Thompson, N. (2003) *Partnership Made Painless*. Lyme Regis: Russell House.

Hasenfeld, Y. (1983) *Human Services Organisations*. Eaglewood Cliffs: Prentice-Hall.

Hawkins, P. and Shohet, R. (2000) *Supervision in the Helping Professions*. Buckingham: Open University Press.

Healey, K. (1998) Participation in child protection: the importance of context *British Journal of Social Work*, 28: 897–914.

Henderson, J. (2003) The consultation process in J. Henderson and D. Atkinson (eds) *Managing Care in Context*. London: Routledge.

Henderson, J. and Atkinson, D. (eds) (2003) *Managing Care in Context*. London: Routledge.

Henderson, J. and Forbat, E. (2003) Relationship-based social policy: personal and policy constructions of 'care', in M. Robb, S. Barrett, C. Komaromy and A. Rogers (eds) *Communication, Relationships and Care: a Reader*. London: Routledge.

Heron, J. (1997) *Helping the Client*. London: Sage.

Hetherington, A. (2001) *The Use of Counselling Skills in the Emergency Services*. Buckingham: Open University Press.

Hill, M. and Meadows, J. (1990) The place of counselling in social work, *Practice*, 4(3): 156–72.

Hinds, A. (2003) Just Chatting? *Community Care*, 27 February–5 March: 40.

Hollins, S. and Sinason, V. (forthcoming) *Psychoanalytic Snapshots: Three Moments of Transition*.

Hooks, b. (1991) *Yearning: Race Gender and Cultural Politics*. London: Turnaround Books.

Hollis, F. (1964) *Casework: a Psycho-Social Therapy*. New York: Random House.

Honey, P. and Mumford, A. (1982) *The Manual of Learning Styles*. Maidenhead: Ardingley House.

Hornby, S. and Atkins, J. (2003) The environment of collaborative care in J. Reynolds, J. Henderson, J. Seden and J. Charlesworth (eds) *The Managing Care Reader*. London: Routledge.

Horwath, J. (2001) (ed.) *The Child's World*. London: Jessica Kingsley.

Howe, D. (1987) *An Introduction to Social Work Theory*. Aldershot: Wildwood House.

Howe, D. (2003) Assessment using an attachment perspective in M.C. Calder and S. Hackett (eds) *Assessment in Child Care*. Lyme Regis: Russell House.

Howe, D., Dooley. T. and Hinings, D. (2000) Assessment and decision making in a case of child neglect and abuse *Child and Family Social Work*, 5(2): 143–55.

Hudson, B. (1991) Behavioural social work in J. Lishman (ed.) *Handbook of Theory for Practice Teachers in Social Work*. London: Jessica Kingsley.

Hudson, B. (1998) *Primary Health Care and Social Care: Working across Organisational and Professional Boundaries, Briefing Paper*. Leeds: Nuffield Institute for Health.

Hudson, B. and MacDonald, G.M. (1986) *Behavioural Social Work: an Introduction*. London: Routledge.

Hudson, B., Hardy, B., Henwood, M. and Wistow, G. (2003) In pursuit of inter-agency collaboration in the public sector: what is the contribution of theory and research? in J. Reynolds, J. Henderson, J. Seden and J. Charlesworth (eds) *The Managing Care Reader*. London: Routledge.

Hugman, B. (1977) *Act Natural*. London: Bedford Square Press.

Humphries, B. (ed.) (1966) *Critical Perspectives on Empowerment*. Birmingham: Venture Press.

Humphries, B. (2004) An unacceptable role for social work: implementing immigration policy *British Journal of Social Work*, 34: 93–107.

Hunter, M. (2003) One for all *Community Care*, 3–9 July: 30–1.

Huntley, M. (2002) Relationship based social work — how do endings impact on the client? *Practice* 14(2): 59–66.

Inskipp, F. (1986) *Counselling: The Trainers Handbook*. Cambridge: National Extension College.

Isaacs, W. (1999) *Dialogue and the Art of Thinking Together: a Pioneering Approach to Communicating in Business and in Life*. New York: Random House.

Jacobs, M. (1982) *Still Small Voice*. London: SPCK.

Jacobs, M. (1985) *Swift to Hear*. London: SPCK.

Jacobs, M. (1988) *Psychodynamic Counselling in Action*. London: Sage.

Jacobs, M. (1991) *Insight and Experience*. Buckingham: Open University Press.

Jacobs, M. (ed.) (1995a) *Charlie, an Unwanted Child?* Buckingham: Open University Press.

Jacobs, M. (ed.) (1995b) *Jitendra, Lost Connections*. Buckingham: Open University Press.

Jacobs, M. (1996) *The Care Guide*. London: Cassells.

Jacobs, M. (1998) *The Presenting Past*. Buckingham: Open University Press.

Jay, R. (1995) *Build a Great Team*. London: Pitman.

Jones, D.P.H. (2003) *Communicating with Vulnerable Children*. London: Gaskell.

Jones. D.P.H. (2005) Communicating with children in J. Aldgate, D.P.H. Jones, W. Rose and C. Jeffery (eds) *The Developing World of the Child*. London: Jessica Kingsley.

Jones, D.P.H. and Ramchandani, P. (1999) *Child Sexual Abuse: Informing Practice from Research*. Oxford: Radcliffe.

Jones, D.P.H., Hindley, N.T. and Ramchandani, P. (2005) Making plans: assessment, intervention and planning in J. Aldgate, D.P.H. Jones, W. Rose and C. Jeffery (eds) *The Developing World of the Child*. London: Jessica Kingsley.

Jordan, B. (2004) Emancipatory Social Work? Opportunity or Oxymoron? *British Journal of Social Work*, 34: 5–19.

Joyce, B. (2003) Tools that dig deeper *Community Care*, September 4–10: 38.

Kadushin, A. (1995) *Supervision in Social Work*. New York: Columbia University Press.

Katz, J. (2003) Managing loss in care homes in J. Reynolds, J., Henderson, J. Seden and J. Charlesworth (eds) *The Managing Care Reader*. London: Routledge.

Keith-Lucas, A. (1972) *Giving and Taking Help*. Chapel Hill: University of Carolina Press.

Kempshall, H. and Pritchard, J. (1997) *Good Practice in Risk Assessment and Risk Management*. London: Jessica Kingsley.

Killick, J. (2004) Eliciting experiences of dementia in C. Malone, L. Forbat, M. Robb and J. Seden (eds) *Reflecting Experience: Stories from Health and Social Care*. London: Routledge.

Kitwood, T. (2004) The experience of person centred care, in C. Malone, L. Forbat, M. Robb, and J. Seden (eds) *Reflecting Experience: Stories from Health and Social Care*. London: Routledge.

Kolb, D. (1984) *Experiential Learning: experience as the source of learning and development*. New Jersey: Prentice Hall.

Krane, J. and Davies, L. (2000) Mothering and child protection practice: rethinking risk assessment, *Child and Family Social Work*, 5(1): 35–45.

Kovel, J. (1976) *A Complete Guide to Therapy*. London: Harvester.

Lago, C. and Thompson, J. (1996) *Race, Culture and Counselling*. Buckingham: Open University Press.

Laird, J. (1995) Family centred practice in the post-modern era, *Families in Society*, March: 150–62.

Laming, H. (2003) *The Victoria Climbié Inquiry*. London: The Stationery Office.

Lancaster, Y.P. and Broadbent, V. (2003) *Listening to Young Children*. Maidenhead: Open University Press and McGraw-Hill.

Leathard, A. (1994/2001) (ed.) *Going Interprofessional: Working Together for Health and Welfare*. London: Routledge.

Leathard, A. (2003) (ed.) *Interprofessional Collaboration: from policy to practice in health and social care*. London: Routledge.

Lescheid, A.W., Chiodo, D., Whitehead, P.C., Hurley, D. and Marshall, L. (2003) The empirical basis of risk assessment in child welfare: the accuracy of risk assessment and clinical judgement, *Child Welfare*, LXXXII Sept/Oct: 5.

Lhullier, J.M. and Martin, C. (1994) Social work at the turn of the century *Social Policy and Administration*, 28(1) Dec: 359–69.

Lindsey, D. (1994) *The Welfare of Children*. Oxford: University Press.

Lipsky, M. (1980) *Street Level Bureaucracy*. New York: Sage.

Lishman, J. (1991 and forthcoming) *Handbook of Theory for Practice Teachers in Social Work*. London: Jessica Kingsley.

Lloyd, M. and Taylor, C. (1995) From Hollis to the orange book *British Journal of Social Work*, 25(6): 691–707.

Lyons, P., Wodarski, J.S. and Doueck, H.J. (1996) Risk assessment for child protective services: a review of the empirical literature on instrument performance *Social Work Research*, 20(3) September: 143–55.

Maluccio, A. (ed.) (1981) *Promoting Competence in Clients: a New/Old Approach to Social Work Practice*. New York: The Free Press.

Malone, C., Forbat, L., Robb, M. and Seden, J. (2004) (eds) *Reflecting Experience: Stories from Health and Social Care*. London: Routledge.

Marsh, P. and Triseliotis, J. (1996a) abstract of 1996b, HMSO and Scottish Office: 1.

Marsh, P. and Triseliotis, J. (1996b) *Ready to Practise? Social Workers and Probation Officers: Their Training and First Year in Work*, Aldershot: Avebury.

Mayer, J. E. and Timms, N. (1970) *The Client Speaks*. London: Routledge and Kegan Paul.

McGuire, J. (ed.) (1995) *What Works: Reducing Offending, Guidelines From Research and Practice*. Chichester: Wiley.

McLeod, J. (1998) *An Introduction to Counselling*. Buckingham: Open University Press.

Mearns, D. and Thorne, B. (1988) *Person Centred Counselling in Action*. London: Sage.

Meyer, C.H. (1993) *Assessment in Social Work*. New York: Columbia University Press.

Moore, W. (1997) Speak to me before it's too late *Health Service Journal*, 2 Jan: 20–2.

Morrison, T. (1988/1999) *Staff Supervision in Social Care*. Brighton: Pavilion.

Murphy, M. (1993) *Working Together in Child Protection: an Exploration of the Multi-disciplinary Task and System*. Ashgate: Arena.

Murphy Berman, P. (1994) A conceptual framework for thinking about risk assessment and case management in child protective services *Child Abuse and Neglect*, 8(2) February: 193–201.

NSPCC (1997) *Turning Points, a Resource Pack for Communicating with Children*. Leicester: NSPCC, Chailey Heritage and the Department of Health.

Nelson-Jones, R. (1981) *Practical Counselling and Helping Skills*. London: Cassells.

Neville, D. (1996) Skills for empowerment in social work, Leicester: Centre for Fun and Families.

North, S.J. (1996) Stress *Community Care*, 30 October.

Nucho, A.O. (1988) *Stress Management*. Springfield: Thomas.

O'Hagan, K.P. (1986) *Crisis Intervention in Social Work*. Basingstoke: Macmillan.

Open University (1999) *MESOL Materials*. Milton Keynes: The Open University.

Open University (2003) *Managing Care*. Milton Keynes: The Open University.

Open University (2004) *Communication and Relationships in Health and Social Care*. Milton Keynes: The Open University.

Open University, NSPCC, Royal Holloway University of London and Department of Health (2005) *The Developing World of the Child: Training and Resource Pack*. Milton Keynes: The Open University.

Parker, R., Ward, H., Jackson, S., Aldgate, J. and Wedge, P. (1991) (eds) *Assessing Outcomes in Childcare*. London: HMSO.

Parker, J. and Randall, P. (1997) *Using Behavioural Theories in Social Work*. Birmingham: BASW.

Parker, J. and Bradley, G. (2003) *Social Work Practice: Assessment, Planning, Intervention and Review*. Exeter: Learning Matters.

Parton, N. (1998) Risk, advanced liberalism and child welfare: the need to rediscover uncertainty and ambiguity *British Journal of Social Work*, 28: 5–27.

Payne, M. (1992/1997) *Modern Social Work Theory: a Critical Introduction*. Basingstoke: Macmillan.

Payne, M. (2000) *Teamwork in Multiprofessional Care*. Basingstoke: Macmillan.

Pearn, M. and Mulrooney, R.C. (1995) *Learning Organizations in Practice*. Maidenhead: McGraw-Hill.

Pearson, G., Treseder, J. and Yellolly, M. (1988) *Social Work and the Legacy of Freud*. Basingstoke: Macmillan.

Percy-Smith, J. (ed.) (1996) *Needs Assessments in Public Policy*. Buckingham: Open University Press.

Perlman, H.H. (1957) *Social Casework*. Chicago: University of Chicago Press.

Petrie, S. and Wilson, K. (1999) Towards the disintegration of child welfare services *Social Policy and Administration*, 33(2): 181–94.

Piachaud, D. (2001) Child poverty, opportunities and quality of life *The Political Quarterly*, 72(4): 446–53.

Pincus, A. and Minahan, A. (1973) *Social Work Practice: Model and Method*. Ithaca: Peacock.

Pittman, F. S. (1966) Techniques of family crisis therapy in J. Masserman (ed.) *Current Psychiatric Therapies*. New York: Grune and Stratton.

Powell, J. and Goddard, A. (1996) Cost and stakeholder views: a combined approach to evaluating services *British Journal of Social Work*, 26(1): 93–108.

Practice Panel (2004) Working at Cross Purposes *Community Care* 26 Feb–3 March: 42–3.

Prins, H. (1995) Seven sins of omission *Probation Journal*, 42(4) December: 199–201.

Pritchard, J. (ed.) (1995) *Good Practice in Supervision*. London: Jessica Kingsley.

Reder, P., Duncan, S. and Gray, M. (1993) *Beyond Blame: Child Abuse Tragedies Revisited*. London: Routledge.

Reeves, J. (2003) Research into practice *Community Care*, August 7–13: 44.

Reid, W.J. (1963) *An Experimental Study of Methods Used in Casework Treatment.* New York: Columbia University PhD Dissertation.

Reid, W.J. and Epstein, L. (1972) *Task-centred Casework.* New York: Columbia University Press.

Reid, W.J. and Epstein, L. (1976) *Task-centred Practice.* New York: Columbia University Press.

Reid, W.J. and Shyne, A.W. (1969) *Brief and Extended Casework.* New York: Columbia University Press.

Reynolds, J., Henderson, J., Seden, J. and Charlesworth, J. (eds) (2003) *The Managing Care Reader.* London: Routledge.

Richards, M., Payne, C. and Shepperd, A. (1990) *Staff Supervision in Child Protection Work.* London: NISWE.

Richmond, M.E. (1922) *Social Diagnosis.* New York: Russell Sage Foundation.

Roberts, A.R. (ed.) (1991) *Contemporary Perspectives on Crisis Intervention and Prevention.* Englewood Cliffs: Prentice Hall.

Roberts, A.R. (1995) *Crisis Intervention and Time Limited Cognitive Treatment.* London: Sage.

Roberts, R.W. and Nee, R.H. (1971) *Theories of Social Casework.* London: University of Chicago Press.

Rogers, A.M. (2001) Nurture, bureaucracy and re-balancing the mind and heart *Journal of Social Work Practice*, 15(2): 182–91.

Rogers, B. (1992) Transference, counter-transference and a teddy bear *Counselling*, November: 242–3.

Rogers, C.R. (1961) *On Becoming a Person.* Boston: Houghton Mifflin.

Rollnick, M.W. (1996) *Motivational Interviewing.* London: Guildford Press.

Rosenstein, P. (1995) Parental levels of empathy as related to risk assessment in child protective services *Child Abuse and Neglect*, 19(11) November: 1349–60.

Rutter, M. (1985) Resilience in the face of adversity: protective factors and resilience to psychiatric disorder *British Journal of Psychiatry*, 147: 163–82.

Rutter, M., Taylor, E. and Hersov, L. (1994) *Child and Adolescent Psychiatry: Modern Approaches*, (3rd ed.) London: Blackwell.

Rutter, M. and Hay, D. (eds) (1996) *Developing Through Life.* Oxford: Blackwell.

Ryan, M., Fook, J. and Hawkins, L. (1995) From beginners to graduate social worker: preliminary findings of an Australian longitudinal study *British Journal of Social Work*, 25: 17–35.

Ryle, A. (1995) Cognitive Analytic Therapy in M. Jacobs (ed.) *Charlie an Unwanted Child?* Buckingham: Open University Press.

Sale, A.U. (2004) Ready for the worst *Community Care*, 15–21 April: 26–7.

Saleebey, D. (1997) (ed.) *The Strengths Perspective in Social Work.* New York: Longman.

Sang, B. and O'Neill, S. (2002) Patient involvement in clinical governance *British Journal of Health Care Management*, 8: 10.

Sawdon, C. and Sawdon, D. (1995) The supervision partnership: a whole greater than the sum of the parts in J. Pritchard (ed.) *Good Practice in Risk Assessment and Risk Management.* London: Jessica Kingsley.

Schaffer, R.H. (1990) *Making Decisions about Children, Psychological Questions and Answers.* Oxford: Blackwell.

Schon, D. (1983) *The Reflective Practitioner.* New York: Basic Books.

Scott, D. and O'Neill, D. (1996) *Beyond Child Rescue: Developing Family Centred Practice at St Lukes.* St Leonards: Allen and Unwin.

Scrutton, S. (1989) *Counselling Older People.* London: Arnold.

Seden, J. (2001) Assessment of children in need and their families: a literature review in Department of Health, *Studies Informing the Framework for the Assessment of Children in Need and their Families.* London: The Stationery Office.

Seden, J. (2003) Managers and their organisations in J. Henderson and D. Atkinson (eds) *Managing Care in Context.* London: Routledge.

Seden, J. (2004) Showing the working: leadership and team culture in C. Malone, L. Forbat, M. Robb and J. Seden (eds) *Reflecting Experience: Stories from Health and Social Care.* London: Routledge.

Seden, J. (2005) Frameworks and theories in J. Aldgate, D.P.H. Jones, W. Rose and C. Jeffery (eds) *The Developing World of the Child.* London: Jessica Kingsley.

Seden, J. and Katz, J. (2003) Managing significant life events in J. Seden and J. Reynolds (eds) *Managing Care in Practice.* London: Routledge.

Seden, J. and Reynolds, J. (eds) (2003) *Managing Care in Practice.* London: Routledge.

Seligman, M.E.P. (1975) *Helplessness: On Depression Development and Death.* San Francisco: W.H. Freeman.

Sheldon, B. (1982) *Behaviour Modification: Theory, Practice and Philosophy.* London: Tavistock.

Sheldon, B. (1995) *Cognitive-Behavioural Therapy.* London: Routledge.

Shemmings, D. and Shemmings, Y. (2003) Supporting evidence-based practice and research mindedness in J. Seden and J. Reynolds (eds) *Managing Care in Practice.* London: Routledge.

Sinason, V. (1992) *Mental Handicap and the Human Condition.* London: Free Association Books.

Sinclair, R., Garnett, L. and Berridge, D. (1995) *Social Work and Assessment with Adolescents.* London: National Children's Bureau.

Siporin, M. (1975) *Introduction to Social Work Practice.* New York: Macmillan.

Skye, E., Meddings, S. and Dimmock, B. (2003) Theories for understanding people in J. Henderson and D. Atkinson (eds) *Managing Care in Context.* London: Routledge.

Smith, A. (1994) *Social Work Assignment.* University of Leicester: unpublished paper.

Smith, M. (1991) *Analysing Organisational Behaviour.* Basingstoke: Macmillan.

Smith, S. and Norton, K. (1999) *Counselling Skills for Doctors.* Buckingham: Open University Press.

Solomon, B. (1976) *Black Empowerment: Social Work in Oppressed Communities.* New York: Colombia University Press.

Sone, K. (1996) Professional roles *Community Care,* 21–7 November: 19.

Specht, H. and Vickery, A. (1977) *Integrating Social Work Methods.* London: George, Allen and Unwin.

Statham, D. (1996) *Address, NOPT Conference,* Leicester University, 11–13 Sept.

Syer, J. and Connolly, C. (1996) *How Teamwork Works: the Dynamics of Effective Team Development.* Maidenhead: McGraw-Hill.

Taylor, B. and Devine, T. (1993) *Assessing Needs and Planning Care.* Aldershot: Arena.

Taylor-Gooby, P. and Lawson, R. (eds) (1993) *Markets and Managers: New Issues in the Delivery of Welfare.* Buckingham: Open University Press.

Topss (2003a) *The National Occupational Standards for Social Work.* www.topss.org.uk, accessed 1 December 2003.

Topss (2003b) *Statement of Expectations from individuals, families, carers, groups and communities who use services.* www.topss.org.uk, accessed 1 December 2003.

Topss (2003c) *Academic Standards for Social Work.* www.topss.org.uk, accessed 1 December 2003.

Townsend, J. (1987) *The Interviewers Pocket Book.* Alresford: Management Pocket Books.

Trevithick, P. (2000) *Social Work Skills.* Buckingham: Open University Press.

Trowell, J. and Bower, M. (1996), *The Emotional Needs of Young Children and Their Families.* London: Routledge.

Truax, C.B. and Carkhuff, R.R. (1967) *Towards Effective Counselling and Psychotherapy.* Chicago: Aldine Publishing.

Turnell, A. and Edwards, S. (1999) *Signs of Safety: A Solution and Safety Oriented Approach to Child Protection Casework.* London: Norton.

Turnell, A. and Essex, S. (2006) *Working with Denied Child Abuse: The Resolutions Approach.* Maidenhead: Open University Press, McGraw-Hill Education.

Unell, I. (1996) Substance misuse in M. Jacobs, *The Care Guide.* London: Cassell.

Valente, M. (1998) Child protection and inter-agency working: a discussion *Practice* 10(3): 37–43.

Valios, N. (2004) Sounds familiar *Community Care*, 3–9 April: 32–3.

Wald, M. and Woolverton, M. (1990) Risk assessment: the emperor's new clothes? *Child Welfare*, 69: 483–8.

Waine, B. and Henderson, J. (2003) Managers, managing and managerialism in J. Henderson and D. Atkinson (eds) *Managing Care in Context*. London: Routledge.

Walker, M. (ed.) (1995a) *Peta, A Feminist's Problem with Men*. Buckingham: Open University Press.

Walker, M. (ed.) (1995b), *Morag, Myself or Mother Hen?* Buckingham: Open University Press.

Walsh, J.A. (1987) Burnout and values in the social service profession *Social Casework: The Journal of Contemporary Social Work*, Family Service, May: 279–82.

Ward, A. (1993) *Working in Group Care: Social Work in Residential and Day Care Settings*. Birmingham: Venture Press.

Ward, A. (2003) Managing the Team in J. Seden and J. Reynolds (eds) *Managing Care in Practice*. London: Routledge.

Ward, H. and Rose, W. (2002) (eds) *Approaches to Needs Assessment in Children's Services*. London: Jessica Kingsley.

West Social Worker (1996) After West *Social Work*, January: 10.

Whalley, M. (1994) *Learning to be Strong: Setting up a Neighbourhood Service for Under Fives and their Families*. Sevenoaks: Hodder and Stoughton.

Wickham, R.E. and West, J. (2002) *Therapeutic Work with Sexually Abused Children*. London: Sage.

White, M. and Epston, D. (1989) *Narrative Means to Therapeutic Ends*. New York: Norton.

Wigfall, V. and Moss, P. (2001) *More Than the Sum of the Parts? A Study of a Multi Agency Childcare Network*. London: National Children's Bureau.

Williams, B. (1996) *Counselling in the Criminal Justice System*. Buckingham: Open University Press.

Winchester, R. (2003) Protection down the line *Community Care*, 6–12 March: 38–9.

Winchester, R. (2004) Get your act together *Community Care*, 29 January–February 4: 265–7.

Winnicott, D.W. (1960) The theory of the parent-infant relationship *International Journal of Psycho-analysis*, 41: 585–95.

Winnicott, D.W. (1986) *Home is Where We Start From*. Harmondsworth: Penguin.

Yelloly, M. (1980) *Social Work Theory and Psychoanalysis*. New York: Van Nostrand.

Yelloly, M. and Henkel, M. (eds) (1995) *Learning and Teaching in Social Work: Towards Reflective Practice*. London: Jessica Kingsley.

# Index

## Related books from Open University Press
Purchase from www.openup.co.uk or order through your local bookseller

---

**SOCIAL WORK SKILLS**
A PRACTICE HANDBOOK
SECOND EDITION

**Pamela Trevithick**

Written by an experienced academic-practitioner, the new edition of this best-selling text is updated to include the current educational, policy and practice context of social work.

The new edition contains additional material on social work methods and approaches, and revised sections on the importance of psychological and sociological theories, as well as more information on multi-disciplinary working, communication with children, and the use of language and jargon in social work.

The main focus of the book is on how skills can be perfected and made transferable across different contexts, service user groups and countries. The handbook is essential reading for all social work students and a valuable reference tool for practicing social workers and human service professionals.

*Contents*
*Introduction – The importance of communication skills within social work – Creative listening – Observing and analysing non-verbal forms of communication – Using theory and research to enhance practice skills – Evidence-based practice: the importance of assessment, effective decision-making and evaluation skills – Basic interviewing skills – Providing help, guidance and direction – Enabling, empowerment and partnership skills – Dealing with conflict and defining professional boundaries and accountability – Conclusion – Notes – Bibliography – Index.*

c.240pp     0 335 21499 1 (Paperback)     0 335 21500 9 (Hardback)

## COUNSELLING SKILLS FOR NURSES, MIDWIVES AND HEALTH VISITORS

### Dawn Freshwater

Counselling is a diverse activity and there are an increasing number of people who find themselves using counselling skills, not least those in the caring professions. There is a great deal of scope in using counselling skills to promote health in the everyday encounters that nurses have with their patients. The emphasis on care in the community and empowerment of patients through consumer involvement means that nurses are engaged in providing support and help to people to change behaviours.

Community nurses often find themselves in situations that require in-depth listening and responding skills: for example, in helping people come to terms with chronic illness, disability and bereavement. Midwives are usually the first port of call for those parents who have experienced miscarriages, bereavements, or are coping with decisions involving the potential for genetic abnormalities. Similarly, health visitors are in a valuable position to provide counselling regarding the immunization and health of the young infant. These practitioners have to cope not only with new and diverse illnesses, for example HIV and AIDS, but also with such policy initiatives as the National Service Framework for Mental Health and their implications.

This book examines contemporary developments in nursing and health care in relation to the fundamental philosophy of counselling, the practicalities of counselling and relevant theoretical underpinnings. Whilst the text is predominantly aimed at nurses, midwives and health visitors, it will also be of interest to those professionals allied to medicine, for example physiotherapists, occupational therapists and dieticians.

*Contents*
*Introduction – The process of counselling – Beginning a relationship – Sustaining the relationship – Facilitating change – Professional considerations – Caring for the carer – Appendix: Useful information – References – Index.*

128pp      0 335 20781 2 (Paperback)      0 335 20782 0 (Hardback)

# WELFARE STATE AND WELFARE CHANGE

## Martin Powell and Martin Hewitt

This excellent book should be read by students and academics alike. It provides a clear account of the nature of the contemporary welfare state and the 'How, what and why' of welfare state change in Britain . . . Highly recommended.

> Nick Ellison, University of Durham

An excellent guide to the complexities of understanding the British welfare state in the contemporary era.

> Francis G. Castles, Department of Social Policy, University of Edinburgh

. . . a valuable guide for students, attempting as it does to explain and assess the 'production of welfare' in Britain in the context of the wide-ranging, interdisciplinary literature on welfare restructuring.

> Professor Jane Lewis, Barnett Professor of Social Policy, University of Oxford, UK

*Welfare State and Welfare Change* is a textbook written with the undergraduate student in mind. It provides a comprehensive and accessible introduction to one of the most important but relatively neglected issues in social policy. It addresses the 'what, when and why' issues of welfare change. What constitutes a change in the welfare state? Do we have a new welfare state? If so, when did this change occur? What factors influenced change? The book brings together a wide range of diverse material, and provides descriptive, analytical and explanatory perspectives on welfare change. It moves beyond both descriptive, historical accounts of the welfare state, and theoretical, abstract accounts to integrate them within a coherent structure.

This book brings a new perspective to the study of social policy and is designed for students of social policy, social work, politics, policy studies and public administration.

## Contents
*Welfare state – The classic welfare state – The restructured welfare state – The modern welfare state – Economic explanations – Political explanations – Organizational explanations – Social explanations – Welfare change – Further Reading – References – Index.*

224pp      0 335 20516 X (Paperback)      0 335 20517 8 (Hardback)

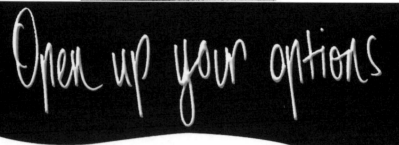

 Education

 Health & Social Welfare

Management

Media, Film & Culture

Psychology & Counselling

 Sociology

Study Skills

for more information on our
publications visit **www.openup.co.uk**

**OPEN UNIVERSITY PRESS**
McGraw - Hill Education